CORPORATE FINANCE, MERGERS & ACQUISITIONS

CORPORATE FINANCE, MERGERS & ACQUISITIONS

J. Scott Slorach MA(Hons), Solicitor
Principal Lecturer in Law and Head of Corporate Training Design,
Nottingham Law School,
Visiting Professor, Strathclyde University

BLACKSTONE
PRESS LIMITED

Published by
Blackstone Press Limited
Aldine Place
London
W12 8AA
United Kingdom

Sales enquiries and orders
Telephone +44-(0)-20-8740-2277
Facsunuke +44-(0)-20-8743-2292
e-mail: sales@blackstone.demon.co.uk
website: www.blackstonepress.com

ISBN: 1-84174-204-X

First edition, 1994
Second edition, 1995
Third edition, 1996
Fourth edition, 1997
Fifth edition, 1998
Sixth edition, 1999
Seventh edition, 2000
Eighth edition, 2001

British Library Cataloguing in Publication Data
A catalogue record for this book is available from the British Library

Typeset in 10/12pt Palatino by Style Photosetting Limited, Mayfield, East Sussex
Printed and bound in Great Britain by Antony Rowe Limited, Chippenham and Reading

CONTENTS

PREFACE

Apparently, it is no longer 'cool' to be a 'hep cat'. Such is the pace of modern life that fashion and phraseology can change overnight. So, farewell to the Yellow Book and hello to The Listing Rules. It seems the new volume is not yet to be known as the Purple Book, its new colour following the corporate colours of the Financial Services Authority. The latter now has the function of the UK Listing Authority, with the effect that shares are now required to be admitted separately but simultaneously to listing and trading. And, at some point in the near future, the Financial Services and Markets Act 2000 (FSMA) will come into effect as next year's 'big thing'. All of this in vogue and in perspective in the latest edition of *Corporate Finance, Mergers and Acquisitions* . . . 'daddy-o'.

J. Scott Slorach
December 2000

TABLE OF CASES

TABLE OF STATUTES

European legislation

ABBREVIATIONS

ABI	Association of British Insurers
AGM	annual general meeting
AIM	Alternative Investment Market
ASB	Accounting Standards Board
CC	Competition Commission
CCD	concentration with a Community dimension
CGT	capital gains tax
DTI	Department of Trade and Industry
FIMBRA	Financial Intermediaries, Managers and Brokers Regulatory Association
FRRP	Financial Reporting Review Panel
FRS	Financial Reporting Standard
FSA	Financial Services Authority (formerly SIB)
FS Act	Financial Services Act 1986
FSMA	Financial Services and Markets Act 2000
IMRO	Investment Management Regulatory Organisation
LAUTRO	Life Assurance and Unit Trust Regulatory Organisation
LIBOR	London Inter-Bank Offered Rate
LIFFE	London International Financial Futures Exchange
LR	Listing Rules
MBO	management buy-out
NAPF	National Association of Pension Funds
OFT	Office of Fair Trading
PAL	provisional allotment letter
PIA	Personal Investment Authority
RIE	recognised investment exchange
RLA	renounceable letter of allotment (or acceptance)
RPB	recognised professional body
SARs	Rules Governing Substantial Acquisitions of Shares
SD	stamp duty
SDRT	stamp duty reserve tax
SEAQ	Stock Exchange Automated Quotations
SFA	Securities and Futures Authority
SIB	Securities and Investments Board (now FSA (see above))
SRO	self-regulating organisation
SSAP	Statement of Standard Accounting Practice
UKLA	UK Listing Authority
USM	Unlisted Securities Market

ONE

THE REGULATORY SUPERSTRUCTURE

This book is not primarily about regulation. It is about the core corporate finance transactions which lawyers are called to advise on. One particularly modern feature of these transactions is the regulation to which they are subject. The focus here is always on the underlying 'deal', though the regulation can never be all that far behind.

This order of priorities reflects the way in which regulation is often perceived, as something which does not tend to facilitate business activity: all the transactions we will look at could be done before regulation arrived. Regulation usually appears to control or systematise an area of corporate finance activity which has flourished in the absence of regulatory constraint – and perhaps because of that!

This is not to say that regulation is necessarily a bad thing. It does after all seek to create order where before there was none or little. It does aim to protect those who might otherwise be the victim of malpractice and to prevent abuses which are deleterious to the reputation of the market. All of these are obviously good things. But it is important to bear in mind that regulation is almost always superimposed over existing market practice. It may change it in the process – indeed, it is often intended to do precisely that – but you will not be able to understand how things are done in the corporate finance world simply by reading the regulations. They do not tell you how to do a deal. They will tell you what are the boundaries of acceptable conduct in the course of doing that deal. Therefore, this book will examine the transaction first, and regulation second.

This has at least two important consequences for us. The first is that much of the law relevant to the transactions discussed in this book is already familiar to you. The word 'transactions' implies give and take, and, indeed, we will see that most of the activities we look at here are constructed on the foundations of the law of contract. For instance, the sale and purchase of a business or shares is governed principally by the contract for the sale. An issue of shares is governed by the contract entered into between company and investor and underpinned by the underwriting contract between company and underwriter. An offer by one company to acquire the shares in another company, if accepted by the shareholders, will create an enforceable contract. Hence much of what we will focus on is the special nature of those contracts and the effect their various provisions are intended to achieve. But for you, the important consequence is that you are not entering waters entirely uncharted.

Second, the transactions have developed to achieve the business ends of the parties. If regulation emerges to intervene in that contractual relationship in some way, the parties can respond either by complying with the regulatory constraints, or by finding some way to achieve the same end but in a way that is not caught by the regulation. This is not because of a law-breaking mentality or even bloody-mindedness, but a recognition that regulation creates cost. This is the cost of delay, of completing the required paperwork, of the necessary professional advice, possibly of changing established business and working practices. If there is still a compelling business reason to enter into the transaction, there will also be very strong business sense in trying to do it at the cheapest price – which means avoiding the regulatory net.

There are in turn different ways of doing this. One is to exploit the holes in the net and escape through them. Another is to adapt the transaction so it still attains the desired outcome but assumes characteristics sufficiently distinct for it to avoid the clutches of the regulators and swim round the net altogether. There is therefore always a demand on the lawyer to be inventive.

Having said all this, the impact of regulation in this area is highly significant and we need to achieve some better idea of how it operates and when. Let us get a better idea first of what regulation actually is.

1.1 What is Regulation?

'Regulation' in this book refers to any body of rules which has developed or is created to authorise or control business conduct or activity. The term does not embrace existing common law principles or precedents as these cannot properly be said to have been codified in any form, though their application and effect is sufficiently well established for us to be able to identify a body of law. Regulation, though, is pre-eminently codification. This is not to say that it comes into existence from nowhere and is then a static, once-and-for-all phenomenon. It may be the crystallisation of best practice which has been in existence for some time. Once it is introduced, it will evolve with changing conditions and new market practices.

Therefore, regulation for these purposes refers to statute first and foremost. Though far from complete, the Companies Acts represent an attempt to codify the formation and functions of companies and those persons connected with them. The Financial Services Act 1986 is an attempt to build the foundation for the regulation of activity relating to investments. Of course these statutes and the others discussed in this book have effect as Parliamentary legislation. Their status as 'law' is therefore unquestioned.

There are other forms of codification which we will be looking at which are not statutory. There are the rules administered by the Takeover Panel in relation to takeovers of public companies. The rules, known as the City Code on Takeovers and Mergers, are not law but something like rules for a professional sport. If you want to play the game, you have to play by the rules; if you break the rules, then the chances are you will not be allowed to play again. This is an oversimplification, but it introduces an important point.

When you break the law set out in a statute, you know that sanctions will follow if the breach is detected and enforced. When you break rules like those of the City Code, there may be sanctions provided for as part of the rules, but these lie essentially at the discretion of the regulator, the body which made the rules in the first place. And one thing is certain: those sanctions will not be criminal, as no such power is vested in these regulators. This is not to say the sanctions will not be serious – they are simply of a different order.

Beyond these non-statutory regulations (of which the City Code is only an example) there are other attempts at codification which amount to no more than principles of best practice. These could not properly be described as rules. This book refers to them as 'guidelines'. The critical distinction between them and rules is the absence of formal sanctions.

An example of such guidelines is the Investment Committee guidelines, which stipulate (amongst other things) what investing institutions regard as acceptable limits on the issue of shares by companies listed on the Stock Exchange. There is no formal sanction for failing to observe the guidelines, but any company which does so can be sure eventually to incur the wrath of its institutional shareholders who may accordingly use their influential power to show their displeasure (for example, by voting against company resolutions).

This kind of regulation is very easy to dismiss as inconsequential as it has no teeth. In fact, though its teeth are less visible, they can still give a company a nasty bite, and such guidelines are treated with care by companies anxious to show they are responsible.

1.2 What is Regulation For?

This section looks briefly at the purpose of regulation so that when we come later to examine the application of regulations in practice, what we are looking at does not seem a senseless piece of rule-creation but rather something with a point.

As we have seen, regulation comes in different flavours and with different objectives. These are some of the most significant:

(a) *Protecting the public*

This is the background to just about every piece of regulation: the prime example in this context is the Financial Services Act 1986, though it is equally true of the City Code on Takeovers and Mergers. The public in both these cases is the investing public. Preventing the perpetration of abuses is likewise the primary motivation behind the Companies Act 1985.

(b) *Licensing*

This is obviously linked to (a), as one way to protect the public is to impose certain thresholds in terms of standards on those who want to enter a market or deliver a product. Again the Financial Services Act 1986 is such an example, as are the Listing Rules administered by the UK Listing Authority (UKLA) which govern what a company needs to do to get its securities listed on the Official List.

(c) *Financing requirements*

We will not be looking at these in the course of this book, but certain businesses clearly need to be properly financed to provide a proper service to clients: banking is a good example and banks regulated in the UK under the Banking Act 1987 need a certain amount of capital to obtain and retain their licence (a requirement known as 'capital adequacy').

(d) *Compulsory insurance*

Again linked to (a), the assumption behind this is that some businesses in an industry will fail or make errors and be forced to compensate those who have suffered loss as a result of their failings. For the better protection of the investor, and shoring up the reputation of the industry in question, a fund needs to exist to which all market operators contribute (including those who never fail) so there is always money available for compensation. We will not look at this further in this book, but an example is provided by the solicitors' profession in the form of the Solicitors' Indemnity Fund.

(e) *Disclosure of information*

This applies to much of the regulation we will see. The idea is to improve the position of those investing in or affected by the business entity by obliging it to make adequate disclosure of relevant information. The investors and others are then free to make decisions based on 'transparency', i.e., the availability of clear data. Much of the Companies Act 1985 deals with disclosure requirements. The UKLA Listing Rules, the Stock Exchange Admission and Disclosure Standards and the City Code also place great emphasis on the accurate and prompt disclosure of information.

(f) *Fairness*

Some regulation aims to ensure the so-called 'level playing field', so that everyone competes by the same rules. Some of the regulations imposed under the Companies Act 1985 are a response to EC requirements which in turn are driven by the desire to harmonise regulatory obligations across the European Community so that companies in one jurisdiction are subject to no more or less regulation than their internal market competitors in other jurisdictions.

(g) *Competitiveness*

Ensuring competitiveness is again in the public's best interests. Antitrust regulation such as the Fair Trading Act 1973 is designed to give protection to consumers against the dangers of monopolies being formed which may lead to higher prices and less choice.

(h) *Systemic failure*

Another common reason for the existence of regulation is to guard against the collapse of a part of the financial system. Safeguarding the viability of an industry is in the best interests of the industry and vital if public confidence in it is to be maintained. The development of the City Code was a response to a growing number of scandals in the unregulated takeover market in the 1960s which threatened a state of chaos. The Code was the solution to the survival of the market: there is always a risk if a market is excessively volatile or prone to abuse that investors will simply stay away.

1.3 What Form Does Regulation Take?

Related to the question of what we mean by regulation is the form in which it comes. We have already seen the layers of statutes, rules and guidelines. But who is responsible for drawing up these codes and enforcing them?

To answer this question, we need to reflect for a moment on what brings about the call for regulation in the first place. Usually, in spite of all the good things which regulation may engender (see **1.2**), most regulatory regimes surface after the inadequacies of what existed before are revealed, generally through scandals or exposed inefficiencies.

The philosophy that has tended to hold sway in response to these crises or imposed obligations is that the best people to sort the mess out or decide what is needed are not government ministers or civil servants but the industry itself. Its self-interest may of course impede any genuine reform but that can be accounted for by making some form of regulation obligatory. This was essentially the way in which the City was finally persuaded to adopt the regulatory system now installed by the Financial Services Act 1986. Normally, when faced with a choice, the City's institutions have opted for getting their own house in order.

The result is that those who bring the codes into being are those whom the codes will regulate. This approach has attracted the label 'self-regulation', in contrast to the alternative of directly imposed governmental regulation sometimes called 'statutory regulation'.

This emphasis is one reflected throughout the City. Its great strength is the responsiveness of such regulators to the needs of the market, simply because they are close to it. The philosophy is that regulation will be less of a costly imposition if those who understand the market develop the rules: they can then do so in a way which is sensitive to the market's needs.

The effect of this approach is that each industry within the City regulates itself separately from every other industry (though there may be some overlap). The Stock Exchange does not regulate anything outside activities on the Stock Exchange. The Takeover Panel does not regulate anything outside public company takeovers.

What follows from this is the need for securities industry professionals to be aware of the overlap between regulators. Companies may find that some of the corporate finance activities or transactions they want to pursue will give rise to the intervention or involvement of more than one regulator at a time. There is no central regulatory unit to which a company can go to get all its regulatory problems handled at once. They have to be confronted on a market-by-market basis.

The consequence, to take an example, is that a public company takeover offer involving the issue of securities to be listed on the Official List as consideration for the offer will be regulated by the UKLA, the Stock Exchange and the Takeover Panel simultaneously: the UKLA, because of the listing of securities, the Stock Exchange for admission of securities to trading and the Takeover Panel because of the takeover offer. Both sets of rules will need to be complied with. Other regulators may be involved as well. The checklist in **1.7.4** gives an idea of the questions which arise when a company is faced with such a multi-regulatory transaction. The nature of regulation in the City means that the activities and transactions we are looking at in this book may intersect with any number of possible regulatory issues at any one time, depending on the nature of the deal, the parties involved and so on. A good grasp of the regulatory superstructure and its key institutions is therefore an essential foundation.

1.4 What is Regulated and by Whom?

The checklist at the end of this chapter summarises the ways in which regulation superimposes itself on corporate finance transactions, and indicates which regulators are involved at different points. It is a useful way of seeing in the round the interaction of the various rules to which public company financing is subject. It is not, though, comprehensive: it covers only the most important aspects in passing, as a kind of overview, as other sections of the book (which are referred to where relevant) include a fuller treatment in context.

We concentrate in this book on three aspects of corporate finance regulation:

(a) the regulation of the financial services market as it affects corporate finance work;

(b) the key elements in the regulation of the securities market; and

(c) the regulation of public companies.

The rest of this chapter will look at the first two. Corporate regulation follows in **Chapter 2**.

1.5 Regulation of Financial Services

The term 'financial services' covers three principal types of business activity:

(a) investment business;

(b) banking business; and

(c) insurance business.

1.5.1 THE REGULATORY STRUCTURE

1.5.1.1 Introduction

The regulation of financial services in the UK is currently in the midst of a major reform. A new regulatory regime is being created by the Financial Services and Markets Act 2000 ('FSMA'). This Act was given Royal Assent on 14 June 2000 but it is currently anticipated that it will come into force through statutory instrument in July 2001. (The target date on which the FSA will eventually assume its full powers is being termed 'N2'.) In addition, a great deal of secondary legislation needs to come into force to give effect to the new regime.

Whilst the FSMA creates a new regime, details of which are given below, much of the detailed regulation of corporate work will remain similar to that currently in operation under the Financial Services Act 1986 ('FS Act'). Given this, and the fact that the commencement date for the new regime is not set in stone, references in this text are to the relevant provisions of the FS Act, that is, the law in force at the date of writing.

1.5.1.2 The Financial Services Act 1986

The significance of the Financial Services Act 1986 ('FS Act') in corporate finance work is that shares, debentures, loan stock and various other interests in securities are defined as investments in sch. 1 to the Act. Most corporate finance work will itself fall under the definition of investment activities in the same schedule. Some exemptions and exclusions are offered under sch. 1, so familiarity with it is advisable. For our purposes, however, almost any activity during the transactions described in this book is likely to have an FS Act dimension.

The FS Act was enacted to regulate the conduct of investment business. It does this by requiring anyone wishing to carry on investment business to be authorised. Currently, authorisation is obtained either through application to the Financial Services Authority ('FSA') (formerly the Securities and Investments Board ('SIB') or by membership of an approved body. The latter include self-regulating organisations ('SROs') and recognised professional bodies ('RPBs') such as The Law Society. Any person authorised to carry on investment business is required to comply with the FSA's rules and that of its SRO or RPB. Conducting investment without authorisation is an offence under s. 4 of the FS Act and any agreement entered into by an unauthorised person relating to investments is unenforceable under s. 5.

1.5.1.3 Reform of regulatory structure

As referred to above, the regulatory structure under the FS Act is currently being reformed with the intention that the FSA will become the sole regulator of financial services in the UK. At present, the FSA is the designated agency under the FS Act with responsibility for the overall supervision of investment business. However, three SROs deal with authorisation for and supervision of financial services for particular investment markets. The latter involves them in maintaining their own rules and, where appropriate, taking investigatory and disciplinary action. The three SROs are:

(a) The Securities and Futures Authority ('SFA'), which regulates market makers, brokers and securities dealers, generally those operating through the Stock Exchange, the Alternative Investment Market ('AIM') and futures exchanges such as the London International Financial Futures Exchange ('LIFFE').

(b) The Investment Management Regulatory Organisation ('IMRO'), which regulates investment and fund managers and advisers, including investment trusts and pension fund managers.

(c) The Personal Investment Authority ('PIA'), which regulates the sale to private investors of investment products such as life assurance and unit trusts.

(Currently, some entities may need to be members of more than one SRO to be authorised if they are carrying out investment business in different markets.)

At the date of writing, the SROs continue to be responsible for discharging their regulatory obligations. However, since 1 June 1998, the FSA has provided, under contract, regulatory services to the SROs, to allow them to meet these obligations. In addition, the staff of all the SROs have become employees of the FSA and are located in the same premises. This gradual transfer of regulatory functions from the SROs to the FSA is intended to culminate in the FSA becoming the single regulator of investment business, across all markets, sometime towards the middle of 2000. The ambit of the FSA's powers under the new regime can be seen in the FSMA. In addition, the FSA has proposed a single integrated set of regulatory standards, to consolidate the current collection of principles, rules and guidance issued by the existing regulatory bodies. It remains to be seen whether the reforms will produce a more effective, streamlined system of financial services regulation. Whilst there may be advantages in terms of economy and consistency, there are concerns as to whether a single set of rules can provide equivalent regulation across the various investment markets.

1.5.1.4 Conduct of investment business

The FSA regulates the conduct of investment business by authorised persons in a number of ways. The most important of these from a corporate finance perspective are:

(a) Through s. 47 it regulates statements and conduct which encourage people to buy investments.

Section 47(1) makes it an offence to induce a person to acquire investments by deliberately or recklessly making misleading, false or deceptive statements, promises or forecasts or dishonestly concealing material facts. A misstatement will effectively need to be fraudulent to fall foul of this section.

Section 47(2) makes it an offence to do any act or engage in any course of conduct which creates a false or misleading impression as to the market or the price or value of any securities if the intention is to create that impression and so induce someone to buy those securities. Reasonable belief that the act or conduct would not create such an impression is a defence. The words 'course of conduct' may cover an omission. One important aspect of this offence is that it is the impression which counts: market perception unsupported by hard facts but based on inferences drawn from what a person has done (or perhaps not done in response to rumours in the market) may be sufficient.

(b) Through s. 57 it regulates advertisements which encourage people to buy or sell investments.

Under s. 57, investment advertisements may be issued or approved for issue only by authorised persons. Most documents issued in the transactions described in this book are likely to be advertisements under the definition of investment advertisement contained in s. 57(2) and the definition of advertisement in s. 207(2) as 'every form of advertising'. The process for an authorised person to approve an advertisement is currently governed by its SRO rules.

Breach of this section is an offence and any agreement entered into as a result of such an advertisement is unenforceable.

There are a whole string of exemptions set out in s. 58 and various statutory instruments (SI 1995/1536 and SI 1996/1586). Listing particulars (see **4.2.5.8**) and prospectuses (see **4.3.1.2**) are exempt. Documents sent by companies to their own shareholders are exempt – this helps rights issue circulars (see **3.6.4**). Advertisements sent to investment or securities professionals only are exempt.

(c) Through s. 56 it regulates unsolicited calls.

These are calls on the telephone or in person made without invitation, for example, attempts made to sell life insurance to you over the telephone or through a visit to the front door. Any agreement relating to investments entered into as a result of such calls is unenforceable. Certain exemptions are available. Professional investors are not protected from such calls and calls to existing customers are exempt.

Under the FSMA there is proposed a single regime for investment advertisements and so-called 'cold-calling'. This is because the distinction between the two is becoming blurred with the use of e-mail and the internet for the promotion of financial products.

1.5.2 BANKING REGULATION

1.5.2.1 Authorisation and supervision of banks

Until recently, the Bank of England was responsible for the authorisation and supervision of UK banks. However, on 1 June 1998, this responsibility was transferred to the FSA. This change was implemented by the Bank of England Act 1998 and is part of the government's aim to have a single regulator of all financial and banking services. To this end, the staff of the supervision and surveillance division of the Bank of England became employees of the FSA.

Under the Bank of England Act 1987, all those who wish to carry on banking business are required to be authorised to do so. Banking business is defined as accepting deposits in the UK whilst carrying on a deposit-taking business anywhere in the world (s. 3 of the Banking Act 1987). A deposit, broadly speaking, is money paid on terms that it will be repaid. To become authorised, a business must show that it will conduct its banking business prudently and that it has a certain amount of minimum net assets. Once authorised, the FSA supervises the operation of the bank. In particular, it oversees capital adequacy (sufficiency of capital reserves against potential losses), liquidity (sufficiency of cash) and large exposures (substantial losses to individual borrowers). These are monitored principally through reporting requirements.

1.5.2.2 The Bank of England

The Bank of England is owned by HM Treasury and governed by the Bank of England Act 1946. It is the UK central bank, in which capacity it manages the UK national debt, the issue of currency and the foreign exchange reserves. It also advises the government on economic and monetary policy. Since 1997, it has had the power to set interest rates.

1.5.3 INSURANCE REGULATION

This is another feature of the regulatory landscape, which is covered here to complete the picture. Once again, we will not be returning to this subject.

The Insurance Companies Act 1982 states that no person shall carry on any insurance business in the United Kingdom unless authorised to do so. Various categories of such business are set out in schs 1 and 2 to the Act. The regulator under the Act is the Department of Trade and Industry ('DTI'). Failure to obtain authorisation when required is an offence.

The DTI sets out to ensure that insurance companies, like banks, have adequate resources available to meet the financial demands placed on them. In addition, the Insurance Companies Act 1982 imposes certain requirements on the conduct of insurance business by those authorised (including such things as the issue of insurance advertisements).

1.6 Regulation of the Securities Market

There are two main markets in company securities. The first of these is the stock market, regulated and supervised by the UKLA and the Stock Exchange. In this section, we shall examine the general roles and functions of the UKLA and the Stock Exchange. In addition, we shall examine the CREST (see **1.6.2**) electronic framework for share trading. The second market is the takeover market. Unlike the stock market, the takeover market is not centred around a formal exchange. However, takeovers are still subject to regulation, in the form of the City Code on Takeovers and Mergers, and governance by the Takeover Panel. The nature of the City Code and the role of the Takeover Panel are also examined below.

1.6.1 THE UK LISTING AUTHORITY

On 1 May 2000, responsibility for the admission of shares to the Official List was transferred from the London Stock Exchange to the FSA, which is now the 'competent authority' for listing under the FS Act. The FSA, in its guise as the UKLA, has re-issued The Listing Rules, the rules under which companies may apply for their securities to be listed and which impose a series of continuing obligations on those companies whose shares are admitted to the Official List. (These rules were formerly issued by the Stock Exchange and were contained in the 'Yellow Book', so named because of its colour. The Listing Rules are now contained in a purple volume, reflecting the corporate colour scheme of the FSA. There is currently little evidence that 'Purple Book' is being used in market parlance.)

As a result of the transfer of responsibility for admission to the FSA, companies wishing to have their securities listed and traded on the Stock Exchange must now apply to the UKLA for admission to listing and to the Stock Exchange for admission to trading (see **1.6.1.2**).

1.6.2 THE STOCK EXCHANGE

The London Stock Exchange, as a term, refers both to the market in which securities are exchanged and to the body which oversees the operation of that market.

1.6.2.1 The market

Looking first at the market, there are a number of separate markets comprised within the Stock Exchange:

(a) the UK equity market, in which shares are bought and sold in UK companies either listed on the Stock Exchange itself or admitted to the Alternative Investment Market (see **4.1.1**);

(b) the international equity market for trading in shares in overseas companies and companies listed on exchanges outside London (such shares can be bought and sold through the Stock Exchange); and

(c) the debt market in which debt securities issued by the government and other bodies (known as 'gilt-edged securities' or 'gilts' for short) are traded.

1.6.2.2 The regulatory body

The Stock Exchange is governed by a Board of Directors, which is assisted by a series of departments. As a body, it has a number of functions:

(a) It admits securities to trading (such securities having been admitted to the Official List by the UKLA) and imposes disclosure requirements to be observed by companies seeking admission whose shares are already traded. These are set out in the Admission and Disclosure Standards issued by the Stock Exchange. Sanctions for breach of these rules include private or public censure, suspension of trading and, ultimately, cancellation of the right to have securities traded.

(b) It monitors share price activity on the equity market to identify evidence of possible insider dealing (see **8.14**).

(c) It regulates those who wish to become members of the Stock Exchange and buy and sell shares through it. These trading members are distinct from the companies listed on the Stock Exchange whose shares are actually bought and sold.

(d) It sets the rules for share trading and the settlement of payment on trades (see **1.6.3**).

(e) It supervises the development and operation of the various computer systems and services needed to support the markets referred to above.

The London Stock Exchange as a market revolves around broker dealers. Often referred to as 'brokers', they act for investors who want to buy and sell securities. Traditionally, brokers have not themselves bought and sold — they have done this through market makers. Market makers (who 'make markets' in the securities they are prepared to buy and sell) are broker dealers who specialise in the dealing function. They quote prices for UK equities through an electronic price display system called SEAQ (Stock Exchange Automated Quotations). The brokers select the appropriate market maker for the shares they want and the market maker trades the shares. This is known as quote-driven trading. Settlement and physical transfer of the shares follow later. The overseas equity market uses a similar system known as SEAQ International.

The Stock Exchange is replacing this system with what is called order-driven trading. This was introduced in October 1997. The system has initially been introduced for trading in the shares of the FTSE 100 index companies but is intended to expand over a period of time to cover more quoted companies. The SEAQ system will be replaced with an automated order book. Investors place orders for the purchase and sale of shares at a stated price through Stock Exchange member firms for inclusion in the order book. Orders will remain on the book until either a counterparty emerges at the desired price (in which case the trade will be executed automatically), the order is cancelled or the order expires. This system known as SETS (Stock Exchange Electronic Trading Service) should enhance the efficiency and price competition of the market. By the end of 1998, around 56 per cent of trades in the FTSE 100 companies were being made through SETS.

Although the London Stock Exchange is the principal market through which equities are traded, Tradepoint was established as a recognised investment exchange in June 1995. This has been set up principally to facilitate secondary market trading between institutional fund managers and broker dealers. This new market enables these institutions to deal directly with each other without using a market maker. The commercial benefit of this is that it should reduce the cost of trading in equities. Issues relating to the regulation of this market are in the process of resolution.

The scale and importance of the London Stock Exchange is illustrated by the fact that the turnover of UK and international equities traded on the Exchange was over £3200 billion in the course of 1998. The average daily turnover of UK equities alone is around £4.1 billion.

1.6.3 CREST

CREST is a computerised system for the settlement of stock transfer transactions on the Stock Exchange. Settlement is the way in which the stock is transferred from seller to buyer and payment is transferred from buyer to seller. CREST commenced operation in July 1996 and has now fully replaced the Talisman, paper-based, system run by the Stock Exchange. It is now a condition for listing that all listed securities of a company incorporated in the United Kingdom should be eligible for electronic settlement. Amongst the intended benefits of CREST are quicker settlement and guaranteed payments to sellers.

1.6.3.1 Uncertificated Securities Regulations 1995

The operation of CREST has been facilitated by the Uncertificated Securities Regulations 1995. These regulations:

(a) set out the legal framework for CREST;

(b) set out the conditions on which companies can allow their securities to participate in CREST;

(c) amend the requirement in s. 207 Companies Act 1985 that shares need to be evidenced by a share certificate, thus allowing shares to be held electronically, in a dematerialised form; and

(d) provide for the transfer of securities without a written instrument such as a stock transfer form.

1.6.3.2 How dematerialised shares can be held in CREST

There are three ways in which a shareholder can hold dematerialised shares in a company through CREST:

(a) as a member;

(b) as a sponsored member; and

(c) through a nominee.

Member

Members are electronically linked to CREST. The cost of this is likely to be prohibitive for small private shareholders. In practice, therefore, members tend to be brokers, market makers and institutions. Each member has an account which records the shares held within the system. Members' names will appear as shareholders on the relevant company's register. A member is required to appoint a settlement bank through which payments on transfers will be made.

Sponsored member

Sponsored members will not be electronically linked to CREST but will use a sponsor (who will be a member of CREST) to provide this service for them. The latter will charge them for this service. Sponsored members will have an account in the same way as members. Their names will also appear as shareholders on the relevant company's register. It is envisaged that those who opt for this method of holding shares in CREST will tend to be the more sophisticated investors, who hold a portfolio of shares and trade on a regular basis.

Nominee route

A shareholder using this route to hold their shares within the system will appoint a nominee who will be a member of CREST. The latter will be electronically linked to CREST and have a nominee account, which can be used for a number of shareholders. Due to this, the nominee route will be the cheapest way in which shares can be held under CREST. However, it will be the name of the nominee CREST member, not that of the shareholder, which will appear on the company' s register. The shareholder will not, therefore, be prima facie entitled to receive shareholder notices and dividends, since these will be directed by the company to the nominee as the shareholder noted on the register. Separate arrangements would have to be made between the nominee and the shareholder to deal with these matters.

It will not be mandatory for a shareholder to hold shares in uncertificated, dematerialised form. The option remains to have a shareholding evidenced by a certificate. The company's register will have to show which shares are certificated and which are dematerialised. Certificated shares are still traded through CREST, although this will be slower and more expensive. This is because such shares will first have to be dematerialised in order to be processed through the system and then rematerialised.

1.6.3.3 Transfers of shares under CREST

If a company decides to make its shares eligible for the system and shareholders decide to hold their shares in one of the uncertificated, dematerialised forms set out above, an electronic record of shareholdings will be held within an account on CREST. Transfers of shares can be made through this account. For example, a private investor holding shares through a nominee will instruct the latter to sell a number of shares. Once the nominee finds a market maker (also a CREST member) to purchase the shares, both the nominee and the market maker electronically send details of the transaction to CREST. The latter matches the messages and checks that the nominee holds sufficient shares within its account to make the sale. On settlement, CREST will instruct the market maker's settlement bank to make a payment to the nominee. It will also instruct the relevant registrar to update the company's register of members. CREST will then update its own accounts.

The Government is currently proposing to issue draft legislation to eliminate the gap between settlement and registration. The intention is that legal title will transfer simultaneously with the settlement of a CREST transaction.

1.6.3.4 Other effects of CREST

The advent of CREST and uncertificated securities has implications for other areas of corporate finance covered in this guide. These include rights issues (see **3.6.4.4**), takeovers (see **8.5.7**) and notification of interests in shares (see **8.11**).

1.6.4 THE TAKEOVER PANEL AND THE CITY CODE ON TAKEOVERS AND MERGERS

The Takeover Panel is not a creature of statute or a government agency. It is not owned by anyone – in fact it is not even a legal entity in its own right. It came into existence in response principally to pressure from the Bank of England, but it is not answerable to the Bank. It occupies part of the Stock Exchange's premises, but that is where the formal relationship with the Stock Exchange ends. The Panel is simply a committee of best practice, designated from within the City by City institutions to oversee the takeover market. This committee draws its members from the various City institutions responsible for its inception and support.

A full-time secretariat has been established to oversee the takeovers market on a regular daily basis. This secretariat is known as the Panel Executive. The Executive is the first line of regulatory supervision and the committee, known now as the full Panel, is the second line – for instance, it is available to be summoned to hear appeals from decisions of the Executive (see **8.8.6**).

The nature of the City Code is itself sometimes a source of confusion. The Code began life as a set of guidelines agreed by the same City institutions that set up the Panel, to constitute best practice in the conduct of takeovers. This was a response to questionable activities which took place in the almost unregulated takeover market in the early 1950s. Since these guidelines were not very successful at preventing further takeover-related scandals in the 1960s, these City institutions, at the behest of the Bank of England, revised the guidelines and simultaneously established the Takeover Panel as their 'authoritative interpreter'.

Since then, the Code has expanded enormously and the Takeover Panel has changed in character, but there has been no fundamental shift in the basic nature of the Code. It is not law. It has never been given any direct legal effect by statute in the way the Stock Exchange's Listing Rules have (see **4.2.5.1**). It remains essentially a set of principles as to best practice in these transactions, now regularly updated and refined by the Takeover Panel. The Code is therefore best described as a self-regulatory system. Importantly, though, the City Code and all its Rules (discussed in much more detail in **8.8**) are treated by takeover practitioners and companies operating in the market *as if they have the force of law*, and the Takeover Panel as if it carried the weight and firepower of any other regulatory authority. This system is currently under threat from the proposed Thirteenth Company Law Directive (see **8.8.8**).

There are other financial services and securities markets operating in the City which there is simply not time to consider as they cover fields outside the scope of this book. We have looked at only those elements of the regulatory superstructure which relate most directly to the major aspects of corporate finance activity.

Before we move on, let us look at the work of the lawyer caught in the middle of such a system.

1.7 Regulation and the Role of Lawyers

1.7.1 INTERPRETATION

Advising clients of the meaning and application of the rules in a given situation is the primary skill a lawyer will be expected to exercise. Many of these regulations, though, cannot be viewed or interpreted as a lawyer would view or interpret ordinary statute.

The first reason for this is that they are simply not law in the classical sense. Many are rules which operate like club rules; some are the distillation of best practice. They are not written to be treated like statutes.

The second reason is that, as we have seen, breach of the rules rarely gives rise to either criminal or civil liability. The sanctions are at the behest of the regulators. This is explained further below.

The third reason is that regulators may not draft to the standards of Parliamentary drafting.

These three factors mean lawyers have to take a different approach when interpreting regulation. The approach must be to discern the intention behind the regulation. The interpretative discipline is purposive, not literal. When you consider that generally the sanctions are exercised at the discretion of the regulator, there is really no point in attempting cleverly to circumvent a rule through a deftly constructed argument about its language. If the regulator considers that the spirit of the rule has been flouted, that will be conclusive. When you add to this the other factors mentioned above, there is really no alternative but to suspend classic legalistic analysis and concentrate on the underlying objective of the rule in deciding whether your client's conduct will be acceptable.

Where, however, you are dealing with a statute, normal principles of interpretation apply.

1.7.2 UNDERSTANDING THE MARKET

Since the rules are written to make the relevant market operate prudently, efficiently and fairly, to understand and therefore interpret the rule properly, you need to understand the market. To determine whether your client's proposals or conduct can be accommodated within the rules, you need to understand the nature of what your client wants to do. Getting to grips with the commercial background to the transactions and the markets is consequently absolutely fundamental to the work of the lawyer, hence the focus of this book.

1.7.3 COMPLIANCE

An inevitable role the lawyer is called on to play, alongside that of the interpreter, is that of the compliance officer. Has the client done everything required of him by the rule book? Has everything gone into the relevant document that should be in the document? At times this is laborious and tedious as it requires a checklist mentality. It is nevertheless a crucial task – you are paid to be painstaking.

1.7.4 JUGGLING THE RULES

We have seen an array of different rules from different regulators. Sometimes they intersect, overlap or run parallel to each other. You need to keep all these balls in the air at the same time and not lose sight of any of them. You cannot just be a master of the City Code when doing a public company takeover: you need to understand, amongst other things, the application of The Listing Rules and the FS Act to the transaction. The checklist below will help you to know what is relevant. Advising on regulation is above all the art of the juggler.

Central to corporate finance work is the company which is raising or using its finance. Central to the functioning of a company is its management, owners and those who advise it professionally. We have now seen something of the regulatory superstructure: let us turn our attention to a specific area where regulation plays an important role, and which is relevant in all the transactions which are the subject of this book – the regulation of the governance of the company.

Table 1.1 Who will be the regulator?

	Activity	*Regulator and regulations*	*References*
1	Is investment business to be carried out?	FSA, SRO (Financial Services Act 1986; FSA and SRO rule books)	The FS Act is of major importance in corporate finance work and is covered in **1.5.1** above.
2	Is banking business to be carried out?	FSA (Banking Act 1987 and Bank of England Act 1998)	Banking regulation as a subject in detail is outside the scope of this book. The basic structure of the banking regulatory system is covered below.

	Activity	*Regulator and regulations*	*References*
3	Is insurance business to be carried out?	DTI (Insurance Companies Act 1982)	Insurance regulation as a subject in detail is outside the scope of this book. The basic structure of insurance regulation is covered below.
4	Is a company to be formed?	Registrar of Companies (Companies Act 1985)	The regulation of public companies, insofar as it is different from that applying to companies more generally, is introduced below.
5	Are securities to be issued?	Registrar of Companies (ss. 80 to 89 Companies Act 1985)	This is covered in the *LPC Guide: Business Law.*
6a	Is the company already listed on the London Stock Exchange or admitted to the Alternative Investment Market?	UKLA London Stock Exchange AIM (The Listing Rules) (Stock Exchange Admission and Disclosure Standards) (AIM Rules)	A listing or admission to the AIM for a company doing an issue of securities means there are continuing obligations to observe – see **4.2.10** and **4.3.5.2**.
6b		Investment Committees (IPC Guidelines)	A listed company doing a securities issue must also consider the Investment Committee guidelines (see **3.3.1.3**); the Committees are described below.
7	Is there to be an offer to the public?	Registrar of Companies London Stock Exchange (Public Offers of Securities Regulations 1995) (as amended by the Public Offers of Securities (Amendment) Regulations 1999)	An offer to the public is discussed in **3.5**.
8	Are the securities to be admitted to the AIM?	London Stock Exchange (Public Offers of Securities Regulations 1995) (as amended by the Public Offers of Securities (Amendment) Regulations 1999) (AIM Rules)	The Alternative Investment Market regulation is discussed in **4.3**; the Stock Exchange administers the AIM.

	Activity	*Regulator and regulations*	*References*
9	Are the securities to be listed on the London Stock Exchange?	UKLA (Part IV FS Act) (The Listing Rules) London Stock Exchange (Stock Exchange Admission and Disclosure Standards)	Obtaining a listing is discussed in **4.2**; the UKLA's and the Stock Exchange's overall function is described above.
10	Is the company listed and making a substantial acquisition or disposal?	UKLA (The Listing Rules) London Stock Exchange (Stock Exchange Admission and Disclosure Standards)	Any listed company must observe the UKLA and Stock Exchange requirements.
11	Is there a substantial acquisition of shares?	Takeover Panel (Substantial Acquisitions Rules) (Part VI Companies Act 1985)	The Takeover Panel administers the Substantial Acquisitions Rules (SARs). These are described in **8.9**. The Takeover Panel is discussed above. Part VI of the Companies Act 1985 is discussed in **8.11**.
12	Is a public company being acquired?	Takeover Panel (City Code)	The Takeover Panel is responsible for the City Code on Takeovers and Mergers. It is mentioned above and in much more detail in **8.8.5**.
13a	Is there a referable merger?	Office of Fair Trading, Competition Commission (Fair Trading Act 1973)	The merger control regime in the UK is discussed in **8.16**.
13b	Or a concentration with a Community dimension or n anti-competitive arrangement or abuse of a dominant position?	European Commission (EC Merger Regulation; arts 81 and 82 Treaty of Rome (formerly arts 85 and 86))	The EC merger control regime is explained in **8.16.2**.

TWO

CORPORATE GOVERNANCE

Public companies have a wider range of opportunities open to them than private companies. They may offer their shares to the public. Their shares may be traded on the stock market. These offer the benefits of greater access to sources of finance. But they come at a price, in the form of more rigorous regulatory obligations. These tougher demands affect everyone connected with the company: the company itself, its directors, its shareholders and its advisers.

2.1 Companies Act Regulation for Public Companies

The Companies Act 1985 applies of course as much to public companies as to private companies. There are, though, a number of additional requirements imposed on public companies by the Act which do not apply to private companies, and a number of requirements imposed on all companies but more stringently on public companies. This section contains only a summary of some of the most important – many of these are covered in detail later on.

The abiding policy underlying all these provisions is to build in extra safeguards for investors, given the greater liabilities likely to be assumed by public companies.

2.1.1 SHARE CAPITAL REQUIREMENTS

Section 117 of the Companies Act 1985 prohibits a public company (unless it has converted from being a private company) from trading without a certificate from the Registrar of Companies, which he will only issue if the company has the authorised minimum share capital of £50,000 (s. 118). At least one-quarter of the nominal value of the shares must be paid up (s. 101).

2.1.2 PAYMENT FOR SHARES

Public companies cannot accept payment for shares in the form of an undertaking from a person to perform work or services (s. 99) – the risks are that such an undertaking may never be performed and that its value is intangible and may be difficult to compare with the value of a share.

Non-cash payments for shares in public companies are not allowed if they are subject to an undertaking to be fulfilled more than five years after allotment (s. 102). This strikes at payment by way of assets to be transferred to the company in the future, as these assets may decline in value.

Non-cash payments for shares in a public company must in any event be valued under s. 103. Exceptions exist where the company is issuing its shares in exchange for shares in another company (s. 103(3)) or is merging with another company by acquiring all its assets and liabilities (s. 103(5)). Section 108 sets out the required valuation procedure. Though often a mere formality this is time-consuming and expensive. Companies generally seek to avoid it wherever possible. In practice, for acquisitions or takeovers involving the issue of shares as consideration, the two exceptions mentioned usually provide the escape route needed.

2.1.3 DIRECTORS

Public companies must have at least two directors (s. 282), while private companies can have one. Other regulatory impositions to which directors of public companies are subject are covered in **2.2**.

2.1.4 MAINTENANCE OF CAPITAL

If a public company's net assets are half or less of its called-up share capital, the directors must call a meeting of shareholders to consider what to do (s. 142). This became a common phenomenon in the recession when property companies in particular had to devalue their assets substantially. At the general meeting, directors will usually seek approval from shareholders for their strategy for survival.

2.1.5 FINANCIAL ASSISTANCE FOR THE ACQUISITION OF SHARES

Two additional restrictions apply to public companies. The first is that a public company cannot take advantage of the so-called 'whitewash' procedure under ss. 155 to 158. The second is that the exemptions under s. 153 (for example, permitting financial assistance for an employee share scheme) apply to a public company only if it does not thereby reduce its net assets, or it provides such assistance out of distributable profits. The financial assistance restrictions are discussed in more detail in **8.12**.

2.1.6 PURCHASES OF OWN SHARES

Companies may buy back their own shares under certain conditions. A public company may not do so out of capital, unlike private companies (s. 171).

2.1.7 DISTRIBUTIONS

A public company may pay dividends only if the amount of its net assets is not thereby reduced to less than the value of its share capital and undistributable reserves (s. 264). This prevents public companies from paying out dividends against unrealised profits made from their assets, such as revised property values.

2.1.8 ACCOUNTS

A public company must put its annual accounts and directors' report to a general meeting, usually the AGM, and send them to the Registrar of Companies within seven months of the end of its accounting reference period (or six months if the company is listed on the London Stock Exchange), not 10 months as in the case of a private company (s. 244). The relaxations from the accounting requirements for small and medium-sized companies in s. 246 do not apply to public companies.

2.1.9 NOTIFICATION OF INTERESTS IN SHARES

Shareholders acquiring an interest in 3 per cent or more (or in some cases 10 per cent or more) of a public company's shares must notify the company within two days (s. 198). This requirement and the ensuing provisions are designed to help the company identify substantial and possibly hostile shareholders on its register. They are covered in much more detail in the context of takeovers (see **8.11**), when they are particularly important.

2.2 Statutory and Regulatory Controls on Public Company Directors

Directors face an array of duties and controls at common law and under statute. These have already been examined in *LPC Business Law*. This chapter looks at the additional regulatory restrictions to which directors of publicly traded companies are subject.

Broadly, these additional regulatory controls on directors affect two things: their dealings in securities and the composition and functioning of their own boards.

2.2.1 DIRECTORS' DEALINGS: DISCLOSURE

You will already be familiar with what the Companies Act 1985 requires of a director and his family when he or it owns, acquires or sells securities in his company or group company: s. 324 and associated provisions require notification of such transactions to the company and the maintenance of a register which may be inspected by the public. In addition, the directors' annual report must effectively relay to shareholders the information regarding directors' shareholding interests in the company or its group companies.

Where the company is listed, and the director notifies the company under s. 324 of a relevant interest, the company must transmit this to the Stock Exchange (s. 329) and the Stock Exchange publishes such data to the market through its Regulatory News Service. Furthermore, The Listing Rules (para. 12.43(k)) ask that the annual report for a listed company distinguishes between each director's beneficial and non-beneficial interests in the company's securities so that shareholders can get some idea of the voting control which directors actually have.

These provisions ensure a degree of transparency in directors' dealings in their own or related companies. The concern remains that directors, given their access to so much privileged information about these companies, should be allowed to deal in their securities in the first place.

2.2.2 DIRECTORS' DEALINGS: PROHIBITIONS

Again, we have already seen in the *LPC Guide: Business Law* and later in **8.14** how the Criminal Justice Act 1993 remedies this by making it an offence for directors to deal in their company's securities where they possess inside information about it, and for them to pass on such information improperly.

As far as listed companies are concerned, however, the UKLA is concerned that directors are seen to be above suspicion in their share dealings. Preserving the integrity of the market is crucial. Acting on inside information erodes that integrity. Directors are most obviously party to inside information, and so the UKLA has a rigorous code to clamp down on the freedom of directors to deal in their own company's securities. The UKLA is not out to prevent directors holding shares in their companies – in fact, this is something it encourages, as it (a) gives their directors a stake in the future of their companies as owners as well as managers, and (b) it is healthy for the company as it sends out positive signals to investors about its directors' view of its investment potential. There must be no suggestion that these shareholdings are acquired or sold with the benefit of privileged information.

2.2.2.1 The Model Code (on directors' dealings in securities)

The Listing Rules, accordingly, contain the Model Code which is to be found in the appendix to ch. 16. To use The Listing Rules' own language, it 'imposes restrictions beyond those that are imposed by law'.

A listed company must, by para. 16.18 of The Lisiting Rules, require its directors to comply with a code of dealing in terms no less exacting than those of the Model Code. The same duty extends to requiring compliance by employees who are not directors but are likely to possess unpublished price-sensitive information about the company. In each case, the company must take all proper and reasonable steps to secure compliance. Para. 16.18 should therefore be seen as a continuing obligation of the company.

The rules in the Model Code provide that the director of a listed company should not deal (i.e., essentially, buy, sell or exercise an option) in his own company's securities (which are traded on the Stock Exchange or the Alternative Investment Market) where he has unpublished price-sensitive information about the company. In addition, he should not deal in his company's securities in the two-month period before annual or half-yearly results are announced. Any dealing must in any event receive clearance from the company chairman or a director appointed to do this job. In addition to these 'close periods', clearance will be refused when the dealing would take place after the need for an announcement to the market of unpublished price-sensitive information about the company has become reasonably probable. A director may, however, sell securities to meet a 'pressing financial commitment'. This would have to be exceptional to qualify.

Where a director advises a company that he intends to deal in shares, the company must maintain a written record of such advice and any clearance given. The company must also provide the director with written confirmation that such recording has taken place.

Where directors cannot themselves deal, they must seek to prohibit such dealings by their families and connected persons (Companies Act 1985 definition – see s. 346) and various other institutions connected with them, such as their investment managers.

The Model Code also provides for a series of exceptions to its terms including an exercise of share options during a prohibited period but approved beforehand, and taking up entitlements under a rights issue (see **3.6.4**).

The point of real importance is that the UKLA is looking for compliance with the spirit, and not simply the letter, of the Code.

2.2.2.2 What if the Model Code is breached?

A breach of the Code will give rise to the same consequences as would apply to non-observance of any of The Listing Rules (on which see **4.2.10**). Note in particular that the failure by a director to discharge his responsibilities under the Model Code may lead to censure by the UKLA and possibly suspension or cancellation of listing (para. 1.8).

Of course, a breach of the Model Code may be a breach of the insider dealing legislation in the Criminal Justice Act 1993, which carries much more serious connotations. This will not always be the case, though, given that the Code's provisions are more extensive than the legislation, and certainly a breach of the Model Code is not to be treated as a presumption of insider dealing. A technical breach of the Code does occasionally arise as a result of a dealing within one of the prohibited periods by an institution connected with the director, often because of a misinterpretation of the application of the Code (and the provisions are certainly quite complex) – but no insider dealing offence will have been committed.

By the same token it is dangerous to assume that compliance with the Model Code will automatically take particular conduct outside the insider dealing regime or act in any way as a defence to charges brought under it. Passing information on outside the course of the director's employment is not a breach of the Code but may fall foul of the Criminal Justice Act 1993.

2.2.3 CORPORATE GOVERNANCE: THE COMBINED CODE

2.2.3.1 Introduction

Listed companies are required to state in their annual report and accounts the extent to which they have applied the principles and provisions set out in section 1 of the Combined Code ('the Code'). The Code is a set of principles of good governance and code of best practice prepared by the Committee on Corporate Governance chaired by Sir Ronald Hampel, and published in June 1998. They are appended to, but do not form part of, the Listing Rules.

The Code is effectively a consolidation of the work of three committees, each taking their name from the relevant chairman: Cadbury, Greenbury and Hampel. The Cadbury Committee reported in 1992, producing a code to govern financial reporting and aspects of management. This was followed, in July 1995, by the Greenbury Code on good practice in relation to the determination of directors' remuneration. The Hampel Committee produced a set of principles and a code which embraced the two earlier codes and the committee's own work. From this, following some changes made by the Stock Exchange, has come the Code.

2.2.3.2 Content of the Code

The Code comprises two sections, each of which contains a number of principles. In relation to nearly all of the principles, there are then a number of provisions dealing in more detail with the relevant area. Section 1 of the Code contains the corporate governance principles and provisions. These can be summarised as follows:

(a) *The Board*

Every listed company should be headed by an effective board which should lead and control the company.

The roles of chairman of the board and chief executive of the company should, if possible, be separate. If this is not the case, the company should be able to justify publicly the decision to combine the roles. Also, there should be a strong, independent non-executive element on the board, with a recognisable senior member other than the chairman.

The board should have a balance of executive and non-executive directors such that no individual director or group of directors can dominate the decision-making process.

The board should be supplied in a timely manner with information in a form and of a quality appropriate to enable it to discharge its duties.

There should be a formal and transparent procedure for the appointment of new directors to the board, involving (unless the board is small) a nomination committee.

All directors should be required to resubmit themselves for re-election at regular intervals and at least every three years.

(b) *Directors' remuneration*

Levels of remuneration should be sufficient to attract and retain the directors needed to run the company successfully, but companies should avoid paying more than is necessary. A proportion of executive directors' remuneration should be structured so as to link rewards to the performance of the company and the individual director.

There should be established a formal and transparent procedure for developing policy on executive remuneration and for fixing the remuneration packages of individual directors. This should involve the setting-up of a remuneration committee of independent non-executive directors to make recommendations to the board.

The company's annual report should contain a statement of remuneration policy and details of the remuneration of each director.

(c) *Relations with shareholders*

Companies should, where practicable, be prepared to enter into dialogue with institutional shareholders based on the mutual understanding of objectives.

Boards should use the AGM to communicate with private investors and encourage their participation.

(d) *Accountability and audit*

The board should present a balanced and understandable assessment of the company's position and prospects.

The board should maintain a sound system of internal control to safeguard shareholders' investment and the company's assets.

The board should establish formal and transparent arrangements for considering how they should apply the financial reporting and internal control principles, and for maintaining an appropriate relationship with the company's auditors.

Appendices to the Code set out provisions on the design of performance related remuneration and the contents of the remuneration report to be presented in the company's annual report.

Section 2 of the Code contains principles and provisions applicable to institutional shareholders with regard to their voting, dialogue with companies and evaluation of a company's corporate governance arrangements.

2.2.3.3 Compliance with the Code

Paragraph 12.43A of the Listing Rules requires all listed companies incorporated in the UK to include in their annual report and accounts:

(a) a narrative statement of how it has applied the principles set out in Section 1 of the Code, providing an explanation which enables shareholders to evaluate how the principles have been applied; and

(b) a statement either confiming that it has complied with the Code provisions or, where it does not, giving reasons for such non-compliance.

In addition, paragraph 12.43A(c) requires companies to report to shareholders on directors' remuneration, giving details of, *inter alia*, the following:

— the company's policy on executive directors' remuneration

— the amount of each element of each director's remuneration package (including salary, benefits in kind and bonuses)

— share options for each director

— any service contracts with notice periods in excess of one year

— early retirement rights and options

Companies are not required to report on whether and how they have complied with the provisions set out in Section 2 of the Code. It was thought that the matters covered in this section were inappropriate to be included within the Listing Rules disclosure requirements. However it is hoped that at least major institutions will disclose to their clients and the public the extent to which they are able to give effect to the provisions of Section 2.

The overall intention is that the Code and the Listing Rules reporting requirements should together result in high standards of corporate governance, transparent to shareholders and other outsiders. The main area where reporting requirements have been made more onerous is that of directors' remuneration. Where previously companies were only required to state that they had considered the Greenbury guidelines in formulating their remuneration policy, they are now required to state how they have applied all the principles. However, it should be remembered that the Code does not form part of the Listing Rules: only the reporting requirements are mandatory. Surveys on the earlier codes showed that many companies were either ignoring guidelines or complying with them only to a limited extent. Companies have been loath to put their remuneration policies before shareholders: it remains to see whether the Code will change this.

2.2.4 COMPOSITION OF THE BOARD: NON-EXECUTIVE DIRECTORS

In addition to the Code, we should also consider PRONED's Guide to Recommended Practice on Non-Executive Directors. PRONED, the Promotion of Non-Executive Directors, exists to do exactly what its name suggests and offer non-executive directors guidance on performance of their functions. Its Guide is no more than a code of best practice, and it acknowledges that it is primarily designed for directors of listed companies (though its principles extend to other companies as well). Non-compliance brings with it no sanctions, but it is a set of criteria to which your corporate clients will pay some attention, and so it is advisable to be familiar with it in outline.

Much of the Guide reflects what is in the Code. Where the Guide supplements what is in the Code, it recommends that:

(a) as they have a contribution to make to the development of corporate strategy and can give independent advice in situations where the board's interests might otherwise be in conflict with those of shareholders (examples are takeover offers and management buy-outs), they should be involved in the board's affairs and kept properly informed;

(b) there should be an element among the non-executive directors which is clearly independent of the existing board or shareholders (though there may be non-executives who retain an allegiance of some description to board or shareholders);

(c) there should be at least three non-executives, and independent non-executives should comprise at least one-third of the board;

(d) non-executive directors should be appointed for an initial period of three years, renewable for a further three-year term if agreed.

The Guide therefore is another source to be considered when advising either companies or their non-executives on their appointment and functions.

2.2.6 OTHER RESTRICTIONS

Directors are subject to a number of other regulatory constraints on their conduct which are addressed elsewhere in this book and so are mentioned here only for the sake of completeness:

(a) Any transaction between a listed company and one of its directors or his associates will be classified as a transaction with a related party under The Listing Rules (ch. 11). Typically, this will catch sales of assets to directors or their associates by listed companies. Exceptions include an issue of shares or options to a director by his company, or a company giving a director an indemnity. Small transactions are also exempt. If the transaction is caught, a circular to shareholders and their consent in general meeting will normally be required (unless the UKLA is prepared to grant a waiver). This subject is covered in more detail in **5.6.4.1**.

(b) Any securities offering or takeover by a company will require the issue of some sort of public document regarding the transaction (prospectus, listing particulars or an offer document respectively). The UKLA and Takeover Panel respectively require the directors of the company to accept and declare publicly their responsibility for these documents on their face. The precise effect this has on their legal liability is considered in **4.2.5.7**. The point to note for the time being is that the regulators place directors firmly in the firing-line in these major corporate finance transactions, irrespective of executive or non-executive status. This provides a useful stick (or carrot, depending on your point of view) with which occasionally to remind directors of the importance of their role in these transactions.

These points are in addition to any relevant statutory obligations directors may face.

2.3 The Role of Shareholders in Corporate Governance

There are two aspects to this:

(a) the regulation of shareholder activity in the affairs of a public company; and

(b) the influence which shareholders can exert over the affairs of a public company.

2.3.1 THE REGULATION OF SHAREHOLDER ACTIVITY IN PUBLIC COMPANIES

Although it seems less obvious, since good corporate governance is intended primarily for the benefit of shareholders, they too are subject to laws and regulations which aim to assist the effective and fair management of corporations. There are two particular areas to note:

(a) The provisions of the Companies Act 1985 which deal with the notification by shareholders of interests they hold in shares in public companies (ss. 198 to 220). These have nothing to do with the obligation of directors to disclose their own or their families' interests under s. 324 Companies Act 1985 and related provisions. Sections 198 to 220 are examined in **8.11**. Their purpose is to help companies keep a close eye on developments on their share registers, so that any potentially controlling influence can be speedily identified. This is supported by the information requirement in The Listing Rules, para. 12.43(1), that any shareholding interest of 3 per cent or more in a listed company be disclosed in the annual report and accounts.

(b) The provisions in The Listing Rules described in **2.2.5** regarding transactions with related parties (between listed companies and their directors) apply equally to transactions between such companies and their substantial shareholders or their associates. Substantial shareholders are those currently holding, or in the past year, held a 10 per cent interest or more in the company. The idea of this is to offer smaller shareholders the right to object to deals involving their company which favour larger shareholders. Similar exemptions to those mentioned in **5.6.4.1** apply, including that for small transactions.

2.3.2 INVESTMENT COMMITTEES

These are committees of the Association of British Insurers ('ABI') and the National Association of Pension Funds ('NAPF'). The ABI is the trade body for the insurance company market, the NAPF the equivalent for pension funds. They are very large organisations – the ABI comprises over 450 insurance companies. They were formed to represent the interests of their members, and these interests include their substantial holdings of shares in UK-listed companies. Though there has been a very significant growth in recent years in the number of private investors holding shares, the total number of shares held by private individuals has declined as institutional share ownership has increased. Roughly 80 per cent of all listed shares in the UK were held by institutional shareholders in 1993.

These stakes are held for investment purposes. The investment potential of shareholdings can be affected quite significantly by such things as fresh issues of shares, as these dilute the value of existing shares, and repurchases of shares, which require the company to spend money it might otherwise distribute by way of dividend. Hence the Investment Committees seek to capitalise on their powerful and often controlling position in listed companies by issuing guidelines expressing their members' views on questions such as new issues of shares (see **3.3.1.3**) and share repurchases. The Committees will also indicate their views on such aspects of corporate governance as the acceptability of proposed revisions to articles of association (which will of course require shareholder approval).

The nature of these guidelines is to alert companies to situations which the associations are likely to find unacceptable, so that a negotiation can be initiated with the association to arrive at a compromise. Sometimes the Committees insist on their guidelines being observed. The sanction they can exercise is their members voting against a resolution required to approve the proposed action. The guidelines are therefore of real concern to listed companies with significant numbers of institutional shareholders, though in practice they are usually observed by all listed companies.

2.4 The Role of Advisers in Corporate Governance

Advisers may seem an odd category of person to whom corporate governance principles should apply, for they are neither manager nor owner of the company. They do, though, play a significant and sometimes crucial role in its management and development and it is therefore in the company's best interests that this role is exercised responsibly.

You will already have seen in the *LPC Guide: Business Law* various legal provisions which affect the activities of a company's advisers.

2.4.1 NEGLIGENCE

There is obviously the influence of the common law duty to take reasonable care in the advice proffered. This is considered particularly in the context of equity issues in **4.2.5.7**. Auditors have no greater duty than any other adviser, but their duty of care has recently been the subject of judicial analysis in cases referred to in that section.

2.4.2 SHADOW DIRECTORS

Statute imposes certain duties. Any adviser may be found to be a shadow director where the directors of the company are accustomed to act in accordance with the adviser's instructions or directions (s. 741 Companies Act 1985). This brings with it the liabilities associated with acting as a director. Accordingly, advisers would be well advised themselves to issue advice to their corporate clients in their professional capacity only and to take no managerial or supervisory role in the company's operations.

2.4.3 AUDITORS

Auditors are under a statutory duty pursuant to s. 237 Companies Act 1985 to carry out investigations into, and report on the propriety of, the company's accounting records.

Section 235 requires auditors to report in particular on whether the company's balance sheet and profit and loss account at the end of each financial year give a true and fair view respectively of its state of affairs and profit and loss.

In the past, the accountancy profession established a series of accounting standards to assist the profession in determining what is true and fair. These are SSAPs, or Statements of Standard Accounting Practice. They are not law, but the major professional accounting bodies, such as the Institute of Chartered Accountants, will penalise any accountants who do not follow them. Essentially, therefore, they are statements as to best practice for auditors and their corporate clients, supported by the certainty of disciplinary action in the event of non-compliance.

Like all such statements, they are capable of differing interpretations, and this has given rise to considerable debate about the accuracy of some public companies' financial statements. In an attempt to improve public confidence in the quality of financial reporting, a new self-regulatory regime was introduced in 1990, under which the Accounting Standards Board (ASB) has become responsible for the issue of new standards. These standards are called Financial Reporting Standards (FRSs). They are the contemporary equivalent of SSAPs. The old SSAPs have stayed in existence and are still referred to as SSAPs. FRSs have no greater legal effect than SSAPs.

Should a company depart from the SSAPs or FRSs, a Financial Reporting Review Panel (FRRP) may question and examine such a policy and publicise any such departures. The FRRP is part of the same self-regulatory regime to which the ASB belongs. Statutory procedures exist under ss. 245A–C of the Companies Act 1985 to enable the Secretary of State for Trade and Industry or the FRRP to obtain a court order stating that a company's accounts do not comply with the Act and requiring the preparation of revised accounts. This supports the FRRP's enforcement role. Companies and their auditors will seek to avoid such public exposure of possible peculiarities in their accounting records, and this strengthens the regulators' arm in ensuring the 'true and fair view'.

2.4.4 INSIDER DEALING

Advisers are in a privileged position. They have access to confidential information about the company's strategy, products, financial status and so on. They could obviously benefit from that information if they chose. The Criminal Justice Act 1993 extends as much to them as to directors of companies. It prohibits advisers with access to information from dealing in securities of the company, and prevents them from passing the information on otherwise than in the proper performance of their job. Certain exceptions apply which will assist dealings by advisers in connection with certain transactions by the company in which they have been instructed to act, for example, acquisitions or disposals (see **8.14** where this is explained fully).

2.4.5 PROFESSIONAL STANDARDS

The regulatory authorities expect advisers to act with probity and the highest standards of professionalism and care.

The Listing Rules indicate the importance the UKLA attaches to the role of a company's sponsor when it seeks admission to listing: this is examined in much more detail in **3.3.4**.

The City Code on Takeovers and Mergers (r. 3) stresses the importance of independent and competent professional advice for both sides in the course of a takeover bid.

Breaches of either the City Code or The Listing Rules are taken very seriously by the self-regulatory authorities which supervise the investment business activities of member firms under the Financial Services Act 1986 (see **1.5.1.2**). Almost all merchant banks are members of the Securities and Futures Authority. Accountants and lawyers are regulated by their own professional bodies, which impose demanding standards of professional care on their members and take disciplinary action against them in the event of misconduct.

All these elements reinforce the common law remedies available to companies which receive negligent or incompetent advice or are the victims of malpractice.

THREE

SECURITIES OFFERINGS

This chapter considers the various ways in which securities are offered to investors by companies raising finance from the stock market. These offerings may be by companies which do not yet have their shares traded on the market and which may therefore seek approval to have them admitted to the market at the same time as they offer them to the public. This is generally referred to as a 'primary offering'. Once their shares are admitted and trading, further issues of shares to raise additional capital are called 'secondary offerings'. This chapter looks at both types of offering.

The company will need to address at an early stage of any primary offering the question of which market it wants to join. In the UK, it is a choice between the Stock Exchange (a 'full listing' as it is sometimes described) and the Alternative Investment Market ('AIM'). The choice and considerations relevant to each are discussed in **chapter 4**, as are the risks and legal liabilities attendant on these public share issues.

A preliminary subject to address is the nature of the securities the company is offering.

3.1 What are 'Securities'?

'Securities' is not a term defined in the Companies Act 1985, though definitions exist in the Stock Transfer Act 1963 and the Criminal Justice Act 1993 which broadly include shares, stocks, debentures, bonds, warrants, options and the like. In general commercial usage, a security is some form of instrument representing an interest in a company. In ordinary company law terms, we are most likely to think of a share or a debenture when the term 'security' is used. The instrument here is the share or stock certificate representing the interest held by the investor in the company. The nature of that interest will vary, depending on the type of security in question.

The security the investor gets is literally the security of something in return for cash. The security is a necessary evil for the company. Ideally, the company would like to be given money for nothing! In reality, it has to give something back to the investor by way of rights or entitlements as a means of attracting capital in the first place.

We will look here at some of the questions relevant when choosing one type of security to issue rather than another.

The basic choice is between debt or equity, though we will see later how this boundary may be blurred.

3.1.1 DEBT

The characteristics of a debt instrument are primarily a defined life and an agreed interest rate, referred to as the coupon. Debt is capital which is paid over on the understanding that it will be repaid (or redeemed) at a fixed point in time and in priority to shareholders on a winding up. That understanding is usually recorded in a contract between investor and issuer, and sometimes that contract may provide for an element of security in the form of a charge over assets. More usually, debt instruments will be unsecured.

A typical debt instrument in the UK market is loan stock. This is something like a single huge debenture carved into a number of separate debentures, each issued individually to different investors. A trustee is appointed to represent the collective interests of the assorted stockholders and ensure that the company complies with its obligations. A price may be quoted for the loan stock on the stock market so it can be traded.

A loan stock may be convertible into ordinary shares (see below) of the company. This is usually at the choice of the holder of the loan stock, who may choose to exercise this right when the ordinary shares are appreciating faster than the return on the loan stock.

Just as shares fluctuate in value on the stock market relative to both their nominal value and issue price, so traded debt instruments will at any point in time be worth more or less than their basic value at redemption, depending on the interest rate they carry in the current market and the underlying value of the company which issued them.

3.1.2 EQUITY

Equity does not have to be repaid to investors, save on a winding up (and even then shareholders usually come last in the priority of claims). The finance paid by an equity investor is available to the company for all time – unlike the finite life of debt capital. This has obvious attractions for the company.

The attraction of equity to an investor is the prospect of a return through a dividend, essentially a distribution from available profit, and capital appreciation of the equity interest (or share) as the company's performance improves. Ordinarily, there is no legal entitlement to receive a dividend. If the profit is not there to pay one out, the investor has no claim on the company. The dividend will be paid out after the company has met its interest payment obligation on outstanding debt.

Equity comes in a number of different forms.

3.1.2.1 Ordinary shares

As well as the right to receive a dividend when it is declared, and the right to receive on a winding up the proportion of capital represented by the size of the equity interest, an ordinary share also carries the right to vote at shareholders' meetings. Occasionally, a company may choose to have different classes of ordinary shares to represent different rights – this may be useful in a joint venture company (see **chapter 6**) or where family members wish to retain enhanced voting rights. For companies seeking admission to the Official List, it is as well to be aware that the UKLA and the Investment Committees do not like a share capital structure in which some of the shares carry restricted voting rights (though the possibility of that is specifically contemplated in The Listing Rules, 6.B.5).

Ordinary shares may be issued as redeemable so that the shares may be bought back by the company. Sometimes the price and date of this redemption is fixed at the time of issue, though this is unusual (see **9.8**).

The great majority of shares traded on the Stock Exchange are ordinary shares. Usually the liquidity in the preference share market is quite low. This tends to depress their share price in comparison with the much more extensive market for ordinary shares. Ordinary shares may therefore have more appeal to the investor.

3.1.2.2 Preference shares

Holders of preference shares are entitled to receive a fixed dividend in priority to ordinary shareholders. This dividend is usually based on a percentage of the nominal value of the shares. It is also cumulative so that if the company has insufficient profits to pay out one year the right accumulates until there is enough money to satisfy the deferred entitlements. In practice, this cumulative right is attractive to companies as they are not obliged to pay out a dividend every year (as compared with the need to make an annual interest payment on debt instruments). Of course, deferring the dividend payment is often unpopular with the shareholder.

Preference shares also generally precede ordinary shares in the priority of claims in a winding up of the company if this is expressly provided in the terms of issue.

Preference shares may also be redeemable, that is, they can be bought back at some date in the future at their nominal value (i.e., a fixed price). They will then generally carry a lower dividend as the guarantee of redemption is felt to be a significant investment inducement.

Preference shares may be convertible into ordinary shares at a definite future date and price. Usually the right to convert is exercisable at the discretion of the investor.

Participating preference shares have the right to receive an additional dividend on top of their fixed dividend. The additional dividend is usually a proportion of the dividend paid out to ordinary shareholders, so the preference shareholders are 'participating' in the profit performance of the company.

One of the characteristics of these more specialised instruments is that they confuse the boundary between debt and equity. An example is the redeemable preference share, which confers on the investor the right to be repaid a fixed amount in the future and an entitlement to a fixed dividend (not unlike interest). This is why it matters much less what an instrument is called and much more what rights it carries.

In view of this plethora of differing rights and interest, what factors will influence the decision as to which instrument to choose?

3.1.3 DEBT OR EQUITY?

3.1.3.1 Interest rates

If interest rates are high, that will make the issue of debt more expensive for the company. When they are low, conversely it may be difficult to get investors excited about debt capital.

3.1.3.2 Cash flow

Interest payments need to be made regularly on debt instruments. If the company has limited supplies of cash, the interest obligation will prove difficult to service.

3.1.3.3 Market conditions

If the company's existing share price is depressed relative to the company's true value, raising finance through the issue of equity will be an expensive choice – it is better to issue equity when the company is able to get full value for each share. The overall state of the stock market may have an influence on this. Clearly there is little to be gained from attempting an equity issue in the wake of a significant fall in stock market values generally.

3.1.3.4 Cost

Different types of instruments may carry broadly comparable rights – we have already seen the similarities between the redeemable preference share and a debt instrument. However, in this case, a redeemable preference share will be more expensive to service as the dividend cannot be set off against tax, unlike interest on a debt instrument. It is this tax benefit which often makes debt attractive to the issuer.

Set against this, of course, is the fact that an ordinary share theoretically carries no cost: the dividend is not an enforceable entitlement. The reality is slightly different. Attempts by companies to suspend or reduce dividend payments are often met with hostility from the Investment Committees (see in particular **2.3.2**).

The size of a dividend on a convertible or redeemable preference share is generally lower than for a normal preference share, and this may sway the issuer in their favour if the difference in cost is significant.

3.1.3.5 Flexibility

Equity offers flexibility in that dividends may be deferred in a bad year, both for ordinary and preference shares, whereas the interest on debt must always be paid because of the consequences for the company if it goes into default.

Convertible instruments, whether preference shares or loan stock, offer a 'hybrid' interest to investors which allows them some choice between the security of the fixed entitlements of debt or preference shares, and the greater risk but possibly greater rewards of equity.

3.1.3.6 Voting power

Preference shares are attractive to some companies in that they do not dilute the voting power of ordinary shareholders (most preference shareholders have an entitlement to vote only at their own meetings and not the company's general meetings). Debt instruments generally carry no voting rights at all (save that some loan stock instruments entitle the holders to vote at stockholders' meetings).

3.1.3.7 Accounting factors

A factor in selecting debt or equity is how it will be accounted for on the issuer's balance sheet. This is now governed by FRS 4. In essence, this requires securities to be accounted for not simply in accordance with their legal form but in a way that reflects the obligations of the issuer. It used to be relatively easy for a company to issue an instrument which carried debt obligations but, by virtue of a right of conversion into the company's shares, was treated as if it was share capital. FRS 4 requires that any security which 'contains an obligation to transfer economic benefits' (including a contingent obligation) be classified as a liability, rather than an equity interest. Thus, a convertible debt instrument would now have to be treated as a liability.

The point of this is that classification of a security as a liability rather than an asset (which would be the case with a share) will worsen the company's debt-equity ratio, which has an impact on its credit rating, and so affects its general standing in the financial markets. It may also raise questions in the minds of investors about the long-term viability and security of the business. FRS 4 therefore effectively requires a company choosing to issue debt to classify it as such on its balance sheet.

3.1.3.8 Conclusion

There is no right answer to which is the best sort of security to plump for. The important thing is to understand the issues relevant to this choice and the options available.

This chapter will leave debt instruments aside and focus instead on the issue of equity securities, and primarily ordinary shares.

3.2 Underwriting and Placing

In looking at issues of equity securities, we begin with underwriting and placing as these concepts underlie almost all the types of offer considered here.

3.2.1 UNDERWRITING

A company issuing new securities on the Stock Exchange or the Alternative Investment Market is looking to raise a fixed amount of money, namely the full value of the securities on offer. Its objective is not just to see how well it can do, and take only whatever it persuades investors to stump up. It has a reason for raising that amount of money, generally to finance identified investment or expansion in particular areas, and anything less than that amount of money will mean that the relevant corporate strategy cannot be implemented.

To avoid this problem, underwriting exists. It is essentially a form of insurance or guarantee. In the event that investors cannot be found to take up all the securities the company is offering, an underwriter agrees to step in and acquire whatever is left. In that way, the company's securities are always paid for by someone, hence securing for the company the total amount of the funds it is looking for from the offer. The quid pro quo is that the underwriter charges a commission for the service, which the company pays whether or not it has to ask the underwriter to take up the shares. A merchant bank will normally play the part of underwriter in the offers we look at below (see **3.3.5**).

No underwriter is likely to feel comfortable in taking on the full risk of a multi-million-pound securities offer alone. He therefore lays off the lion's share of his own risk to a series of sub-underwriters, who perform the same service for him as he has undertaken for the company – in other words, to take up an agreed proportion of the company's securities in return for a commission. Sub-underwriters are generally other merchant banks or firms of stockbrokers who also have experience of arranging sub-underwritings of their own, or institutional investors such as pension funds, unit trust managers, insurance companies and the like.

3.2.2 EXAMPLE OF UNDERWRITING

A company wishes to make an offer of new securities (100 million ordinary shares) at £1.00 each. The company appoints U to underwrite the offer and U appoints 25 sub-underwriters, each of whom agree to sub-underwrite up to 1/25th of whatever is left of the ordinary shares after they have been offered to the public.

Assume the offer is a total failure and not a single share is acquired by a member of the public in the offer. U has agreed with the company to acquire all 100 million shares in this event, but, through its sub-underwriting arrangements, it can require each of the 25 sub-underwriters to take (and pay for) 4 million shares. U has 'laid off' the risk entirely. U and each of the sub-underwriters will receive a commission for their commitment.

If the public had acquired 50 million shares in the offer, leaving 50 million shares to be taken up under the underwriting, each sub-underwriter would have been left with 2 million shares (the appropriate proportion of its 1/25th commitment).

Ordinarily, the underwriter (U) will not lay off all its risk, but, as a sign of its commitment to the offer, will hold some shares back for its own account in the event that not all the shares are wanted by the public.

The important characteristic of underwriting is that it depends entirely on the success of the offer with the general public whether the underwriters and sub-underwriters end up with any of the securities on offer.

3.2.3 PLACING

A placing may work in a number of ways, some of which produce results similar to those produced by the underwriting of a public offer.

A company issuing its securities will appoint its merchant bank to arrange the placing. As you will see below (**3.3.5**), this means that it is the merchant bank's job to identify and target particular potential investors and get them to commit to take some of the securities on offer. These investors are then known as 'placees'. Placees are typically drawn from the same ranks as are sub-underwriters – but do not let this confuse you! In this case, they are the primary investors and are not acting as sub-underwriters. If sufficient interested investors cannot be found, the merchant bank may agree to acquire the shares itself – effectively, it underwrites the placing. The company is therefore still guaranteed to get the money it is seeking. This is often referred to as a 'best efforts' placing and is the common form adopted.

Alternatively, and more unusually, a merchant bank may agree only to act on a 'reasonable endeavours' basis to secure placees for the offer. This means he will do what he can to find placees, but if he is not successful, then that is the end of his responsibility: he has no further obligation regarding the shares left and does not underwrite the offer. Obviously this is a less attractive option for the company issuing the securities. Notwithstanding these terms of art, the specific obligations of the merchant bank will be set out in a placing agreement made with the company.

In a placing with clawback (see **3.6.5.2**), the placees will effectively act as sub-underwriters. This is because the securities are placed conditionally with the placees and offered to other investors first (generally the company's shareholders): the placees only end up with securities if the other investors are not keen on the offer. The merchant bank continues to act as an 'underwriter' in this kind of offer.

Placings are considered in more detail in **3.5.6** below.

3.2.4 BOOKBUILDING

Bookbuilding is a method of underwriting an offer of securities which is used for international equity offerings and increasingly on large initial and subsequent offerings in the UK market. It is in fact closer to a placing in structure.

With a traditional underwriting, the underwriter approaches sub-underwriters to lay off his risk in advance of the offer, but since the issue price is only determined on the day of the offer, sub-underwriters will only be contractually bound to take the risk they have agreed on the day of the offer itself. When bookbuilding is used, potential investors (usually the same institutions and individuals approached in a placing (see **3.2.3**)) bid in advance of the offer for the securities which are to be issued. Their bid, which is not legally binding, is an indication of the number of shares they would be prepared to take up and the price at which they would do so. The potential investors will assess any bid they make on the basis of a preliminary offer document called a 'pathfinder' prospectus. This may often indicate the range within which the final offer price will be set.

The level of demand shown by potential investors will eventually determine the issue price of the securities on the day of the offer: effectively the underwriter (known as the manager) has conducted an auction of the securities and 'run a book' – hence bookbuilding – on the interested investors and the price they will pay. The manager continues to act as underwriter of the offer in the event that investors cannot be found or do not pay for the securities they have agreed to purchase. The underwriting agreement is signed following the bookbuilding process and the setting of the issue price just before commencement of dealings. The period of underwriting risk for the merchant bank is therefore much shorter than on a traditional underwriting.

The bookbuilding process carries with it a number of advantages. In theory, it generates a higher offer price for the company's securities because the price can be fixed accurately on the basis of demand shown, in contrast with the traditional underwriting where the underwriter may suggest a lower price to sub-underwriters to ensure a successful issue. The bookbuilding route also ensures greater transparency in identifying investors, as they are selected by the underwriter (the manager) rather than the broker (contrast the sub-underwriting process). Since bookbuilding has developed as the typical form of underwriting for international equity offerings (principally because it is the traditional marketing method for securities offerings in the USA), it affords UK companies who conduct their issues through the bookbuilding process an opportunity to access an international investor base. This means a broader range of potential investors and a greater profile, which may be valuable where the company is intending to expand its business overseas.

Section **3.5.4** describes the typical structure for a UK securities offering. This is still the conventional route, but you should be aware that increasing use is being made of the bookbuilding route as an alternative vehicle in the domestic UK market. The underwriting agreement (see **3.5.4.1**) will be very similar in a bookbuilt offering.

3.3 The 'Players'

This section is devoted to the 'football team' of participants and advisers in issues of equity securities. The intention is to give you a picture of who is involved and who does what to help you understand what is going on in these transactions.

3.3.1 THE COMPANY

It is important to remember that the company is a separate legal entity from its directors and other managers. There may be situations in these issues where the directors' interests and the company's are quite different (for example, where the directors are to dispose of or acquire large shareholdings in the course of the offer), in which case separate advice will be needed for company and directors.

There may be a great deal of preliminary legal work needed to get a company ready for an issue of securities to the public. Much of this preparation can be ignored by a company which is already listed on the Stock Exchange or has its securities dealt in on the Alternative Investment Market, as it will have taken care of them prior to initial listing or entry onto the AIM. The number of things to deal with will depend largely on the individual nature and circumstances of the company making the issue, hence the following are offered by way of illustration only.

3.3.1.1 Plc status

The company must be registered as a public limited company before it can make an offer to the public (LR, para. 3.2 require this, quite apart from s. 81(1) Companies Act 1985). Time will be needed for the company to register or re-register as a public company (see ss. 117 and 118 CA 1985).

3.3.1.2 Transferability of securities

For a company to have its securities listed, they must be freely transferable (LR, para. 3.15). Hence, fully paid shares must be free from all liens and from any restriction on the right of transfer (save for any restriction imposed for failure to comply with a notice under s. 212 Companies Act 1985). Only in exceptional circumstances will the UKLA allow a company the power to disapprove the transfer of shares, provided that this did not affect the market in such shares.

3.3.1.3 Allotment and issue of securities: statute

The company will need to think about the following requirements of the Companies Act 1985 before it goes ahead with the issue.

(a) *Section 121 Companies Act 1985*

The company will probably need to increase the amount of its authorised share capital to cover the new securities to be issued (s. 121(2)(a)).

(b) *Section 80 Companies Act 1985*

Directors must have authority from the company to exercise the power to allot new securities (see *LPC Guide: Business Law*).

(c) *Section 89 Companies Act 1985*

The issue of equity securities must be on a pre-emptive basis (ie, to existing shareholders in proportion to their existing holdings) unless the company has empowered its directors to do otherwise, either by virtue of the articles or by means of a s. 95 CA 1985 special resolution disapplying s. 89. The use of the s. 95 special resolution procedure is the normal route (see *LPC Guide: Business Law*).

3.3.1.4 Allotment and issue of securities: regulation

More important for listed companies, in some ways, are the non-statutory restrictions on the allotment and issue of securities which apply to them. These are derived from The Listing Rules (LR, ch. 9), and guidelines issued in 1988 by the Investment Committees (see **2.3.2**). They apply to s. 80 authorities, and s. 89 disapplications.

Breach of the Stock Exchange's restrictions will be a breach of its Continuing Obligations and so subject to the same risks as described in **4.2.10**. Breach of the Investment Committee guidelines runs the risk of incurring the institutional investors' displeasure and so having the offending s. 80 or s. 95 resolution voted down at an annual or extraordinary general meeting. If there is any risk of this, it is therefore vital to discuss the position with the Investment Committees first.

As far as s. 80 authorities are concerned, the Investment Committees guidelines look to restrict them to the lesser of the amount of authorised but unissued share capital of the company, *or* one third of the company's issued ordinary share capital.

As far as s. 89 disapplications are concerned, the non-statutory restrictions affect any disapplication in place on listing – so existing s. 95 resolutions will need to be reviewed carefully in advance of the listing application.

As for the *amount* of a disapplication, the Investment Committee guidelines state that their members should not oppose proposals for non-pre-emptive issues provided that they do not exceed 5 per cent of its issued ordinary share capital at any one time or $7\frac{1}{2}$ per cent of its issued ordinary share capital over a three-year period.

The guidelines also suggest that companies should restrict any *discount* to market price in an issue of new securities (relevant in secondary offers such as rights issues and vendor placings) to 5 per cent of the market price immediately before the offer is made.

These guidelines apply only to *listed companies*, and remember that they complement, not replace, the statutory provisions in the CA 1985.

3.3.1.5 Company 'audit'

A great deal of information about the company's activities will need to be researched and prepared, ultimately for disclosure in the prospectus or listing particulars (see **4.2.5.6**). It is as well to initiate this process as soon as the decision to apply for listing has been taken. It may then be that various disclosures which might otherwise have to be made in the prospectus or listing particulars can be avoided (for instance, if the company has failed to keep its filing of returns under the Companies Act 1985 up to date, it may be possible to correct this before the listing process begins). The information to concentrate on includes material contracts, assets and liabilities (particularly any assets which may require valuation, such as real property), any outstanding, pending or threatened litigation and the state of the company's statutory books and registers.

3.3.1.6 Timing notification

Under guidelines issued jointly by the Stock Exchange and the British Merchant Banking and Securities Houses Association, the Bank of England should be informed of the launch date (known as 'impact day') for any new issues exceeding £20 million in value. The idea is to avoid clashes in dates between new issues, on the basis that excessive simultaneous demands for new money from investors will mean that one or both of the competing issuers will inevitably lose out. It would be better in these circumstances if the issuers could agree to come to the market at different times.

The system works by means of a notification from the issuer's sponsor to the Bank of England of the proposed timing of the issue. If there is a clash of dates, the sponsor is informed. The issuer may then choose to go ahead with its selected date regardless, and neither the Bank of England nor the Stock Exchange has any power to force the issuer to do otherwise, though the Bank will inform the other competing issuer. More often than not, however, the sponsor and issuer will agree a revised date for the launch of their own issue which is then communicated to the Bank.

3.3.2 THE DIRECTORS

The directors bear a significant risk of liability for misleading statements in their company's prospectus or listing particulars (see **4.2.5.7**). Consequently the directors will take a close interest in the preparation of the prospectus. In any event, some of the information regarding the company's affairs will be known only to them and so they will have an important advisory role as the prospectus or listing particulars are being drafted. There are a number of other considerations to bear in mind.

3.3.2.1 Service contracts

Where a company is coming to the market for the first time, service contracts between the directors and the company will be put in place where none may have existed before. This is done largely to meet market expectations rather than for any compelling business reason, though the professional investment community see it as one way of securing continuity of management, regulating permitted external business interests and providing a clearer basis of remuneration and benefits than would otherwise be the case. The prospectus or listing particulars will have to make various disclosures about directors' remuneration, as will annual reports and accounts in the future, so clarity in this area is important.

3.3.2.2 Non-executive directors

The effect of PRONED's Code (see **2.2.4**) and the Combined Code (see **2.2.3**) is that a company coming to the market for the first time will need to appoint a number of non-executive and independent directors to the board, if it does not already have them. In compliance with the Combined Code, it will also need to establish a series of committees staffed by non-executive directors to review the company's audit procedures, the remuneration of directors and the future nomination and appointment of non-executive directors. The non-executive directors are expected to bring a more objective eye to the company's decision-making process.

3.3.3 SELLING SHAREHOLDERS

At the same time as the company issues new securities and applies to have them listed, existing shareholders may decide it is time to realise the whole or part of their shareholding interest in the company. Their securities can then be sold in conjunction with the issue of the new shares (see **3.5.3.1**). If this is to be the case, it needs to be built into the arrangements early on.

3.3.4 SPONSOR

The UKLA requires an applicant for listing to appoint a sponsor for its application (LR, para. 2.3). Where a company is seeking a listing it must also seek admission to trading from the Stock Exchange. The Stock Exchange Admission and Disclosure Standards do not require a sponsor but do require companies to select a nominated representative. It is likely that the sponsor required by The Listing Rules will fulfil this role. The Alternative Investment Market requires the appointment of a 'nominated adviser' (see **4.3.5.1**) which performs the same role as a sponsor. The sponsor must be a person fulfilling the qualification requirements under para. 2.1 of The Listing Rules. There are over 100 approved sponsors. Often it will be a firm of brokers which is also a member firm of the Stock Exchange. It is referred to variously as the issuer's 'sponsor', 'sponsoring member firm', 'brokers' and 'sponsoring brokers'. The sponsor has a number of responsibilities, encapsulated more generally by the undertaking to the UKLA which it has to give (LR, sch. 1). A failure to fulfil such responsibilities may give rise to Stock Exchange sanctions such as censure or a ban on future sponsoring (LR, para. 2.24). These responsibilities are:

(a) To liaise with the UKLA regarding the listing application, to ensure that it has all the information it needs to consider the application, and to lodge with the UKLA all the documents relevant to the application (LR, para. 2.8(b) and see **4.2.6.5**): the sponsor is the UKLA's first port of call if it has any questions or problems relating to the application.

(b) To submit to the UKLA, at an early stage, a declaration of interests in the form of LR, sch. 1A.

(c) For a new applicant, to satisfy itself that the company has satisfied all relevant conditions and requirements for listing (LR, para. 2.7) and then to complete a declaration in the form of LR, sch. 4A, saying that everything relevant to a decision regarding the company's suitability for listing has been disclosed to the UKLA. This may be a responsibility jointly shared with the issuing house where one is appointed (see LR, para. 2.18, and see **3.3.5**).

(d) To ensure the company's directors understand the responsibilities expected of them once the company is listed, and to report this to the Stock Exchange (LR, para. 2.9).

(e) Where consulted by issuer on the application or interpretation of The Listing Rules, to give proper guidance and advice, exercising reasonable care and skill (LR, para. 2.7A).

(f) To introduce the company to the market maker(s) who will trade the company's securities on listing.

(g) To advise the company on the appropriate price at which to offer its securities: it will do this jointly with the issuing house where one is appointed (see below).

(h) To secure placees or sub-underwriters for the issue.

(i) In the case of a new applicant for listing, the sponsor must obtain written confirmation from the company that the directors have established procedures which provide a reasonable basis for them to make proper judgments as to the financial position and prospects of the company and its group. The sponsor must be satisfied that this confirmation has been given after due and careful inquiry by the company (LR, para. 2.11). In all cases where a prospectus or listing particulars are produced, the sponsor must report to the Stock Exchange that any profit forecast made by the company has been prepared after due and careful inquiry by the company, and that the company's confirmation that it has sufficient working capital has also been given after due and careful inquiry and has been supported by any institutions providing the finance.

(j) To report on the market's response to the proposed issue of securities for which the application is being made and, in particular, to stimulate market interest by preparing a report (sometimes known as a 'broker's circular') which is circulated to professional investors. This report will contain a detailed analysis of the company's history, performance, products, competitors and future potential. It is not a document required by the listing application, nor is it referred to in the prospectus or listing particulars. It does, however, contain a significant amount of information which will also appear in the prospectus or listing particulars, and it is released to the market prior to the launch of the offer through a controlled distribution process (essentially to the broker's clients, though often also to the media). Consequently, it is important to ensure that what is said in the circular is not significantly at variance with what is said in the prospectus or listing particulars. This is often difficult: the lawyers do not have a role in the production of the circular and often will not see it before it is distributed. As a result, it is important that the circular should contain a disclaimer of liability for the company and its directors.

In addition to the above, if the sponsor is the nominated representative of the company for the purpose of admission to the Stock Exchange, it will carry out additional functions. It may liaise with the Stock Exchange on regulatory matters, agree the timetable for admission to trading and otherwise deal with the documentation required by the Stock Exchange.

Where the company does not also appoint a merchant bank to act for it (see below), the sponsors will also fulfil its functions in addition to any of those mentioned above.

3.3.5 MERCHANT BANK

The main business of a merchant bank is to provide advice on raising finance and otherwise developing a business through, for example, acquiring other businesses. In a listing, where a company is raising finance through the issues of shares, a merchant bank will frequently be involved.

However, not all issues of shares will involve a merchant bank. Smaller offers will only need the sponsoring brokers. It is in relation to the bigger issues that the marketing and organisational expertise which a larger organisation like a merchant bank can offer is necessary. In addition, the merchant bank will often act as underwriter.

In the context of a listing 'issuing house' is the formal term used for the company's merchant bank. This is simply because the merchant bank is a securities house making an issue of shares on behalf of its corporate client.

Where a a merchant bank is appointed, a decision should be taken whether it will also be regarded as a sponsor to the issue in the same way as the sponsoring brokers. If so, LR, para. 2.18, requires the company to indicate which sponsor has primary responsibility and how the responsibilities referred to in **3.3.4** are to be allocated between them. Hence the merchant bank may be referred to, confusingly, as the company's 'sponsors', 'issuing house' or simply as its 'merchant bank'. In fact in roughly half of all primary offers, the broker also plays the role of sponsor, while in another third of such offers, the merchant bank assumes the role of sponsor alone, leaving the broker to its own functions. Roughly one tenth of these transactions involve the merchant bank and broker acting as joint sponsor. The merchant bank's responsibility is as follows:

(a) To fulfil whatever duties under The Listing Rules it agrees with the sponsoring brokers.

(b) To organise the flotation and coordinate the activities of the other parties involved: the company essentially delegates the management of its equity offering to the merchant bankers on the basis that they have the experience necessary to make it a success. In particular this means that the merchant bankers will be the prime movers behind the preparation of the prospectus or listing particulars.

(c) To advise the company on the appropriate price at which to offer its securities: it will do this jointly with the sponsoring broker (see above).

(d) To act as underwriter and/or placing agent (that is, the agent of the company in arranging the placing): this will involve instructing the sponsoring brokers to secure sub-underwriters or placees and liaising with them on this. Acting as underwriter means that the merchant bank will be shouldering the primary risk if the issue is a failure with investors.

3.3.6 REPORTING ACCOUNTANTS

An issuer must appoint accountants to produce financial information about it (LR, ch. 12, and see **4.2.6.3**). Usually the company's existing auditors will play this role unless either they do not have the experience necessary for preparing such a report, or the company's financial affairs require a completely fresh reappraisal (for example, where it has just reorganised its business structure). Accountants appointed for this task will then generally work alongside the company's existing auditors. The responsibility of whoever plays this role is:

(a) To prepare what is known as the 'accountants' long-form report': this is not required by the UKLA and will not be disclosed in the prospectus or listing particulars. It is a confidential report prepared for the directors, not potential investors, containing a detailed review of the financial information available to the management, including financial controls and reporting systems. It will comment on the adequacy of the company's accounting systems and may suggest improvements. As such it can contain material of a highly sensitive nature which it would not be prudent to reveal to the company's competitors. It will be a valuable source for much of the initial drafting of the listing particulars.

(b) To prepare the financial information for inclusion in the prospectus or listing particulars in accordance with ch. 12 of The Listing Rules (see **4.2.6.3**).

(c) Where the company is a new applicant and is presenting its financial information in a comparative table (see section **4.2.6.3**), to file a report with the UKLA that the company's accounts have been audited in accordance with international accounting standards.

(d) To include a report in the prospectus or listing particulars on the company's profit forecast.

(e) To report to the company and its sponsors in the form of a comfort letter that the company has sufficient working capital to meet its needs.

(f) To check any other financial information presented in the prospectus or listing particulars for accuracy and consistency.

3.3.7 SOLICITORS

What you do as a lawyer in these issues depends to some extent on whether you are appointed to act for the company or the merchant bank, although the functions of the two sets of solicitors will often overlap.

Solicitors to the company will be responsible for ensuring the company is ready for the issue, as described above (see **3.3.1**): this will often be the lion's share of their work. They will also spend time advising the company and directors (provided there is no conflict between them) on their liabilities in the issue.

Solicitors to the merchant bank (also known as 'solicitors to the issue' or 'solicitors to the offer') will be responsible for preparing the first draft of the underwriting or placing agreement and supervising the sub-underwriting documentation (though this may in fact be produced by the brokers). Of course, this will all need to be negotiated with the company's solicitors. As with the company's solicitors, the merchant bank's will need to consider their client's legal liabilities carefully throughout.

The solicitors to both parties spend a significant amount of their time in these issues advising on the drafting of the prospectus and usually take responsibility for preparing some parts of it.

The initial draft of the prospectus is generally prepared by the merchant bank, often drawing on the accountant's long-form report for inspiration. Thereafter the prospectus will go through numerous drafts, with the bulk of the attention focused on the description of the company's business. The drafting process is by committee, with merchant bankers, representatives of the company, solicitors to both sides and sometimes the accountants and sponsoring brokers present. The solicitors are often relied on for their views on the accuracy or suitability of certain words and phrases in the draft.

The solicitors to the company are very often left to produce the so-called 'back end' or 'boiler plate' of the prospectus or listing particulars, namely the detailed information on the company required by The Listing Rules (see **4.2.6.3**): particularly, details on the company, its share capital, directors' interests, the terms of material contracts and relevant extracts or summaries from the company's articles of association. This information will be obtained through carrying out the legal due diligence exercise (see below).

In view of the range of potential liabilities which all parties may be exposed to in an issue (see **4.2.5.7**), an elaborate and painstaking ritual has developed to check thoroughly the accuracy of statements made in the prospectus or listing particulars and other documents arising from the issue – this is known as the 'verification exercise' and it is a critical part of the company's solicitor's task to make sure this is done to the highest standards. In carrying out this exercise, the solicitors involved will owe a duty of care to the company and its directors, though the exercise serves everybody's interests.

The purpose is simple enough: by checking the accuracy of every statement in the prospectus or listing particulars, to minimise the risks of any liability for false, misleading or negligent statements made in them or omissions from them. It is important to be clear, and make clear to all parties, that verification is not due diligence. Verification checks the accuracy of information contained in the particulars; due diligence is a more taxing examination of the company to establish whether it is suitable for admission to listing in the first place. Due diligence may very often precede verification; but it is important that the relatively limited scope of the verification exercise is understood.

How is this done? This varies, depending on the practice of the firm of solicitors running the exercise and the particular approach of the individual solicitor who is responsible for it. Broadly, though, the idea is to prepare a document which literally asks a question about every statement in the prospectus. The questions are put to the company's directors for them to answer: in practice, they delegate members of their management team to respond. The questions need to test not only the factual accuracy of statements, but also whether information has been omitted and whether any inferences drawn from statements are correct.

A satisfactory response to a verification question is one which does not simply parrot back the relevant sentence in the prospectus or listing particulars, but which gives detailed reasons for the statement and provides supporting documentation. Specified directors or members of the management team should take responsibility for each verification question. For some questions, for instance on future corporate strategy, the only answer possible will be that the statement in the prospectus or particulars represents the reasonable belief or best judgment of the board (and only the board can confirm this).

Ultimately the completed verification answers must be presented to the board for it to consider prior to approving the draft prospectus or particulars: the directors will need to be completely satisfied that the answers are correct before they can give approval. Since the verification notes are produced by the company's solicitors for the benefit of their client and its directors, they are not public documents, and so are not disclosed during the offer but should be retained by the solicitors at its conclusion.

The same process will be needed for the other public statements made in connection with the issue, particularly any advertisements or publicity material.

The degree of verification required for different issues varies. A company coming to the market for the first time would be expected to go through a rigorous verification exercise. A company making a rights issue and seeking to have the new shares admitted to listing need not be subjected to such an intense examination in view of the amount of information already available to the market: however, a company in financial difficulty attempting a rights issue would need to be vetted much more carefully than on a typical rights issue because of the enhanced risks of possible liabilities arising in the future.

3.3.8 RECEIVING BANK

Where the issue involves an offer to the public as in an offer by subscription or for sale (though not a placing – see **3.5.6**), a receiving bank is generally appointed by the merchant bank and the company. It has a number of tasks:

(a) to receive the application forms for securities from the general public: hence 'receiving bank', as most receiving banks are also high-street clearing banks;

(b) to process and clear cheques from applicants;

(c) to allocate securities to succesful applicants and send out share certificates.

The main point of having a receiving bank to do these apparently simple tasks is that, in large issues, the volume of paperwork to be handled in the form of applications, cheques, share certificates and the like is enormous, and the resources of the company and merchant bank are simply inadequate.

3.3.9 REGISTRARS

It is usual for a listed company to contract out the task of maintaining its register of members to a firm of professional registrars, which is often a different division of the same organisation which acted as receiving bank for the company. Their task is principally to record share transfers on the register, send out notices to members as required and process dividend payments on behalf of the company. They will usually be appointed to assume their duties when the offer closes and so will need to compile their first register to include all the new investors. Once again, in large offerings, this can be a major undertaking, one for which the company secretary's department is often simply not equipped.

3.3.10 PUBLIC RELATIONS ADVISERS

Public relations advisers are generally appointed on large public offerings to advise the company on the protection of its image to the investing public to ensure the issue's success. They will supervise the company's advertising and marketing campaigns, and the lawyers will need to work closely with them to ensure that all publicity material is accurate and not misleading, and consistent with the information presented in the listing particulars (not always the easiest of tasks to perform without killing off a good advertisement).

There may be other parties involved, depending on the nature of the company: property valuers, expert consultants and overseas lawyers are some examples of others who may be brought into play. From a practical point of view, it is vital to make sure that adequate and timely communication takes place between all these parties and that everyone understands what everyone else is doing. This seems trite: but management of the team is as much the key to success in these issues as any other factor.

3.4 Admission to Listing and Trading

Since 1 May 2000, responsibility for the admission of securities to official listing in the United Kingdom has been vested in the FSA as the UK Listing Authority. Previously, this was the responsibility of the Stock Exchange. However, the Stock Exchange retains responsibility for admission of securities to *trading* on the Exchange. There is now a distinction between being admitted to the Official List maintained by the FSA and being admitted to trading on the Stock Exchange (or any other recognised investment exchange, within the meaning of the FS Act). The consequence is that where a company wishes to have securities admitted to listing and trading, either by way of an initial public offering or otherwise, it has to make two applications: one to the UKLA and the other to the Stock Exchange. These applications have to be coordinated such that admission to listing and trading take effect simultaneously, admission to trading being dependent on admission to the Official List.

3.5 Initial Public Offerings

Initial public offerings are issues of securities by companies coming to the market for the first time, that is, companies which do not already have securities listed on the Official List or which do not already have their securities dealt in on the Alternative Investment Market.

3.5.1 METHODS OF BRINGING SHARES TO LISTING

For companies seeking to have their securities admitted to listing for the first time, LR, para. 4.2, sets out the methods which can be used. These are:

(a) an offer for sale;

(b) an offer for subscription;

(c) a placing;

(d) an intermediaries offer;

(e) an introduction; or

(f) such other methods as may be accepted by the Exchange either generally or in any particular case.

The structure of each of (a) to (e) above will be described below (see **3.5.4** to **3.5.8**). The most common methods used for an initial public offering are placings and offers for sale or subscription. A combination of these methods may also be used.

In 1998, the total amount raised by companies (both UK and international) obtaining listings of their equity securities on the London Stock Exchange for the first time was around £11.2 billion. Of the 155 companies involved: 21 per cent used a public offer; 35 per cent used a placing; 6 per cent combined a placing and a public offer; and 38 per cent used an introduction, as the method by which their shares were admitted to listing.

Prior to 1 January 1996, companies seeking to have their securities admitted to listing for the first time could use the placing only in small-scale offers. These restrictions have now been entirely removed. Companies can use whatever method of marketing they prefer, whether it be an offer for sale, a placing or intermediaries offer. The only general requirement which still applies is that the securities must be sufficiently widely held that their marketability when listed can be assumed (see **3.5.2**). There has been criticism that this will work against the interests of wider share ownership, in that companies will prefer to use placings rather than offers for sale (and placings inevitably concentrate shares in the hands of fewer investors).

3.5.2 MARKETABILITY OF SHARES WHEN LISTED

Whatever method is chosen for an initial listing, the securities must be sufficiently widely held that their marketability when listed can be assumed. Prior to the UKLA considering an application, the sponsor must submit a statement summarising shareholdings in the company for which listing is sought. The statement, in the form set out in LR, sch. 2, must include details of the percentage of shares in public hands. One of the conditions for the listing of shares is that 25 per cent of the shares to be listed must be in the hands of the public no later than the time of admission to listing (see LR, paras 3.18 and 3.19). There are circumstances in which a percentage lower than 25 per cent will be allowed (see LR, para. 3.19). Circumstances in which shares *will not* be regarded as being in public hands are set out in LR, para. 3.20.

3.5.3 PRINCIPAL OR AGENT

Whether it is a placing or an offer for sale or subscription which is being used, the company will appoint a merchant bank (in larger offerings) or a broker (in smaller offerings: see **3.3.4** and **3.3.5** for a description of their respective roles) to arrange and effect the offer of securities. In this section, they are both referred to as 'the sponsor' for convenience. The legal relationship of the sponsor in the offer is central to the way it is structured.

The sponsor is an intermediary between the company and the investors. The immediate assumption is therefore likely to be that the sponsor will, on a legal analysis, always act as the company's agent in organising the offer. But consider the effect of the underwriting or 'best efforts' placing described in **3.2.3**: the sponsor agrees to take on to its own shoulders all the primary risk of the issue failing. Of course, as we have seen, it takes steps to cushion itself from that risk by sub-underwriting in the case of the offer for sale or subscription – but the ultimate risk is still the underwriter's in the event that one of the sub-underwriters is unable to honour its commitment.

An alternative approach to the sponsor acting as agent in this role as intermediary would be for the sponsor to acquire all the shares from the issuer in the first place, and then sell them on to the investing public as principal. The sponsor can still arrange a sub-underwriting to protect itself if the offer to the public does not succeed. All the sponsor has done is to convert its conditional primary risk when an agent to an unconditional primary risk when it acquires the securities outright – but it has not changed its fundamental risk at all. Nor does the sponsor thereby change its costs or benefits: the sponsor will still charge the same commission even if it acts as principal.

3.5.3.1 What is the legal effect of the sponsor acting as principal rather than agent?

(a) If there is a false or misleading statement in the listing particulars, the sponsor is at no greater risk of liability under the principles derived from *Hedley Byrne & Co. Ltd* v *Heller and Partners Ltd* [1964] AC 465 or *Caparo Industries plc* v *Dickman* [1990] 2 AC 605 (see **4.2.5.7**) than if acting as an agent. Under s. 150 FS Act, the sponsor's risk of liability is likely to be greater if it acts as principal (see **4.2.5.7**) because it will issue the listing particulars in its own name.

(b) Of course the investor acquires its shares from the sponsor and its contract is with the sponsor, hence it is the sponsor and not the company whom the investor will sue under s. 2(1) Misrepresentation Act 1967 and for breach of contract. The sponsor is therefore in theory marginally more exposed as principal than agent.

(c) Where some or all of the company's existing shareholders are to sell their securities as part of the offer (the rest of it being made up of the company's issue of entirely new securities) and they appoint the sponsor to act as their agent in doing this, there is the theoretical risk that different investors could end up with different roots of title to their securities, depending on whether they acquired them from the company or its shareholders. This could be important where there is a question over the legitimacy of a selling shareholder's entitlement to the securities being disposed of. This risk will only arise if the sponsor acts as agent; if the sponsor is a principal, all investors buy from the same seller and so a common root of title prevails.

(d) The other potential difficulty for the investor where the sponsor is the selling shareholders' agent is that the agency may terminate if the shareholder goes bankrupt, dies or becomes insane in the interim – all of which are such unlikely eventualities, and can in any event usually be accommodated through devices such as taking powers of attorney from the selling shareholders, that the risk is generally regarded as sufficiently remote not to affect the decision whether to act as principal or agent.

The trend of the argument is broadly that, where there are selling shareholders, there is a good case (in the interests of general convenience) for the sponsor to act as principal provided it is happy to carry the additional legal risk this brings.

3.5.3.2 What is the tax effect of the sponsor acting as principal rather than agent?

The principal tax issues to consider are stamp duty ('SD') and stamp duty reserve tax ('SDRT'). To understand these in this context, it is worth recapping on the nature of the two taxes.

(a) SD is chargeable on documents conveying or transferring property (including shares) on sale, not on transactions.

(b) SDRT is imposed on transactions, not on documents. Those transactions are where A agrees to transfer to B chargeable securities for consideration in money or money's worth. Chargeable securities for our purposes include shares and loan capital.

Both SD and SDRT attract a $\frac{1}{2}$ per cent charge on the value of the shares being transferred.

Applying these to an offer for sale and offer by subsciption, we see the following results:

(a) Where the merchant bank acts as agent, no SD or SDRT is payable. The shares are never transferred to the merchant bank as agent – they are simply issued direct into the hands of the investors.

(b) Where the merchant bank acts as principal, neither SD nor SDRT is payable on the issue of shares to the merchant bank (this is an issue and not a transfer), but when the merchant bank sells the shares on to the investors, then the sale attracts both SD and SDRT. The SDRT charge is treated as 'franked' by the SD, and so only the SD is payable.

There is an exemption available under s. 89A Finance Act 1986 which allows the merchant bank acting as principal to be treated in exactly the same way as if it were acting as agent, provided the securities are to be listed on the Stock Exchange and the merchant bank is making an offer to the public. (The exemption is therefore effectively not available for an AIM offering or a private placement.)

(c) Where selling shareholders are involved, the tax analysis is more complex as there will be SD and SDRT on the transfer of the existing shares from selling shareholder to merchant bank. The SDRT charge can be relieved through the 'franking' exemption.

These tax issues apply equally in the context of secondary offerings (see **3.6**).

The conclusion from this tax analysis is that, provided the 'public offer' exemption is available, there is no difference in tax treatment between the merchant bank acting as principal and agent.

Assuming the decision of principal or agent can then be resolved, how do the offering structures actually work? You will find the following descriptions are simplified accounts of typical transactions. In real life, they may look quite different from this – but these, if you like, are the 'role models'.

Whether the company is coming to the Stock Exchange or the AIM, these offering structures will be equally relevant, as they are determined by market considerations and not regulation.

3.5.4 PUBLIC OFFERS FOR SALE OR SUBSCRIPTION

In an offer for sale, the public is invited to purchase securities which have already been issued or allotted by the company.

An offer for subscription is one in which the public is invited to subscribe for new securities of the company.

These methods are often combined: selling shareholders use the prospect of listing as an opportunity to realise their investment by offering their shares to the public whilst the company seeks to increase its share capital by offering the public new shares.

Figure 3.1 assumes a merchant bank has been appointed as well as a broker. The following description is based on **Figure 3.1**:

Figure 3.1 Offer for sale or subscription

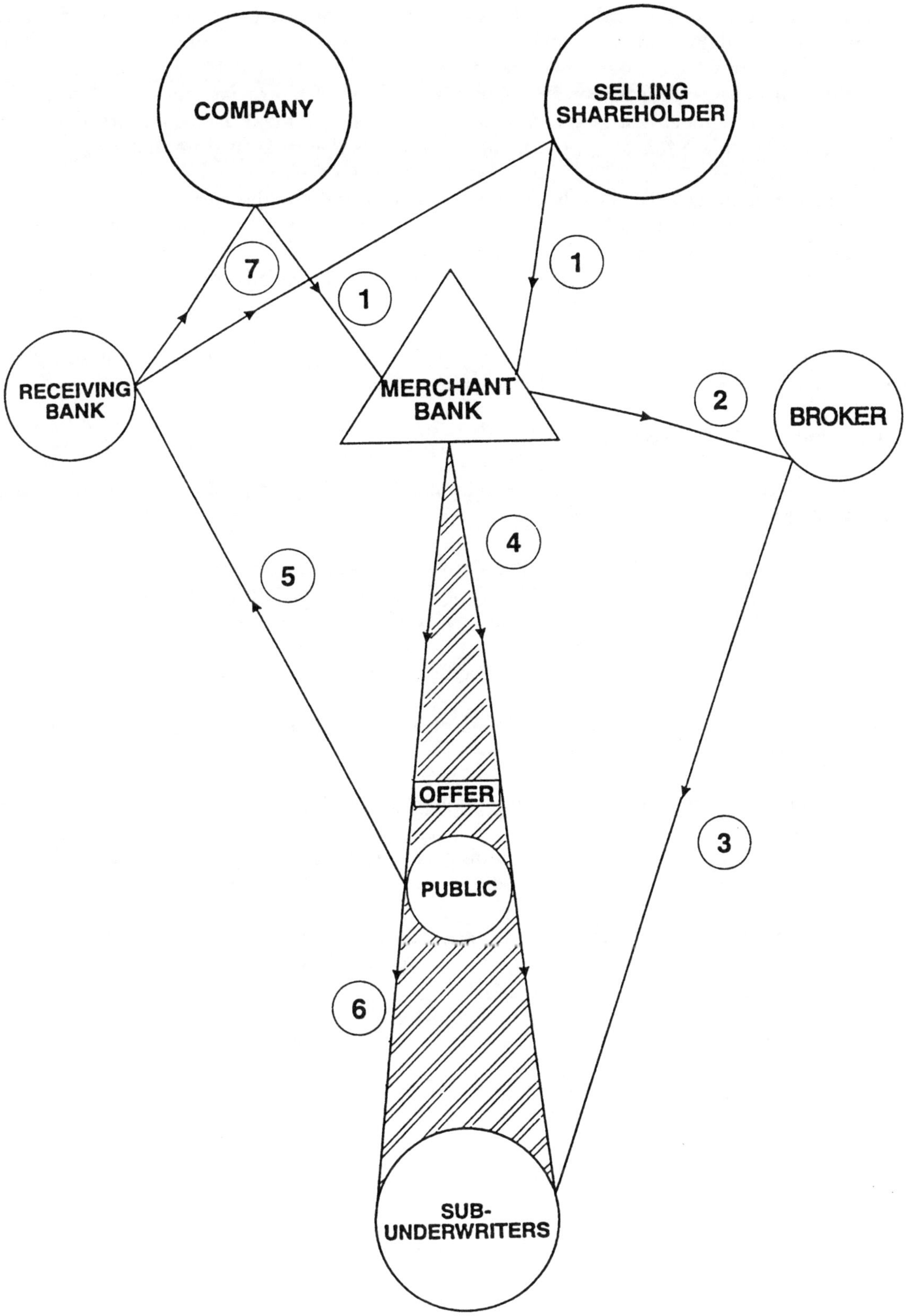

(1) The company (and in this case the selling shareholders as well) appoint the merchant bank to arrange the offer and act as underwriter to it. This appointment and the merchant bank's responsibilities will be recorded in an underwriting or offer for sale agreement. It is usually known as an underwriting agreement where the merchant bank is acting as agent and as an offer for sale agreement where the bank is a principal, but terminology can vary so it is important to analyse the text of the agreement to determine the precise role of the merchant bank. Sometimes the appointment is also reflected in an engagement letter or a letter of appointment, though this is not always the case.

Any underwriting agreement is likely to be negotiated fiercely by the parties to it. The 'typical agreement' set out here will therefore vary with the respective bargaining power of the parties. For instance, in privatisations, HM Government (the selling shareholder of the relevant State enterprises) has forced underwriting commissions down to well below the 'market norm' because of the size of such offerings and its own negotiating strength.

The description below also excludes any mention of the typical 'boiler plate' (assignment, waivers etc.) you would expect to find in such agreements.

3.5.4.1 Underwriting agreement

(a) The merchant bank agrees with the company and the selling shareholders to underwrite the issue and sale of securities.

(b) The agreement is conditional on the securities being admitted to listing or the AIM, on approval, registration and distribution of the prospectus listing particulars (see **4.2.5.4**) and on passing of any necessary shareholders' resolutions.

(c) The company (and sometimes the directors) warrant to the merchant bank that:

  (i) the prospectus or listing particulars (including the profit forecast) are true and accurate in all material respects,

  (ii) the company's latest accounts present a true and fair view of its financial position,

  (iii) the company has the constitutional power and authority to enter into and effect the issue, and

  (iv) the company has taken on no onerous liabilities or been threatened with any material litigation otherwise than as reported in the prospectus,

  and indemnifies the merchant bank against any loss resulting from breaches of these warranties.

(d) The merchant bank may terminate the agreement (usually, at any time up to admission) if:

  (i) the company materially breaches any provision in the agreement, including the warranties; or

  (ii) there are changes in the UK or international financial, economic or political conditions which may have a material adverse impact on the success of the offer (the *force majeure* provision, often hotly contested).

(e) Commissions payable to the merchant bank and other parties are set out: these are usually percentages based on the market value of the underwritten securities, paid out in the following proportions:

$\frac{1}{2}$ per cent to the merchant bank,
$1\frac{1}{4}$ per cent to the sub-underwriters,
$\frac{1}{4}$ per cent to the brokers,

amounting to 2 per cent in total. The merchant bank may receive an advisory fee on top of its commission payment. Commissions will usually be payable even if the agreement terminates *unless* by reason of *force majeure* or the merchant bank's own default.

The Office of Fair Trading has recently concluded that the total 2 per cent fee often amounts to overcharging for underwriting, so having the effect of making raising capital more expensive for UK industry than is necessary. It is difficult for companies to create competition by shopping around for lower fees because of the long-term relationship most companies have with their particular merchant bank. The OFT concluded that there was a competition problem but it recommended that companies and underwriters took their own steps to tackle it. By the end of 1996, there was some evidence that more competitive structures were developing, involving the use of, for example, tenders. However, the OFT referred the matter to the Monopolies and Mergers Commission (now the Competition Commission) in November 1997. At the date of writing, no firm conclusions had been reached on its investigation.

The Competition Commission found that two complex monopoly situations exist. First, the supply of lead underwriting services at standard fees and, secondly, the supply of sub-underwriting services at standard fees. In relation to lead underwriting services, the Commission concluded that competition among financial advisers and brokers is reasonably vigorous. As a result, the fees retained by the lead underwriter (i.e., the merchant bank) and those paid by it to brokers were not viewed as being higher than they would be in the absence of standard fees. Although it was thought that the fees should be more transparent, the Commission did not find that the lack of transparency operated against the public interest. In relation to sub-underwriting, the Commission discussed whether it should make mandatory the tendering of sub-underwriting. However, this was rejected on the grounds that it would restrict market flexibility and the right of companies to choose the share-issuing method they thought was in their best interests. The most appropriate remedies were seen as those which increase transparency and the information available to companies. The main recommendation of the Commission was therefore that The Securities and Futures Authority issue guidance to corporate financial advisers reminding them of the application of the FSA's principle on information for customers and recommending that they should advise their clients of alternatives to underwriting at standard fees. In addition, it was recommended that The Bank of England publish guidance for companies on share-issuing good practice, including encouraging the use of tendering and explaining when deep discounting (see **3.6.4.2**) is likely to be advantageous.

(Commissions on a bookbuilt equity offering (see **3.2.4**) will generally be a higher overall percentage, normally between 3 and 5 per cent. This reflects the fact that the merchant bank will usually have to spend a large amount of time marketing. Commissions are split between the managers of the so-called underwriting syndicate so that about 20 per cent of the total commission represents a fee for the management of the underwriting, 20 per cent of the total is a fee for underwriting the issue (agreeing to take securities if there are no interested investors) and about 60 per cent of the total is for selling securities on to interested investors. The total is split between the managers depending on the separate roles they have performed.)

Returning to the figure:

(2) The merchant bank appoints the broker its agent to arrange the sub-underwriting.

(3) The broker will contact potential sub-underwriters by telephone and extract a provisional commitment from them to take a proportion of the securities if the investors are not

interested. On the morning the price of the securities is announced ('impact day' and also the day the prospectus or listing particulars are published and sent to potential investors), the broker contacts the potential sub-underwriters again and confirms their commitment at the announced issue price.

The sub-underwriters are sent a sub-underwriting letter which they sign in acknowledgement and a contract is concluded between merchant bank and sub-underwriter. The sub-underwriting letter must be on all fours with the underwriting agreement – that is, must be subject to the same conditions and have the same commissions payable. You do not want to find the sub-underwriting letter failing because of unfulfilled conditions but the merchant bank still liable under the underwriting to take the shares because the agreement is not caught by the same condition – particularly if you are acting for the merchant bank!

(4) The prospectus or listing particulars are sent or made available to potential investors (see **4.2.6.4** for a summary of the typical content of a prospectus). Legally, they constitute an invitation to those investors to subscribe for the company's securities at the advertised price. Interested investors complete the application form contained in the prospectus or listing particulars (which, legally, constitutes an offer).

(5) The offer is sent by investors to the receiving bank, which processes all the forms and attached cheques. The receiving bank is usually appointed by the merchant bank in a separate receiving bank agreement. Sometimes applications have to be scaled down or eliminated because of excessive demand for available securities. Successful applicants are sent an interim document of title for the securities allocated to them which they can trade in the market. Compilation of the new register of members, followed by preparation and distribution of the formal share certificates, usually takes some time – hence these temporary documents (typically referred to as renounceable letters of allotment or acceptance – RLAs for short).

(6) The receiving bank notifies the merchant bank of the number of securities taken up by the public. If there are securities left outstanding in the offer (the 'stick'), the merchant bank instructs the broker to allocate these to the sub-underwriters pro rata to their respective sub-underwriting participations. The merchant bank will be left with any securities it has not sub-underwritten.

(7) The proceeds from the issue (less commission and fees) pass up to the company and selling shareholders: the offer has completed its course, and the company's securities are now publicly traded.

3.5.5 TENDER OFFERS

The description above assumes an offer of securities at a fixed price. An issuer may choose to offer its securities to the highest bidders on an auction basis. The same structure as above applies, but investors are invited to bid for shares at or above a 'minimum tender price', and the underwriting and sub-underwriting takes place at this price. Securities are allocated to those with the highest tenders at the price at which they bid, and so on down, until the point at which all the securities have been taken up. The purpose behond this is to realise maximum value from the offering. Sometimes a common striking price is selected (the highest price common to all bids at which the entire issue will succeed), and this is the price which everyone ends up paying for their securities. The important point to note is that in all other respects this method replicates the offer for sale or subscription route.

3.5.6 PLACINGS

LR, para. 4.7, describes a placing as 'a marketing of securities . . . to specified persons or clients of the sponsor . . . which does not involve an offer to the public'. In legal terms, it may in fact be an offer to the public (see LR, para. 3.20). In concept though, it is not an offer by general invitation but to selected persons, usually institutional investors.

The merchant bank is faced with the decision in a placing whether to act as agent or principal, in exactly the same way as for the offers considered above. The same legal and practical considerations apply. There is no difference in terminology here, however, between placings for sale or subscription.

A company coming to the market for the first time is typically faced with the choice of launching itself through an offer for sale or subscription, or a placing. To understand how it makes this decision, let us look first at how a placing works. **Figure 3.2** assumes a merchant bank has been appointed alongside a broker.

(1) The company (and in this case the selling shareholders as well) will appoint the merchant bank to arrange the placing. Invariably, where these placings are in connection with an application for a full listing or admission to the AIM, the merchant bank will be acting on a 'best efforts' basis and so will be underwriting the offer of securities. As with the offer for sale or subscription, the merchant bank's responsibilities may be recorded in an engagement letter, and will always be set out formally in a placing agreement.

The terms of the placing agreement will closely resemble what you will find in an underwriting agreement (see **3.5.4.1**). Obviously any descriptions of the mechanics of the offer will vary to reflect the placing's differences. The parties to the agreement will be the same: the company and the merchant bank, with the selling shareholders and the directors parties to some (or perhaps all) of the warranties.

The major difference between the underwriting and placing agreements is in the commission payable:

$\frac{1}{2}$ per cent to the merchant bank,
$\frac{1}{2}$ per cent to the placees (as compared with $1\frac{1}{4}$ per cent to the sub-underwriters),
$\frac{1}{4}$ per cent to the broker.

The higher commission paid in an offer for sale or subscription is because of the open-ended nature of the risk which sub-underwriters take on. Placees are able to decide definitively in advance how many securities they are prepared to take.

(2) The merchant bank appoints the broker its agent to arrange the placing.

(3) Usually the broker will have solicited informal indications of interest in the company's securities from potential placees before the placing is launched. When the placing is announced, the broker will renew contact with the potential placees over the telephone, announce the price at which the securities are to be issued and then confirm the placees' interest. The broker will follow up this conversation with a placing letter, which will be accompanied by a placing memorandum (though the placees will have already seen a draft version of this).

A placing letter resembles a sub-underwriting letter. The placee agrees to subscribe for or buy the securities at the issue price, on conditions that are identical to those contained in the placing agreement (for example, that the securities are admitted to listing). Legally, the placing letter constitutes the offer of securities to the individual placee.

A placing memorandum is the term, in the context of a placing, for the offer document, which will also invariably be the listing particulars or prospectus. As with the offer for sale or subscription, this will be an invitation to treat.

The placee signs the letter of confirmation attached to the placing letter, indicating acceptance of the offer, and returns it with payment to the broker. Occasionally, the proper contractual analysis is that the contract with the placees has been concluded in the telephone conversation

Figure 3.2 Placing

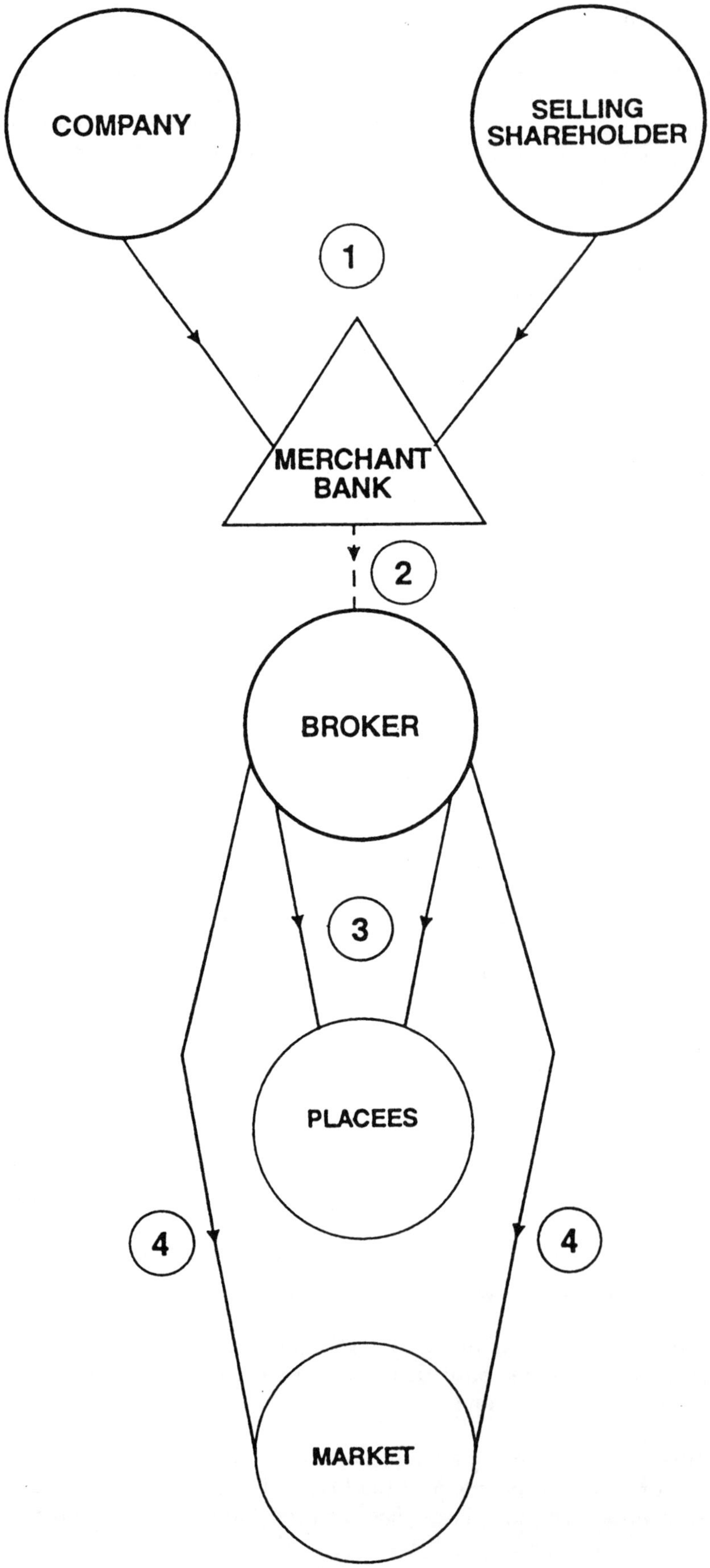

between broker and placee, with the exchange of letters merely confirming an existing agreement.

The securities are then allotted in the name of the placee, and documents of title are sent to him in exactly the same way as described in **3.5.4** for offers for sale or subscription.

(4) If potential placees contacted by the broker over the telephone are not willing to take up securities in which they originally expressed interest, the broker's task is to identify other investors in the market who would be prepared to take up shares as part of the placing syndicate. If this fails, the merchant bank is of course the ultimate back-stop.

What, then, are the principal distinguishing features of a placing and what are its merits?

(a) A placing is clearly more appropriate where the company wishes not to throw itself into the arms of the public at large, but rather to persuade the professional investing community to take a more serious interest in the company. There are all kinds of circumstances where this may make commercial sense.

An example is where the company's business is relatively high-risk (for instance, businesses with high environmental exposure, such as waste management operations, will be perceived as risky). The general public is unlikely to be attracted to such investments.

Where the conditions for launching new issues are volatile or poor, it will be much harder to secure the success of an offer for sale or subscription than a placing.

A placing is cheaper, and this may be compelling particularly where the total value of the offering is relatively low and the company therefore wishes to keep the costs of the issue down.

(b) Since the number of investors taking up securities will be significantly less than for an equivalent offer to the general public, there is no need for a receiving bank. The broker is able to handle the applications for securities from the placees.

(c) The marketing of the securities is essentially performed by the broker over the telephone with its contacts. There is no need for a campaign to raise investor awareness of the issue.

(d) The commissions payable to placees are less than those the sub-underwriters in an offer for sale or subscription would normally expect to be paid (see **3.5.4**).

This amounts to a cheaper offering. The placing is therefore most attractive to companies anxious to bear down on the costs of the offering.

Before we leave the placing, it is worth re-emphasising that many primary offerings are a mix of offer for sale or subscription and placing. In other words, a portion of the securities to be offered are kept aside for the institutions to acquire through a placing, and the rest are sold to the general public through an offer for sale or subscription. Technically, the public offer and placing structure and mechanics will simply work alongside but apart from each other (though both offers will use exactly the same prospectus or listing particulars). Sometimes arrangements are made which allow for securities allocated to the placing to be 'clawed back' in favour of the public offer if demand there is higher than anticipated.

3.5.7 INTERMEDIARIES OFFER

The intermediaries offer is available as an alternative to an offer for sale or subscription or a placing. The way the offer works is that securities are allocated to intermediaries, who then sell them on to their own clients (at a commission). Intermediaries for this purpose are Stock Exchange member firms and other securities houses selected by the sponsoring broker. The idea is that this achieves a wider spread of investors than would be the case with a placing: you can imagine that the offer structure looks something like **figure 3.3**, with the securities passing down the pyramid.

Figure 3.3 Intermediaries offer

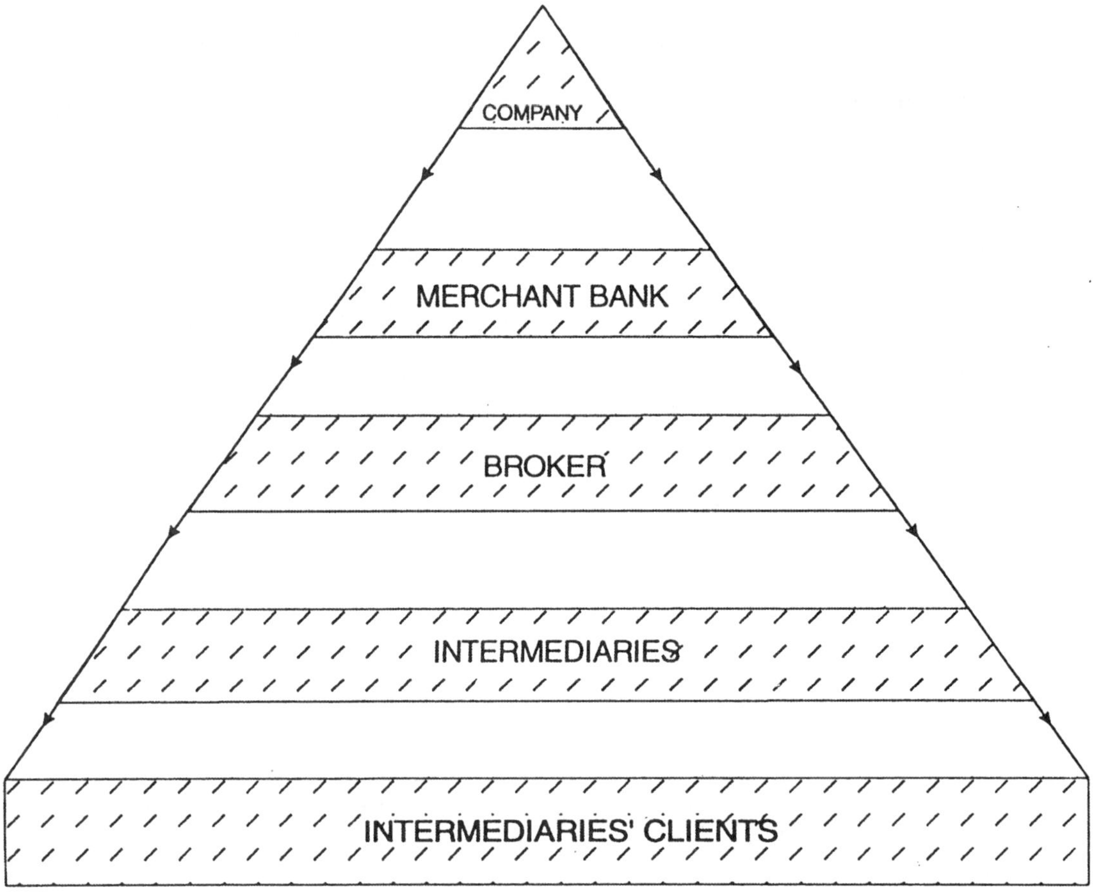

In terms of mechanics, the intermediaries offer otherwise works very much like a placing (see **3.5.6** and **figure 3.2**), with the sponsoring broker initially making informal contact with the potential intermediaries (who are here the equivalent of the placees) and then making the allocations to them when the offer is announced. The UKLA may require a list of the names of the intermediaries to whom shares were allocated and the names and addresses of the clients to whom each intermediary passed shares (LR, para. 4.11).

Depending on the scale of the transaction, there may or may not be a merchant bank coordinating the transaction and acting as co-sponsor with the brokers. The issuer and the sponsor will enter into an offering agreement which sets out the sponsor's responsibilities and contains some of the standard warranties from the company we have seen in the context of underwriting agreements (see **3.5.4.1**). There have been comparatively few of these offers so far.

3.5.8 INTRODUCTION

A company may also obtain a listing on the Official List (and also technically on the AIM, though this would be very uncommon) by means of an introduction. To call this an issue of securities is something of a misnomer, as no issue of securities is actually involved. An introduction is an acknowledgement, as The Listing Rules say at para. 4.12, that 'the securities are already widely held by the public' – it is simply that they have not been formally listed.

When will this be the case? There are two likely situations. The first is where the company has an overseas listing so that its securities are already being traded internationally, and the second is where the company's securities are being dealt in on the AIM and the company wishes to transfer to a full listing.

The process of seeking an introduction involves an application for admission to listing of the company's securities (as with any other offer), save that this application relates only to securities already in existence. The application will of course require the production of a prospectus or listing particulars.

The company, as with other offers, needs to appoint a sponsor, which will handle the mechanics of the introduction, and the sponsor will need to identify potential market makers who will be prepared to buy and sell the company's securities on the Stock Exchange.

No actual offer or issue of new securities takes place: on admission of the securities to listing, it becomes possible to trade the securities on the Stock Exchange in exactly the same manner in which they were traded up to that time on the AIM or the overseas stock exchange. In a sense, a new market has been opened up to existing investors in the company.

3.6 Secondary Issues

We mean by this expression issues of securities by companies already listed or whose securities are already being dealt in on the AIM. Further issues of securities take place to raise extra working capital, fund acquisitions, finance growth, and so on. During 1998, over £6 billion was raised by UK companies through 851 secondary issues. Once again, there are some commonly accepted offering structures for these kinds of issues, which will be used on whichever market the issue takes place. The full range is set out in LR, para. 4.1. This section will look at the commonest of them. Before we do, there are two preliminary points to observe.

3.6.1 PRE-EMPTION RIGHTS

You will be familiar with s. 89 Companies Act 1985, which requires offers of new securities to be made on a pre-emptive basis to the company's existing shareholders in proportion to their existing holdings. You will also have encountered the additional layer of regulation which listed companies face when contemplating further issues of securities (see **3.3.1.4**).

It is worth noting that the UKLA supports s. 89 by making it a basic condition of listing that issues for cash of securities having an equity element must, unless shareholders otherwise permit, be offered in the first place to the existing equity shareholders in proportion to their holdings (LR, para. 9.18). The same condition applies to AIM companies.

The presumption, then, is that a company seeking to raise further capital through an issue of securities will do so through an offer to its existing shareholders.

One of the consequences of this presumption is that companies frequently use their annual general meetings each year to obtain and then renew disapplications of s. 89 under s. 95 (within the restrictions laid down by the Investment Committees). This then confers on them the flexibility to launch a non-pre-emptive issue in the ensuing year and still operate within the UKLA's basic conditions.

3.6.2 PROSPECTUS REQUIREMENTS

Section 144(2) of the FS Act requires as a condition for admission the publication of a prospectus where securities are offered to the public in the UK for the first time before admission. This applies where there is a subsequent issue of shares, even though that class of shares is already listed.

There are a series of exemptions which will take the offering outside the requirement for a prospectus. These include:

(a) Where shares are offered to no more than 50 persons.

(b) Where securities are offered to persons whose ordinary business activities involve them in buying, selling and managing investments.

(c) Where securities are offered to a restricted circle of persons who are sufficiently knowledgeable to understand the risks involved in accepting the offer.

(d) Where the issue is raising less than 40,000 euros in total.

There is accordingly no exception for offers to existing members of the company. Therefore a rights issue by a company already listed will give rise to the need for a prospectus, rather than listing particulars.

The Listing Rules apply to a prospectus in exactly the same way as they apply to listing particulars, but as if references to listing particulars were a reference to a prospectus. Accordingly, the contents requirements for the document will stay exactly the same, and will depend on the type of transaction (see **4.2.6.3** for the contents requirements).

If placing

The Listing Rules contain a list of exemptions from the requirement to issue full listing particulars. These are referred to in **4.2.5.5**. These exemptions do not apply to prospectuses, only to listing particulars. All rights issues therefore require a full prospectus. If the transaction is not a rights issue, but a subsequent placing of securities, the key test is to ask whether or not there is an offer of shares to the public within the meaning of section 144(2). If there is, then the prospectus requirements apply. If not, because one of the exemptions applies, then the provisions relating to listing particulars under The Listing Rules automatically bite. Listing particulars will therefore need to be published in accordance with the Rules. Accordingly, it may be possible, in these circumstances, to take advantage of the exemptions set out in **4.2.5.5** from the requirements to issue full listing particulars.

3.6.3 PLACING

The placing is widely used in both initial public offerings and secondary issues. As we saw in **3.5.6**, the placing is relatively cheap and straightforward as an offering structure. The structure and mechanics of a placing by way of a subsequent offering mirror those for an initial public offering. In addition, if the securities being placed are of a class already listed, the company will have to observe LR, paras 4.8 and 4.9, which regulate the price at which the securities can be placed.

3.6.4 RIGHTS ISSUE

3.6.4.1 Introduction

As **3.6.1** above will have made plain, the rights issue is the offering structure for new issues of securities preferred by the UKLA and the Investment Committees.

The rights issue is an offer of new securities to existing shareholders in proportion to their existing holdings. Those securities may be different in nature to those already held by shareholders. It is possible, for instance, to offer ordinary shareholders new redeemable preference shares by way of a rights issue.

To encourage shareholders to take up the new securities being offered, they are offered at a discount to the market price of the existing securities (assuming they are of the same class and type). Unless the securities are cheaper than those currently available in the market, what point is there in shareholders subscribing to the offer? Discount to par value is obviously not acceptable (see s. 100 Companies Act 1985).

What shareholders are offered is the *right* to take up new securities (hence 'rights issue'). If they choose not to take up the new securities themselves, they are entitled to sell on that right to interested buyers.

3.6.4.2 Procedure

The description below refers to **figure 3.4**.

(1) There is no question with a rights issue of shareholders selling their stake in the company: the issue is by the company alone of new securities.

The issue of whether the merchant bank is to act as principal or agent is also irrelevant. The offer is by the company to its own existing shareholders, so the merchant bank can only act as the company's agent in arranging and facilitating the offer.

The merchant bank's duties will be defined in the same way as for an offer for sale or subscription: there may be a letter of engagement and there will usually be an underwriting agreement with broadly the same terms and conditions as in the offer for sale agreement (see **3.5.4.1**). The only difference will be in the description of the mechanics of the offer. The commissions will be as for offers for sale or subscription.

The circumstance where there would be no underwriting agreement is where the company decides to offer the new securities at such a discount to the market value of the existing securities that there is perceived to be no danger of the issue failing (known as a 'deep discount' issue). This would only happen where the company either is desperate to save the expense which the underwriting commissions otherwise incur or where it needs the money very quickly and cannot afford to wait for the merchant bank to arrange an underwriting.

Assuming this is not a deep discount issue, the merchant bank will agree, exactly as for an offer for sale or subscription, to underwrite the entire issue if it fails.

(2) The merchant bank appoints the broker as its agent to arrange the sub-underwriting.

(3) The broker arranges the sub-underwriting exactly as for an offer for sale or subscription (see **3.5.4**).

(4) The shareholders are sent a circular, usually consisting of a letter from the company's chairman explaining the reasons for the rights issue, and the additional information to be included in the prospectus (see **3.6.2**). The circular sets out the terms and conditions which form the basis of the offer made to the shareholders.

With the circular is a document known as a provisional allotment letter, or 'PAL' for short. This offers the shareholders the right to subscribe for the new securities which have been provisionally allotted to them already. The shareholders must have a minimum of 21 days within which to accept the offer (s. 90(6) CA 1985).

If shareholders choose to pay the subscription price, the securities are theirs upon notification of acceptance and payment to the receiving bank. The PAL will be their temporary document of title until a definitive share certificate can be dispatched.

Figure 3.4 Rights issue

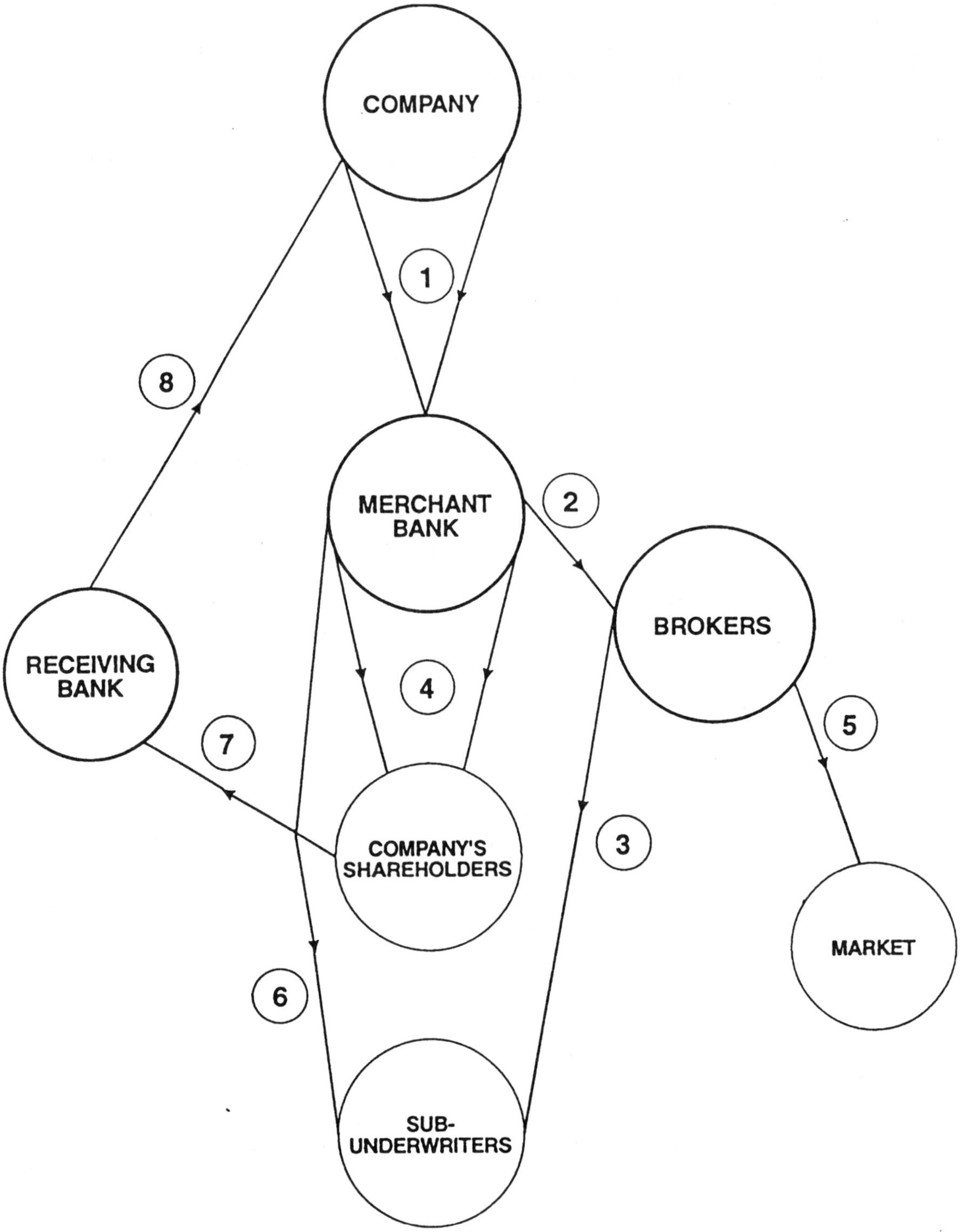

A shareholder who chooses not to pay the subscription price can either do nothing, in which case the PAL is said to 'lapse' (see stage (5) below), or sell the PAL (and hence the right to subscribe for the new shares).

(5) When the 21-day offer period closes, the broker is responsible for attempting to sell the 'lapsed' securities (collectively known as the 'rump') into the market to any interested buyers (usually other professional investors). If the broker can agree a price at a premium to the subscription price, the premium belongs to the 'lapsed' or 'lazy' shareholders, and the rest is obviously the company's.

(6) If the broker cannot sell any of the lapsed shares, the so-called 'stick' (i.e., what is left of the unsubscribed PALs) is taken up by the sub-underwriters in the normal way.

(7) The receiving bank is appointed as most listed or AIM companies have large numbers of shareholders and so only an organisation of the bank's capacity and experience is likely to be able to manage the volume of PALs, cheques and share certificates effectively.

(8) Commissions and fees are deducted before the cash passes up to the company.

3.6.4.3 Trading in PALs

There is one particular problem to watch out for. As the PALs are effectively tradeable documents of title, it is important that they can only be traded when all the conditions to the offer have been satisfied – otherwise there is the danger of the offer terminating and all the sales of all the PALs having to be reversed (which may in practical terms be very difficult). Hence (save in rare cases) sending out the PALs will need to await any EGM resolutions which the offer requires (for instance, giving the directors s. 80 Companies Act 1985 authority to allot the securities or disapplying the statutory pre-emption rights). This is done in order to deal with fractional entitlements, the issue of overseas shareholders and to ensure that the offer period is no longer than 21 days (see the effect of s. 90(2) Companies Act 1985). The only condition which is an exception to this is admission of the securities to listing or admission to the AIM, as this almost always takes place within 24 hours of dispatch of the PALs and is a virtual formality by that stage.

3.6.4.4 Effect of CREST on rights issue

The advent of CREST (see **1.6.3**) will have an effect, on a rights issue, on those members who hold shares in uncertificated, dematerialised form. These members will not receive PALs but will have their nil paid rights credited to their CREST accounts. Instead of the ability to trade their PALs, they will be able to trade the nil paid rights through CREST. They should be able to do this from the morning after the PALs are posted to certificated shareholders.

3.6.5 VENDOR PLACING

One of the possible uses of the funds raised by a rights issue will be to finance an acquisition of another company or business. The vendor placing has developed as an acquisition-financing technique which combines both the raising of finance and the acquisition itself, and rather neatly confers a number of advantages in the process.

What is a vendor placing? LR, para. 4.29, defines a 'vendor consideration placing' as a 'marketing, by or on behalf of vendors, of securities that have been allotted to them as consideration for an acquisition'. To explain in more detail, let us start with a situation and a problem arising from it.

Buyer plc, a listed company, wants to buy Target Ltd, and Seller Ltd, which owns all the shares in Target, has agreed to sell it. Seller wants cash for the sale. Buyer has no cash available and would like to give Seller some of its own securities as consideration for the purchase. How is this mismatch resolved?

If Buyer agrees to appoint a merchant bank to arrange for its securities to be placed into the market (and, let us say, listed and traded on the Stock Exchange alongside its other securities), then Seller agrees to have the securities allotted to it as consideration for the sale of Target and sells them to the merchant bank to be placed. The placing produces cash. This would ordinarily pass into the company's coffers, but here it passes to Seller as its consideration for the transfer to Buyer of Target.

Result: Buyer issues its securities, Seller gets its cash, and Target is sold to Buyer.

If it sounds complicated, it is! The basic idea, though, is very simple. A vendor placing is a placing of securities to raise cash to finance an acquisition – nothing more nor less.

How does it work in more detail? **Figure 3.5** describes a typical transaction. If we ignore the reference to buyer's shareholders for the moment:

(1) The securities which are the consideration for the acquisition are allotted by Buyer to Seller. These two parties also enter into an acquisition agreement which records their deal to sell Target to Buyer. One of the conditions which must be fulfilled before the ultimate transfer of Target is that the securities which are to be placed in the market are admitted to full listing or to the AIM. It would be a disaster if the Seller took the securities as consideration and then discovered they were unmarketable, as they would be impossible to place.

(2) Now that the consideration has technically been paid, Target transfers to Buyer, though this will be conditional on the securities being issued in consideration by the Buyer being admitted to listing or the AIM, as appropriate, and satisfaction of the other conditions to the placing.

(3A) Buyer will have appointed a merchant bank to arrange the placing, usually by a vendor placing agreement. This will contain similar terms and conditions to those found in an underwriting agreement (see **3.5.4.1**), though descriptions of the mechanics will vary. Commissions will be payable as in an ordinary placing.

One of the conditions to the vendor placing agreement will be that the conditions in the acquisition agreement have been satisfied! Although this seems like circularity, this is intended to avoid putting the placing into effect only to find that a vital regulatory approval for the transfer of Target has not been obtained. Hence, when Target is transferred, this will only be after all conditions to the transfer have been satisfied (with the exception of the securities being admitted to listing and the Stock Exchange or the AIM, as appropriate).

The merchant bank in this context will have to decide whether to act as principal or agent, that is, whether it buys the newly issued securities from the seller in its own name or simply acts as agent of the seller in placing them. The same considerations arise as discussed in **3.5.3**.

The merchant bank will invariably agree with the Buyer in the vendor placing agreement to arrange the issue on a 'best efforts' basis: in other words, to underwrite the placing if enough placees cannot be found to take up the securities.

(3B) Seller will transfer its allotted securities to the merchant bank under a sale agreement, in which the seller gives the merchant bank authority to place the securities.

(4) See **3.6.5.2**.

Figure 3.5 Vendor placing

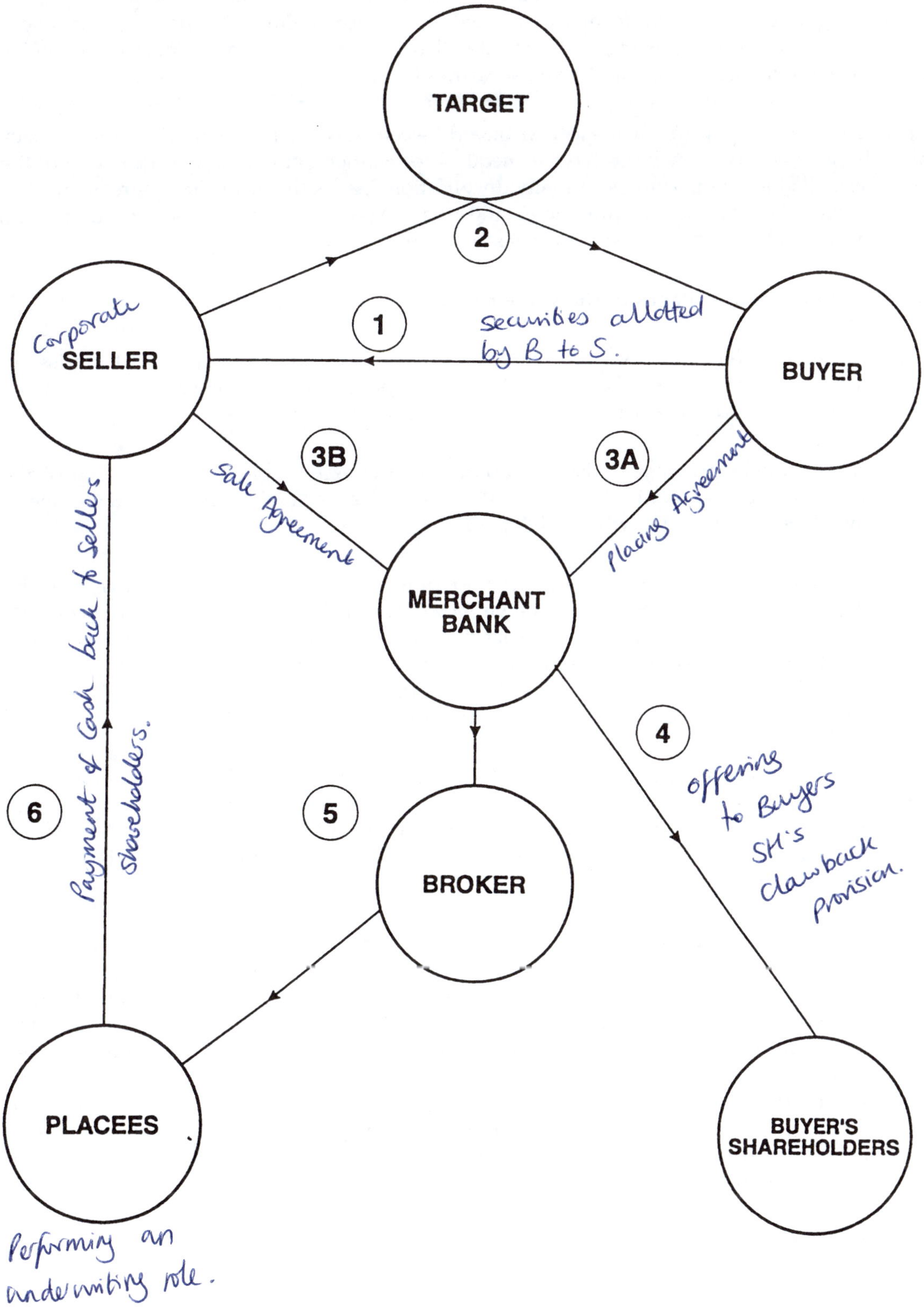

(5) Through the agency of a broker, placees are contacted informally to establish interest and then, when the exact price of the securities is announced, the brokers arrange for them to sign placing letters to confirm formally their willingness to take up securities. This will work exactly as for an ordinary placing, including the distribution of a placing memorandum which will also be the listing particulars for the securities.

(6) The placees pay up their cash to buy the securities. In fact this will pass up back through the broker (who will receive the cheques) to the merchant bank. On admission of the securities to listing, the placing is formally unconditional, as is the acquisition agreement. The bank deducts the various commissions and then passes the cash representing Seller's consideration to Seller and any surplus back to Buyer.

3.6.5.1 Particular advantages of the vendor placing

(a) Section 89 Companies Act 1985 rears its head only where securities are being issued for cash. The particular beauty of the vendor placing is that the securities are being issued for shares or assets (namely Target), hence no s. 89 concerns arise.

A consequent problem is that a valuation of the assets bought for the issue of the securities may be required under s. 103 Companies Act 1985, although usually one of the exceptions to s. 103 will apply (see **2.1.2**).

(b) A vendor placing will often permit the use of merger accounting, where Buyer is using shares to buy at least 90 per cent of Target's share capital. The advantage of this is that Buyer and Target can merge their balance sheets and profit and loss accounts as if they had been one entity. This avoids the creation of goodwill and the consequent need to write that off against the profit and loss or other accounts and so is generally a more attractive option from the accountant's point of view (see **8.6.3.5**).

(c) Even if merger accounting is not available, merger relief generally will be under s. 131 Companies Act 1985. This means there will be no need to set up a share premium account in respect of any premium at which the securities are issued. As a share premium account ties up capital which might otherwise be put to use, that is a benefit (see **8.6.3.7**).

(d) The discount to market price at which securities are issued in rights issues varies (and there are in any event the Investment Committee guidelines to consider), but normally the range is anywhere between 12½ per cent and 20 per cent (more than this in deep discount issues). The discount in vendor placings is usually finer than this (the exception is open offers – see **3.6.5.2** – where the level of discount tolerated by the Investment Committees is between 15 and 18 per cent). This is because LR, para. 4.30(b), makes a discount of more than 10 per cent subject to UKLA permission and, since a placing is a selective marketing to institutions rather than an offer to shareholders whose mood may be unpredictable, there is not the need to be quite so generous with discounts to ensure its success.

The benefit of this is that fewer securities need to be issued to raise the same amount of money, hence it is cheaper for the company.

(e) In recent years it has become standard practice for a new structure to be adopted for a vendor placing arrangement. In this, rather than the Buyer's securities being issued to the Seller of the target, and then sold on in the placing, the securities are issued directly to the placees (or, in the case of clawback, the Buyer's shareholders — see **3.6.5.2**).

The principal reason for this is that it saves stamp duty and stamp duty reserve tax when the securities are transferred by the Sellers. Accordingly, it is a cheaper method of finance-raising.

The effect of these advantages is that the vendor placing is a more attractive route for a company when funding an acquisition than a rights issue.

3.6.5.2 Clawback

To return to figure 3.6 and, in particular arrow 4, the concept of clawback is that, instead of placing the securities into the market, the company offers them, via the merchant bank, to its own shareholders. The broker still identifies placees in the usual way, but their commitment is conditional on the company's shareholders not taking up the offer made to them: in a sense, then, the placees stand almost in the position of sub-underwriters. The only differences in terms of the structure of the offer are that there is an offer of securities to the company's shareholders and, given the likely scale of the offer, it may also be necessary to bring in a receiving bank to handle acceptances and payment from the shareholders.

Why do this when it is not strictly required by s. 89 (see **3.6.5.1**)?

Partly this is due to the influence of the Investment Committees, and partly what the Stock Exchange says in its continuing obligations for listed companies (LR, para. 9.18). The presumption is that further issues of new securities will be to existing shareholders in proportion to their existing holdings *unless shareholders otherwise permit*. It follows that it is very difficult for a listed company to avoid returning to its shareholders to explain why it is proposing to exclude them from its latest issue of securities, and even harder to come up with a very good reason when it does try to explain.

So how is the offer made to shareholders? There are two basic variations.

(a) *Rights offer*

This works almost exactly like a rights issue. The shareholders are offered the securities, in proportion to their existing holdings, on a PAL which they can trade, allow to lapse or take up as they see fit. If the issuer is a listed company, the listing particulars prepared for this offer need only comply with the The Listing Rules' requirements for rights issues. This is the route preferred by the Investment Committees, as it gives shareholders the most favourable deal.

(b) *Open offer*

This looks like a rights issue, but it is subtly different. Shareholders are offered new securities in proportion to their existing holdings, but *not* on a PAL. They get a letter of entitlement which entitles them to a minimum number of securities. They can apply for more if they choose. The letter of entitlement is *not tradeable*, so all that the shareholders can do with it is to let their entitlement lapse or take it up.

For listed companies, UKLA listing requirements are the same for open offers and rights issues. The rationale for this is that, essentially, both are pre-emptive issues to shareholders.

As between these two, there is likely to be some preference on the company's part for doing an open rather than a rights offer, despite the attitude of investors. The reason lies in the letter of entitlement. As it is non-tradeable, there are none of the fears of issuing the letter before all the conditions to the issue have been satisfied – unlike a PAL (see **3.6.4**). Consequently an open offer is speedier than a rights offer, which in turn means that the company obtains its cash faster. The UKLA reinforces this by only requiring that the timetable for an open offer is approved by the relevant recognised investment exchange (e.g., the Stock Exchange) on which the company's securities are traded (LR, para. 4.24). The Stock Exchange requires that an open offer be open for at least 15 business days from the posting of application forms. This compares to the 21-day requirement for rights issues.

With vendor placings, it is important to look out for variations. The transactions are complex and refinements are being devised all the time. Just remember the basic theme of placing a buyer's securities (or offering them to its shareholders) as a way of providing cash to buy shares or an asset from a seller.

3.7 Timetable

The timetable set out below is provided only to be indicative of the typical path of an offer for sale or subscription, where the company is a new applicant seeking an initial listing from the UKLA and admission to trading on the Stock Exchange. That is, it is intended to show the general order of events over an acceptable timescale for a specific transaction. Circumstances may require significant variations in particular cases, where, for example, there are overseas regulatory requirements to take into account. The other transactions described in this chapter will also differ in certain aspects from the model below; for example, post-impact matters on a placing will generally occur within a shorter period of time.

The timetable assumes that any approvals required from shareholders for the issue will be obtained before the run-up to the offer itself. This is usual, and part of the process of preparing the company for the issue (see **3.3.1**). Approvals required include those under the Companies Act 1985, such as an increase in authorised capital (s. 121), or obtaining authority to allot for the directors (s. 80), or under ch. 10 of The Listing Rules (see **5.6.4**).

Remember that the applications to the UKLA and the Stock Exchange have to be coordinated (see **3.4**).

Date	*Events*
By 12 weeks before impact day	Appointment of advisers. Company's solicitors review issuer's constitution. Agree timetable and list of documents.
By 8 weeks before impact day	First draft of prospectus circulated. First drafting meeting (all parties). Accountants' long-form report available. Company's solicitors finalise changes to constitution. Company's solicitors prepare tax clearances.
By 5 weeks before impact day	Drafting meetings on prospectus continue: early draft submitted to Stock Exchange for comments. Tax clearances received. Opening meeting on underwriting agreement. Accountants initiate work on statements of indebtedness and working capital. Company's solicitors submit new or revised constitution to UKLA for comments.
By 3 weeks before impact day	Drafting meetings on prospectus continue. Submit draft prospectus to UKLA (at least 20 clear business days before publication). Initial publicity in newspapers (sometimes earlier).

	Public announcement of offer (sometimes earlier). Accountants finalise long-form report and working capital projections. Company's solicitors prepare first draft of verification notes.
By 2 weeks before impact day	Drafting meetings on prospectus continue. Negotiations on underwriting agreement continue. Accountants finalise short-form report for prospectus and statement of indebtedness.
By 1 week before impact day	All documents substantially agreed with UKLA. Verification meetings to finalise verification notes. Drafting meetings on prospectus continue.
Date	*Events*
By 2 days before impact day	Profit forecast finalised. Prospectus finalised (subject to minor amendments). Documents submitted to UKLA and Stock Exchange.
By 1 day before impact day	Price of securities finalised. Underwriting agreement finalised. Issuer's board meeting approves issue and all documents (underwriting agreement held in escrow).
Impact day	Underwriting agreement released from escrow. Sub-underwriting letters sent to sub-underwriters. Press conference and price announced. UKLA approves prospectus. Prospectus registered at Companies House. Prospectus bulk-printed.
By 1 day after impact day	Application lists open.
By 3 days after impact day	Newspaper publicity. Presentations ('roadshow') to institutions.
By 5 days after impact day	Applications for listing and admission to trading heard
By 7 days after impact day	Close application lists (sometimes earlier). Clear cheques from applicants. Allocate shares.
By 8 days after impact day	Allocations made to sub-underwriters.
By 12 days after impact day	Letters of acceptance or rejection posted to investors. Underwriting and sub-underwriting commissions paid.
By 14 days after impact day	Admissions to the Official List and to trading effective. [n.b. The need to obtain admission to CREST] Dealings in shares commence.
By 6 weeks after impact day	Share certificates posted.

3.8 Documents

This is a summary only of the documents most commonly of importance in these transactions.

3.8.1 STOCK EXCHANGE DOCUMENTS (FOR FULL LISTING OR ADMISSION TO THE AIM)

Prospectus or listing particulars, prospectus, mini-prospectus, circular to shareholders.
Application form(s) for listing.
Derogation and non-applicables letter.
Advertisement for the securities.
Working capital letter.
Profit forecast reports.
Memorandum and articles of association (primary offers only).
Directors' declarations (only primary offers).
Sponsor's declaration.
Temporary and final documents of title (i.e., PALs, letters of entitlement).

3.8.2 STOCK EXCHANGE DOCUMENTS

Prospectus or listing particulars, mini-prospectus, circular to shareholders.
Application for admission to trading.
Copy board resolution allotting the securities or authorising the issue.

3.8.3 AGREEMENTS

Underwriting or placing agreement.
Sub-underwriting or placing letter.
Acquisition agreements (for vendor placings with or without clawback).

3.8.4 SUPPORTING DOCUMENTS

Verification notes.
Completion board minutes.
Material contracts.
Accountants' reports (long and short-form).
Brokers' circular.
Notices and resolutions for any general meetings.

3.9 Checklist

This checklist is no more than a summary of the most important questions you need to ask yourself when acting on an issue of equity securities.

3.9.1 FOR COMPANIES WITH THEIR REGISTERED OFFICE IN THE UK

Q1 Has the company considered its obligations under ss. 80 and 89 Companies Act 1985, and the requirements of s. 121 Companies Act 1985?

See relevant sections in *LPC Guide: Business Law* and (if the company is listed on the Stock Exchange) **3.3.1.4**.

Q2 Have the directors of the company considered whether they are exercising their power to issue securities for a proper purpose?

See relevant sections in the *LPC Guide: Business Law.*

Q3 Is the company public or private?

IF PRIVATE, does it wish to make an offer to the public?

NO: see **4.3.1** and no further questions; the company may be able to issue shares privately to interested institutional shareholders provided the restrictions of s. 81(1) Companies Act 1985 and s. 57 Financial Services Act 1986 are observed.

YES: see **4.3.1** and then Q5.

IF PUBLIC, see Q4.

Q4 If the company wants to make an offer to the public, does it already have securities listed on the Offical List, or are its securities admitted to the Alternative Investment Market?

NO: see Q5.

YES: see **3.6.1** and **3.6.2** and then Q5.

Q5 Has the company appointed advisers for the offer yet?

NO: see **3.3** and then Q6.

YES: establish which ones and then see Q6.

Q6 Has the company notified the Bank of England of the proposed date of the offer?

See **3.3.1.6** and Q7.

Q7 Are the securities to be listed on the Official List?

NO: see Q8.

YES:

(a) If they are already admitted to the AIM, or a foreign stock exchange, and the company wants in future to have them on the Official List and traded on the Stock Exchange instead of or in addition to these other markets, see **3.5.8** and no further questions.

(b) If (a) is not true of the company, see **4.2** and then Q9.

Q8 Are the securities to be admitted to the AIM?

NO: see Q9.

YES: see **4.3** and Q9.

Q9 Is the company planning to issue an advertisement for the securities?

NO: see Q10.

YES: see **1.5.1.4** and then Q10.

Q10 Is the company making an acquisition at the same time as the offer?

NO: see Q11.

YES: see **3.6.5** and then Q11.

Q11 What marketing structure is the company proposing to use for the offer?

See **3.5** or **3.6**.

3.9.2 FOR COMPANIES INCORPORATED OVERSEAS

Q13 Does the company want to have its securities publicly traded in the UK?

NO: no further questions; it can, like UK private companies, seek to raise capital from interested investors privately.

YES: see Q14.

Q14 Does the company have a listing on a recognised overseas stock exchange?

NO: see Q5.

YES:

(a) Does the company want to issue new securities and have them listed on the Official List? See **4.2.9** and **4.2.10.5**.

(b) Does the company want simply to have listed on the Official List its securities already in issue? See **3.5.8**.

FOUR

REGULATION AND LIABILITY IN SECURITIES OFFERINGS

4.1 A Public Market For Securities

The regulation of the securities offerings we have been looking at in **chapter 3** varies, depending on whether the issuer's securities will be traded on a market or not at all. There are three options available:

(a) the company is public and wants its securities listed on the Official List and traded on the London Stock Exchange (see **4.2**);

(b) the company is public and wants its securities admitted to the AIM (see **4.3**);

(c) the company is private and so is not free to make an offer to the public (s. 81 Companies Act 1985) but may still find ways of offering its securities through private subscriptions.

Traditionally the Stock Exchange was the only official market on which securities could be publicly traded and prices quoted for them (see **1.6.2**).

The AIM was formed in 1995 as a successor to the Unlisted Securities Market (USM). AIM is based on the highly successful NASDAQ market in the United States. The objective is to attract new companies and investors at the junior end of the market through a relaxed regulatory regime and with a low cost base. Whereas the USM was seen as a 'feeder' market for listings on the Official List, the AIM is seen as a quite separate market from which companies may choose never to move, though they will be free to graduate to the Official List and Stock Exchange if they choose to do so.

The regulatory regime which applies to the AIM is described in **4.3**.

4.2 Listed Securities on the London Stock Exchange

4.2.1 WHAT DOES 'LISTED' MEAN?

When securities (see **3.1**) are 'listed', this means they have been admitted to the Official List of the UKLA and admitted to trading by the Stock Exchange. A price at which those securities can be bought and sold will be quoted by those who deal, or 'make a market', in them. Those securities can then be bought and sold on the stock market, i.e., through the Stock Exchange's trading procedures and in accordance with its rules. A listing therefore allows a company's securities to be freely traded and publicly priced. It opens up the company's securities to anyone interested in buying shares – the general public and the professional investing community.

4.2.2 WHY OBTAIN A LISTING?

Obtaining a listing is difficult and expensive. A company wanting a listing has a complex series of requirements to satisfy – they are described in **4.2.6**. Once listed, a company has to pay an annual listing fee to stay on the Official List (which rises as the value of its listed securities increases) and is subject to the UKLA's Continuing Obligations and the Stock Exchange's Disclosure Standards (see **4.2.10**). So what are the advantages?

4.2.2.1 Access to capital

One of the objects and requirements of listing is to attract new investors to the company, and their acquisition of the company's securities makes new money available to the company. If the company needs further capital in the future, it has a larger shareholder base from which to obtain those additional funds. In 1998, around £118 billion was raised by companies both joining and already on the Stock Exchange and the AIM, from a combination of equity and debt finance.

4.2.2.2 Liquidity

As a listing means public trading, the company hopes this will generate demand for its securities. The value of securities bought and sold on the Stock Exchange's UK domestic equity market every day is just over £4 billion – again, the size of the potential market is huge. As demand grows, the company will find it easier to make further issues of its securities, hence raising more capital. Increased demand should also enhance the company's share price, which in turn improves the company's buying power if it is using its own securities as an asset in making acquisitions (see **chapter 8** and **3.6.5**).

4.2.2.3 Prestige

The London Stock Exchange trades more equity securities by volume (over £834 billion in 1998) than any other stock exchange in Europe. Although New York trades more securities by value than London, London quotes more securities than any other major exchange worldwide. A quotation in London does not thereby change a company's fortunes overnight, but belonging to a market of this importance raises a company's profile in the eyes of the domestic and international investment community.

4.2.2.4 Investor relations

A listed company must inform the market of its financial performance, business developments and any activities affecting its securities so that investors can constantly appraise the company's value (see **4.2.10.1**). Though onerous, these duties are also an opportunity for the company to secure the future commitment and confidence of its investors. These are in turn vital in the context of access to capital and liquidity.

4.2.3 HOW DOES A COMPANY GO ABOUT OBTAINING A LISTING?

4.2.3.1 Application for admission to the Official List

A company's application to be listed on the Official List must be made through a sponsor by means of the UKLA's Form – Application for Admission of Securities to the Official List (see LR, sch. 3A and see **3.3.4** on the role of a sponsor). It is the company's responsibility to appoint a sponsor (LR, para. 2.3). The sponsor in turn needs to be satisfied it is dealing with a company and directors who understand the obligations and commitments expected of a company seeking listing (LR, paras 2.7 and 2.9). Although the relationship between company and sponsor is sometimes represented by a formal agreement in the shape of an engagement letter, there is no legal or UKLA obligation to do this.

Assuming the company's application presents no problems (on which, see below), the company's securities will eventually be admitted to listing when this is announced to the market as a whole by means of a notice disseminated by the electronic systems used by the UKLA for communications with the public (see LR, para. 7.1). Once a company is listed, the sponsor is expected to advise and assist the company in complying with its continuing obligations (see **4.2.10**).

4.2.3.2 Application for admission to trading on the Stock Exchange

In order to have securities admitted to the Stock Exchange's markets for listed securities, companies must follow a two-stage admission process. In addition to applying for admission to the Official List (see **4.2.3.1**), a company must also seek admission to trading on the Stock Exchange. This is done by means of the Stock Exchange Form — Application for Admission of Securities to Trading (sch. 1 of the Stock Exchange's Admission and Disclosure Standards). There is no Stock Exchange requirement to appoint a sponsor; however, it does recommend that a company appoint a nominated representative from an outside organisation to assist in the admission process. This representative will most likely be the sponsor required by the UKLA.

Admission to trading will occur simultaneously with admission to listing. It becomes effective only when the decision to admit the securities to trading has been announced by the Stock Exchange through the Company Announcements Office.

4.2.4 WHAT REQUIREMENTS MUST A COMPANY FULFIL TO OBTAIN A LISTING?

A company must comply with:

(a) part IV of the Financial Services Act 1986 (see **4.2.5**);

(b) The Listing Rules' provisions on:

  (i) general conditions for listing (see LR, ch. 3, and **4.2.6.2**),

  (ii) specific contents of prospectus or listing particulars (see LR, ch. 6, and **4.2.6.3**),

  (iii) application procedure (see LR, ch. 7, and **4.2.6.5**),

  (iv) publication of prospectus or listing particulars (see LR, ch. 8, and **4.2.6.5**); and

(c) The Stock Exchange's Admission and Disclosure Standards (see **4.2.7**).

4.2.5 PART IV FINANCIAL SERVICES ACT 1986

This section is a description of the legal framework around which a company seeking a listing of its securities and its advisers must work. Any lawyer working in this field must be familiar with this framework; in the actual handling of an issue of securities, however, attention tends to be focused on the detailed requirements laid down by The Listing Rules as to listing (see **4.2.6.2** and **4.2.6.3**), as these will determine the structure of an offering and what can actually be written into the offering and listing document read by investors.

4.2.5.1 Background

The Financial Services Act 1986 ('FS Act') currently governs the admission of securities to listing. Since 1 May 2000, the FSA, acting as the UKLA, has been the 'competent authority' under the Act, with general power to make listing rules (s. 142(6)). The rules it has created are set out in The Listing Rules, which have statutory force by virtue of the FS Act.

4.2.5.2 Why must a company seeking a listing comply with Part IV's requirements?

Under s. 143 FS Act, a company may only apply for listing in accordance with The Listing Rules. Under s. 144, the UKLA cannot admit securities to listing unless The Listing Rules have been fulfilled in respect of those securities.

4.2.5.3 What are the UKLA's listing powers under the FS Act?

The UKLA is the competent authority with power to make listing rules. In practice, it issues occasional amendments to The Listing Rules, usually after prior consultation with affected parties together with their financial and legal advisers.

It is empowered to grant dispensations to its listing rules (s. 156(2): see **4.2.6.1**), and in practice exercises considerable flexibility in the interpretation and application of the rules. The curious result of this is that, though the rules have the effective force of law, they often work in reality more like the rules of the City Code on Takeovers and Mergers: in other words, it is as important to understand the spirit behind the rules as it is to know their letter.

The UKLA has power to refuse an application for listing (s. 144(3)). If it grants approval, its decision is not justiciable (s. 144(6)).

The UKLA is entitled to suspend a listing temporarily or to discontinue a listing altogether (s. 145: this is generally referred to as 'de-listing'). This is the ultimate sanction for companies which fail to comply with the Continuing Obligations in The Listing Rules or commit any other breaches of the rules (for instance, when making a further issue of shares at some future date). Decisions to de-list securities are thought to be susceptible to judicial review applications (for example, by shareholders, see *R* v *International Stock Exchange of the United Kingdom and the Republic of Ireland Ltd, ex parte Else (1982) Ltd* [1993] QB 534). The chances of success are always likely to be slim in view of the need for the UKLA to act quickly and decisively, and the courts' general reluctance to interfere with the decisions made by securities markets regulators (see **8.8.7**).

It is vital, therefore, when acting in a transaction where a company is seeking admission of its securities to listing, to ensure that the company understands what its Continuing Obligations will be (see **4.2.10**), and at no stage prejudices its relationship with the UKLA.

4.2.5.4 The need for listing particulars or a prospectus

As the competent authority, the UKLA can impose requirements on companies seeking admission to the Official List in its Listing Rules. In particular, it requires as a condition of admission the publication of listing particulars (which are the particulars required by The Listing Rules).

Section 144(2) FS Act requires as a condition for admission to listing the publication of a 'prospectus' where securities are offered to the public in the UK for the first time before admission.

There are several exemptions to the requirement to publish a prospectus where there is an offer to the public. These are listed in sch. 11A to the FS Act. The principal exemptions cover the following circumstances:

(a) Where shares are offered to no more than 50 persons.

(b) Where securities are offered to persons whose ordinary business activities involve them in buying, selling and managing investments.

(c) Where securities are offered to a restricted circle of persons who are sufficiently knowledgeable to understand the risks involved in accepting the offer.

(d) Where the issue raises less than 40,000 ECU in total.

If the offer falls within one of these exemptions, the need for a prospectus falls away; the need for listing particulars will still exist by virtue of The Listing Rules. Where, however, the exceptions do not apply, it will be necessary to prepare a prospectus rather than listing particulars. The Listing Rules apply in relation to a prospectus in exactly the same way as they apply in relation to listing particulars, but as if references to listing particulars were a reference to a prospectus. Accordingly, the contents requirements for the document will stay exactly the same (see **4.2.6.3**), and will depend on the type of transaction. It is just the name of the document that will change.

There are exemptions to the need to produce listing particulars (see **4.2.5.5**). These exemptions are not available where the document is a prospectus.

Although the practical difference between publishing a prospectus or listing particulars is therefore small, it is an offence not to publish a prospectus if one is required, and the rules regarding legal responsibility for publication of a prospectus slightly differ from those for listing particulars (see **4.3.4**).

In practice, an offer for sale will almost certainly require publication of a prospectus. In contrast, a placing will normally be exempt on the grounds that securities are offered only to a restricted group of people who are in the investment business or who are sufficiently knowledgeable. By the same token, an intermediaries offer is also likely to be exempt from the prospectus requirements.

Where a company's securities are already listed, and it is undertaking a subsequent offering, the prospectus requirements will also apply. These are described in **3.6.2**.

4.2.5.5 When are listing particulars not required?

NOT APPLY TO PROSPECTUS ONLY IF NEED LISTING P'S.

LR, para 5.23A, indicates that issuers may be exempted from the obligation to publish a prospectus or listing particulars, provided an application for admission of the securities to listing is made, where:

(a) an equivalent document has been published in the previous year as a result of the securities in question having been the subject of a public issue, or issued in connection with a takeover or merger;

(b) the securities have been listed in another Member State of the European Union for the past three years (or, if for less, the relevant local stock exchange has confirmed the issuer has complied with its rules since being listed); or

(c) the securities have been traded on the AIM for at least two years prior to the issue.

In these cases the issuer must produce an exempt listing document. In the case of (a), this should contain details of any material changes since the equivalent document was published, a statement as to the securities being listed, and the directors' responsibility statement (LR, ch. 5, app. 2). In practice, this kind of exempt listing document is rarely possible, because the changes which occur to any listed company in any 12-month period are usually significant enough to merit large-scale revisions to the information presented in the original document.

In the case of (b), the exempt listing document required which is discussed in more detail in **4.2.9.2**.

In addition, LR, para. 5.27 sets out a number of categories of issues for which listing particulars are not required. These include the situations where the new securities would increase a company's listed securities of the relevant class by less than 10 per cent and where shares of a class already listed are allotted to employees. In the cases described in para. 5.27, paras 5.28 to 5.30 prescribe certain information which must be published in printed form.

4.2.5.6 What should prospectuses and listing particulars contain?

ps81

The detailed requirements for the contents of prospectuses and listing particulars are set out in **4.2.6.3**. Section 146 FS Act requires that, in addition to the information The Listing Rules demand, a prospectus shall contain:

> all such information as investors and their professional advisers would reasonably require, and reasonably expect to find there, for the purpose of making an informed assessment of—
>
> (a) the assets and liabilities, financial position, profits and losses, and prospects of the issuer of the securities; and
>
> (b) the rights attaching to those securities.

Section 146 thus imposes a general obligation to disclose in the prospectus or listing particulars facts material to an investment decision about the company's securities. It is an overriding duty *to which the detailed contents requirements in The Listing Rules are themselves subject*. When preparing a prospectus or listing particulars, it is therefore vital always to have the words of s. 146 in mind.

4.2.5.7 What are the risks of civil liability in preparing prospectuses or listing particulars?

Prospectuses and listing particulars make a series of statements about the company's assets, liabilities, financial position, profits and losses, its prospects, the rights attaching to its securities and other assorted details about the company and its performance. These are all made ultimately with a view to attracting investors to acquire those securities. There are the usual risks of civil liability associated with such statements with which you will already be familiar:

(a) *Negligent misstatement*

Liability under the principles derived from *Hedley Byrne & Co. Ltd* v *Heller and Partners Ltd* [1964] AC 465 and *Caparo Industries plc* v *Dickman* [1990] 2 AC 605 will arise if the maker of the statement owes a duty of care to the reader and that duty is breached. The law implies a duty of care where the maker possesses special skills or knowledge and knows or ought to know that the reader will rely for a particular purpose on that skill or knowledge. The reader will, though, have to be within the contemplation of the person making the statement. In the case of prospectuses and listing particulars, new investors will in law be relying on the document. A duty of care may extend to purchasers of the company's securities in the 'after market' where the document specifically or implicitly contemplates this (*Possfund Custodian Trustee Ltd* v *Diamond* [1996] 2 All ER 774). It is important to be conscious of this risk when drafting the document.

Prospectuses and listing particulars are prepared with the clear intention of encouraging people to invest in the company which issues them, so the investor will have little difficulty in showing reliance if they contain a misstatement. If there has been a failure to exercise due care (as described above) in making that statement, the maker will be liable to the investor for any foreseeable loss resulting from it. Liable parties include:

(i) The company itself: the company issues the prospectus or listing particulars and it will clearly be reasonable for an investor to assume the company's expertise in relation to its own affairs!

(ii) The directors of the company: the directors are required to assume responsibility for the contents of a prospectus or listing particulars by virtue of the Listing Rules (LR, para. 6.A.3). Directors, both in practice and law, can usually be taken to possess a reasonable degree of expertise in relation to the affairs of their company on which an investor will almost certainly be entitled to rely, and the responsibility statement makes it clear that the directors have authorised the statements contained in the prospectus or listing particulars: hence they will find it very difficult to avoid liability.

(iii) If the misstatement is contained in financial information supplied or verified by the company's auditors (such as the company's latest audited results), the auditors or the accountants reporting on the financial information would almost certainly be liable.

(iv) The merchant bank appointed by the company to advise it on the offering (see **3.3.5** for a more detailed description of the merchant bank's activities) will probably also be at risk of liability. To some extent, this will depend on the structure adopted for the offering (see **3.5.3.1** on this point).

In all cases, however, the UKLA makes it clear (LR, para. 2.9) that the merchant bank (or 'issuing house') has a responsibility as sponsor to ensure that the directors understand and fulfil their own responsibilities properly, and must be satisfied that the company is suitable for listing. This may not amount to issuing direct statements on the face of the prospectus or listing particulars to this effect; but certainly the professional investment community places considerable importance on the quality of the 'name' sponsoring the company. An investor may therefore be able to show that the bank is so intrinsically associated with the contents of the prospectus or listing particulars that it is legally responsible for misstatements in them.

Quite apart from this, an issuing house as sponsor is required (LR, para. 2.15) to state publicly in respect of any profit forecast made in the prospectus or listing particulars that it is satisfied the forecast has been made after due and careful enquiry: profit forecasts are probably among the most exposed of any statements made (and have been the subject of negligence actions involving merchant banks in a different context (*Morgan Crucible Co. plc* v *Hill Samuel & Co. Ltd* [1991] Ch 295). A merchant bank therefore needs to be particularly careful here.

(v) Other advisers: any other party which is responsible for a statement in a prospectus or listing particulars which turns out to be false or misleading (for example, a firm of surveyors producing a valuation report for a property investment company) will also be exposed to liability. Solicitors also fall into this bracket, though it is almost unknown for a firm of solicitors to authorise a statement: their task is confined to that of advising their clients (typically the company or merchant bank) on the legal accuracy of a statement – hence their liability, if any, will be to their own clients, not investors.

(b) *Misrepresentation*

Misrepresentations in a prospectus or listing particulars will give rise to the following remedies:

(i) *Rescission*

An investor will be entitled to rescind his contract with the company where he is induced to invest by statements of fact made in the prospectus or listing particulars which are untrue. In some issues, the contract will in fact be with the company's merchant bank, in which case the right of rescission is obviously against the bank.

The right applies whether the misrepresentation in the prospectus or listing particulars was fraudulent, negligent or entirely innocent, although the misrepresentation must be material and must be as to fact rather than opinion (for example, production figures for the past year, not the company's prospects in the ensuing 12 months).

Of course the usual limitations as regards the right to rescind apply: in particular, it will not survive if the investor affirms the contract (e.g., by trying to sell the shares), nor will it extend beyond a reasonable period of time following discovery of the misrepresentation by the investor. The courts have in the past held that a two-week delay between discovery and seeking rescission was too long a period.

It is worth bearing in mind that the court may refuse rescission and grant damages instead (Misrepresentation Act 1967, s. 2(2)), though not for consequential losses.

(ii) *Damages*

If the misrepresentation was fraudulent, the investor may sue for all the loss flowing directly from the misrepresentation (whether foreseeable at the time of the misrepresentation, or not), as in any action in deceit. The investor will need to show he was induced to acquire the securities by the fraudulent misrepresentation. The right to sue for damages lies against any person responsible for the misrepresentation (on which, see above).

If the misrepresentation is negligent or innocent, the investor may sue under s. 2(1) Misrepresentation Act 1967, as the company (or merchant bank, as the case may be) will have a contract with the investor. There have been two traditional benefits of pursuing this remedy in preference to an action based on *Caparo Industries plc* v *Dickman* principles, as far as the investor is concerned. The first has been that the skill or knowledge of the maker of the statement does not have to be established, and the second that the maker has to show that he had an honest and reasonable belief that his statement was true.

The damages for a claim under the Act return the victim of the misrepresentation to the position he was in before the misstatement. *Royscot Trust Ltd* v *Rogerson* [1991] 2 QB 297 has made it clear that, as far as the measure of damages is concerned, the maker of a negligent or innocent misstatement is liable to the same extent as for a fraudulent misrepresentation – that is, for all the loss flowing directly from the statement whether foreseeable or not at the time the statement was made. This may therefore confer another advantage on investors pursuing a claim for negligent misstatements under the Act rather than *Caparo Industries plc* v *Dickman*, as damages in tort for misstatements are recoverable only if they are foreseeable.

(c) *Breach of contract*

Damages arising from actions in misrepresentation will put an investor in the position he was in before the misstatement. An investor may in addition seek to recover damages for his loss of bargain, that is, what the securities would have been worth had the misstatement made in the prospectus or listing particulars been correct. This assumes that the misstatement has become a term of the contract, but an investor who takes securities on the strength of what is in the prospectus or listing particulars should be able to treat all material statements in the particulars or prospectus as contractual representations.

The old rule that a shareholder could only sue for damages for breach of contract if he had rescinded his contract of allotment in the first place has been removed by s. 111A Companies Act 1985.

As with rescission, in some offers, the investor's contract will be with the merchant bank and not the company – hence it may be the merchant bank and not the company which will be the defendant in these circumstances.

(d) *Section 150 Financial Services Act 1986*

Although there is no doubt that investors will continue to rely on the various heads of liability described above when suing for misstatements in prospectuses or listing particulars, the Financial Services Act 1986 is likely to be the most powerful weapon in the investor's armoury, because it suffers from none of the constraints of other remedies (for example, the need to show reliance under *Hedley Byrne & Co. Ltd* v *Heller and Partners Ltd* or inducement in misrepresentation). Having said this, it has yet to be tested in the courts. It makes the 'persons responsible' for listing particulars or prospectuses liable to pay compensation to any person who has acquired any securities, and suffered loss as a result of any untrue or misleading statement in the particulars or prospectus or any omission from them of anything which s. 146 FS Act, would require (the general duty of disclosure – see **4.2.5.6**).

Note there need be no reliance on the misstatement, only a causal connection between it and the loss suffered. Note also that a misstatement includes an omission – but an omission which would fall foul of s. 146: hence an omission of detail required by The Listing Rules (see **4.2.6.3**) will not of itself give rise to liability under this section. The remedy is available to subsequent purchasers of the securities as well as the original investors (it will be more difficult for subsequent purchasers to argue this in a claim in negligence), although proving the loss was caused by the misstatement will become more difficult the longer the time elapsed since publication of the particulars or prospectus.

Who are the persons responsible? For *listing particulars*, they are defined in s. 152 FS Act:

(i) The company (the issuer of the securities).

(ii) The directors and anyone who has agreed to become a director following the issue.

(iii) Anyone else who gives the responsibility statement (in the case of an overseas company with an unusual corporate structure, this may be a party other than a director – for example, a general manager).

(iv) Anyone who has authorised the contents of, or any part of, the particulars. This will include the auditors and/or reporting accountants and the financial information in the particulars which they approve. It will also extend to the merchant bank where the listing particulars contain a profit forecast and the bank has to report in the particulars that it is satisfied that the forecast has been prepared after due and careful enquiry. Where the merchant bank issues the listing particulars in its own name (for example, in an offer for sale) it is likely to be treated as having 'authorised' the document and so its risk of exposure under this section will be greater. Surveyors who produce a valuation report on the portfolio of assets held by a property company will be taken to have authorised part of the document.

(v) Solicitors and other professionals will not be persons responsible by virtue of s. 152(8), provided they only advise in a professional capacity.

Defences exist under s. 151 where listing particulars are published without the knowledge or consent of a responsible person, or where a person reasonably believed when the particulars were published that a misstatement was true or that it was proper to leave a statement out of the particulars.

Section 154A FS Act applies all of the provisions relating to responsibility and liability for listing particulars to *prospectuses*. It also extends the reference in s. 152 to the issuer of securities to include the person offering or proposing to offer them. On the face of it, this would extend responsibility for misleading statements in a prospectus to, for example, employees or other individual shareholders offering for sale their shares as part of a public offer. However, s. 154A(2) (inserted by the Public Offer of Securities (Amendment) Regulations 1999) states that a person shall not be responsible where:

(a) he is not the issuer, but is making the offer in association with the issuer; and

(b) the prospectus . . . was drawn up primarily by the issuer, or by one or more persons acting on behalf of the issuer.

Therefore, in the example above, employees would not be held responsible unless they had somehow otherwise accepted responsibility for or authorised some part of the particulars.

To summarise, civil liability for a prospectus or listing particulars may arise through:

(a) negligent misstatement (*Hedley Byrne & Co. Ltd* v *Heller and Partners Ltd*),

(b) misrepresentation,

(c) breach of contract, and

(d) s. 150 Financial Services Act 1986.

4.2.5.8 What are the risks of criminal liability when preparing listing particulars or prospectuses?

(a) *Financial Services Act 1986*

You need to be aware of both s. 47 and s. 57 FS Act (see **1.5.1.4**). As far as s. 57 is concerned, there is a whole range of documents which may fall foul of the definition of investment advertisement (see **1.5.1.4**), but listing particulars are exempt from the investment advertisements regime by virtue of s. 58(1)(d)(ii) FS Act, and prospectuses are exempt by virtue of art. 14 of the Financial Services Act 1986 (Investment Advertisements) (Exemptions) (No. 2) Order 1995 (SI 1995/1536).

(b) *Theft Act 1968*

Section 15 Theft Act 1968 makes it an offence to dishonestly obtain by deception property (including cash) belonging to another. Deception takes place when a person attempts to pass off a statement which is or may be false as being true. Dishonesty is a question left to juries to decide. The same statement may give rise to liability under s. 47(1) FS Act and this provision.

Section 19 Theft Act 1968 makes it an offence for an officer of the company (or person purporting to act as an officer of the company), for example, a director, to publish or concur in publishing a written statement or account which to his knowledge is or may be materially false, misleading or deceptive, if he intends to deceive the company's members or creditors in the process.

Other more minor offences also exist, such as failure to deliver prospectuses or listing particulars to the Registrar of Companies under s. 149 FS Act.

4.2.5.9 Supplementary prospectuses and listing particulars

At any time following the preparation of a prospectus but before dealings start in the relevant securities, a supplementary prospectus will have to be published if there is a significant change affecting any matter mentioned in the original prospectus, or a significant omission appears in the original prospectus (s. 147 FS Act). This and the following provisions apply equally to listing particulars, so prospectus and listing particulars should be read interchangeably in this section.

What is significant? Significance is to be measured against the test of disclosure in s. 146 FS Act – in other words, it depends whether the change significantly affects the information an investor would reasonably require in order to make an informed assessment about the company.

A supplementary prospectus carries exactly the same risks of liability as the original (including the possibility of compensation under s. 150 FS Act).

What form does a supplementary prospectus take? LR, para. 5.16, gives you the answer. It contains a directors' responsibility statement. It states it is to be read in conjunction with the original prospectus. It details the significant changes which have arisen since the original prospectus was submitted to the Stock Exchange and indicates that the directors are aware of no other significant changes on which the company should be reporting.

In practice, everything possible is done to minimise the prospect of having to publish a supplementary prospectus. Partly this is because of the additional work and time involved, not to mention the cost of producing another document. Largely, though, it is because the need to publish a supplementary prospectus is often taken as a sign that all is not well with the issue, and this may affect its success. This may only be a matter of perception, but if the supplementary prospectus was required because the company and its advisers were unable to anticipate new developments or resolve outstanding issues adequately prior to publication of the original prospectus, this may cause them considerable embarrassment.

Submission of the original prospectus for approval by the UKLA will precede commencement of dealings in the securities only by a matter of days, hence the time in which the potential obligation to prepare a supplementary prospectus exists is very short – in practice, therefore, a supplementary prospectus is rarely required.

If the change (or new matter) arises after dealings have commenced, that will not require a new prospectus. The change will, though, affect the price at which the securities trade on the market – and it might give rise to questions of liability as discussed in **4.2.5.7** above if it adversely affects the value of the securities.

4.2.6 THE LISTING RULES

As we have seen, Part IV of the Financial Services Act 1986 gives the Stock Exchange the power to make Listing Rules. The Listing Rules requirements apply equally to prospectuses and listing particulars. References in this section to prospectuses therefore apply to listing particulars as well. The Listing Rules contain provisions on the following:

(a) the general conditions to be satisfied by any issuer (LR, ch. 3, see **4.2.6.2**);

(b) the specific contents requirements for prospectuses (LR, ch. 6, see **4.2.6.3**);

(c) the process through which companies must go to obtain a listing for their securities (application procedure, LR, ch. 7, see **4.2.6.5**);

(d) the requirements applying to the constitutional documents of companies seeking listing for their securities, i.e., articles of association (see **3.3.1.2**);

(e) continuing obligations which listed companies must observe once listed (LR, ch. 9, see **4.2.10**);

(f) rules applying to listed companies involved in acquisitions, sales and takeovers once listed (LR, ch. 10; these are *in addition* to the City Code on Takeovers and Mergers, and are dealt with in that context – see **5.6.4**);

(g) rules applying to the listing of the securities of overseas companies (LR, ch. 17, see **4.2.9**);

(h) rules applying to the listing of eurobonds and other euro-currency debt securities (LR, ch. 23; not covered in this book);

(i) some specific rules applying to certain types of companies seeking listing of their securities, such as property companies, investment trusts, public sector issuers and innovative high growth companies (LR, chs 18–22 and ch. 25; not covered in this book).

4.2.6.1 Status and interpretation of the listing rules

The natural tendency of the lawyer is to treat a book of rules as an inflexible and unyielding set of limitations and prescriptions, particularly when, as here, the rules have been prepared under a statutory power. While an applicant must always assume that compliance with the rules is required, the UKLA is prepared to be flexible in its interpretation and application of the rules (though this may not always be to the applicant's advantage). Hence if a company finds it is unable to comply with a rule, the right course is not to assume that it is automatically disbarred from seeking a listing: its sponsor should discuss the point with the UKLA first to see whether there is scope for relaxing the rule in this case.

The Listing Rules expressly indicate where the UKLA is prepared to deviate from the stated rule, for example, where disclosure of information in the prospectus otherwise required by The Listing Rules would be contrary to the public interest (see LR, para. 5.18).

In any event, the UKLA has the power to grant dispensations from the general duty of disclosure under s. 146 FS Act by virtue of s. 148 FS Act, where enforcing it would be contrary to the public interest, or seriously detrimental to the company.

The process of seeking 'derogations' from the rules is governed by LR, para. 5.21. It is generally handled by the sponsors in writing, though may also be done by another adviser, such as the lawyer. They will prepare a list of derogations wanted by the company, which they submit to the UKLA for approval during the application process. On occasion, the UKLA is not prepared to make a concession and a compromise is needed. Generally, though, requests for derogations with suitable reasons will be received reasonably favourably.

In addition, when checking listing particulars against the UKLA's specific requirements (see **4.2.6.3**), requirements which are not relevant to the company should be listed in a letter to the UKLA. This 'non-applicables' letter is usually prepared by the sponsoring brokers. It is a quite normal part of the procedure (see LR, para. 5.17).

Hence it is important to look at these requirements as a perimeter fence which the UKLA carefully polices but is prepared in appropriate circumstances to snip away at.

4.2.6.2 Basic requirements

The general conditions for listing are set out in LR, ch. 3. These conditions are prefaced by the UKLA's 'health warning' in para. 3.1 that it may apply special conditions to particular issuers where it considers this appropriate in the interests of protecting investors. The Listing Rules are therefore not a comprehensive guide to all the factors which decide suitability. Essentially the UKLA wants to preserve some element of flexibility in its admissions process.

The other basic requirements mentioned below are the most significant.

(a) The minimum expected market value of equity securities for which listing is sought is £700,000 (LR, para. 3.16(a)). In practice, companies seeking listing will require a market capitalisation significantly in excess of this in order to meet typical investor demand and satisfy the required advertising costs – a more usual value would be at least £5 million.

(b) At least 25 per cent of any class of shares for which listing is sought must (by the end of the offering) be in the hands of the public, i.e., not directors, major shareholders of the company or people connected with them, unless widespread distribution of the shares would still be possible with less than 25 per cent in the public's hands (LR, paras 3.18 to 3.20).

(c) The securities for which listing is sought must be freely transferable (LR, para. 3.15), i.e., pre-emption rights on transfer of shares will have to be removed.

(d) The company should have a three-year trading record and should present audited accounts for the latest three years (LR, para. 3.3(a)). This is one of the requirements which the UKLA will relax in particular cases. Financial information submitted must be prepared and audited in accordance with UK, US or international accounting standards (LR, para. 3.3(c)).

(e) The UKLA needs to be satisfied that the company is an independent entity and that it has no conflicts of interest with substantial shareholders. Where a shareholder has more than 30 per cent of the votes in the company, clearance will be needed before listing can proceed (LR, paras. 3.12 and 3.13).

4.2.6.3 Specific requirements

The specific contents requirements for a prospectus or listing particulars are set out in LR, ch. 6. The UKLA will require copies of the prospectus or particulars marked in the margin to indicate where particular items from LR, ch. 6 have been dealt with (see LR, para. 5.11). Partly for this reason and partly to be absolutely sure that The Listing Rules have been complied with, at some stage in the preparation of the prospectus or listing particulars, they will need to be cross-checked rigorously against LR, ch. 6 to be certain that nothing is missing. The sponsoring brokers will prepare the marked-up draft for the UKLA, but it is sensible for the solicitors to check the document as well.

It is not possible to list all the specific contents requirements: only the main features have been covered. There are a number of points to bear in mind before studying the list below:

(a) The general duty of disclosure in s. 146 FS Act is the overriding requirement. The basic rule is: if it is material, it should be disclosed, whether LR, ch. 6, requires it or not.

(b) Not all the specific contents listed in LR, ch. 6, are required for every prospectus or set of listing particulars. The contents requirements are more relaxed for rights issues, other secondary issues and debt securities issues (see LR, ch. 5, app. 1).

(c) Specific exemptions from the requirement to publish a prospectus or listing particulars may apply (see **4.2.5.5**).

There is no need to follow the order in which the requirements are listed in LR, ch. 6, when preparing the prospectus or listing particulars.

The specific contents requirements are divided into a number of parts:

(a) *Part A: the company, its directors and professional advisers*

(i) name and address of company, date and country of incorporation;

(ii) names and functions of directors;

(iii) names and addresses of the company's auditors, bankers, sponsor — this requirement leads to the typical display of the team of advisers at the front of the prospectus or particulars;

(iv) directors' responsibility statement. This should read:

The directors of [the issuer], whose names appear on page [ ], accept responsibility for the information contained in this document. To the best of the knowledge and belief of the directors (who have taken all reasonable care to ensure that such is the case) the information contained in this document is in accordance with the facts and does not omit anything likely to affect the import of such information.

This statement should also be given by those intending to become directors upon listing.

(v) statements of consent from experts; where the prospectus or listing particulars contains a report from an expert, that expert must state his consent to its inclusion, and authorise the relevant part of the prospectus or listing particulars for the purposes of s. 152(1)(e) FS Act (see **4.2.5.7**):

(b) *Part B: the company's securities, and the terms and conditions of any recent marketing of securities*

This is principally a description of the securities for which admission is being sought, their price and their rights.

(c) *Part C: general information about the company and its share and loan capital*

(i) details of the share capital of the company;

(ii) the company's group structure, if relevant;

(iii) substantial and controlling shareholders in the company;

(iv) all material contracts entered into within the last two years will need to be disclosed (including consideration and terms and conditions); this does not extend to contracts entered into in the ordinary course of business;

(v) list of contracts available for public inspection: this includes the material contracts, the last two years' accounts, directors' service contracts and the memorandum and articles of association of the company.

Derogations from the need to put the material contracts on display are quite often sought. The UKLA does countenance this under LR, para. 5.22. It will rarely permit a company to exclude a particular contract altogether, but may allow it to delete from the public eye any sensitive or confidential commercial information, in particular the amount of consideration passing under a contract.

(d) *Part D: information on the company's activities*

(i) a description of principal activities;

(ii) an analysis of sales by geographical area and product group;

(iii) details of land, buildings and principal establishments;

(iv) policy on research and development;

(v) number of employees;

(vi) material investments in other companies;

(vii) information on any pending or threatened legal proceedings which may yet, or in the past year did, represent a significant liability.

(e) *Part E: financial information*

This information is to be provided for the entire group of companies to which the issuer belongs. An accountants' report on a new applicant for listing is not required, unless the last three years' audited accounts no longer present a complete picture because of material changes. A comparative table for the last three financial years can be used instead. The table should compare profits and losses, assets, cashflow, accounting policies and notes for those three years. If an accountants' report is not needed, the sponsor will need to confirm this in writing to the Exchange, and the reporting accountants will have to confirm the three years' accounts were satisfactorily prepared, and the comparative table is a proper extract from them. The detailed provisions on these accounts and tables is contained in LR, ch. 12. The solicitors' function is to check that everything required by ch. 6, part E and ch. 12 has been included. The information required by part E whether a comparative table or accountants' report is produced is:

(i) statement of any significant change in the financial position of the company or group since its last financial statement;

(ii) statement of current indebtedness;

(iii) statement of company or group's contingent liabilities.

This part also requires the directors to state that the company's working capital is sufficient. Working capital is available cash and facilities less immediate cash requirements (eg, salaries). The accountants will invariably produce a report on the adequacy of the working capital to give the directors the comfort they need before making this statement, though this report will not be reproduced in the listing particulars: it is a private document addressed to the directors of the company alone. The merchant bank or sponsoring member firm will also have to confirm to the UKLA (LR, para. 2.14) that the working capital statement has been arrived at by the directors after due and careful inquiry and the person or institution providing the finance has confirmed that the finance exists.

(f) *Part F: the management*

(i) directors' remuneration for the previous and coming years;

(ii) details of directors' existing or proposed service contracts;

(iii) directors' (and their families') interests in the company's securities;

(iv) details of employee share option schemes.

(g) *Part G: information on recent developments and prospects of the company's group*

If the company wishes, it may choose to include a profit forecast in the listing particulars. If it does, that profit forecast must contain:

(i) a report by the accountants on the accounting policies and calculations used in arriving at the forecast (LR, para. 12.24);

(ii) the assumptions on which the forecast is based (for example, that inflation will not rise above 5 per cent next year) (LR, para. 12.27); and

(iii) a statement from the sponsor that the forecast was made by the company after due and careful enquiry (LR, para. 2.15).

Trends affecting the company or group over the next year (in terms of prices, demand for its products, costs, new factors affecting its particular trading activities) will in any event have to be reported on.

4.2.6.4 Typical layout of a prospectus or listing particulars

A prospectus or listing particulars does not have to follow a regimented pattern, only to 'provide factual information in words and figures, in as easily analysable and comprehensible a form as possible' (LR, para. 5.7). In addition, The Listing Rules restrict the use of some techniques for presenting information: for instance, the prospectus or particulars should not contain pictures, graphs or illustrations unless the UKLA is satisfied this is the only way to present the information (LR, para. 5.7). There are also restrictions on the use of text and illustrations on the cover of the document.

In spite of the relative latitude which issuers have in the construction of their prospectus or listing particulars, they do typically follow a particular order.

Front page

'Headline' for the offer and number of shares to be issued.

Statement that an application for listing has been made to the UKLA.

Responsibility statement.

Statement that the prospectus or listing particulars has been delivered to the Registrar of Companies under s. 149 Financial Services Act 1986.

Other wording required to satisfy SFA Rules (the issuing house will almost certainly be an SFA member) and US securities legislation (if there are US shareholders or any risk of the offer being made in the US).

Following pages

Contents, definitions.

Share capital statement – this must appear on the first page.

Indebtedness statement – this must appear on the first page.

Expected timetable.

Directors and advisers.

Key information: this is a summary of the key commercial and financial facts about the issuer, the reasons for the offer and its structure.

Commercial information: the issuer's industry, history, performance and trading record, and strategy.

Management team.

Reasons for the offer and offer structure.

Profit forecast, followed by accountants' and issuing house's letters on the forecast.

Accountants' report.

Information required by The Listing Rules and not included elsewhere (generally referred to as 'additional information' or 'statutory and general information'): details about the company's share capital, subsidiaries, constitution, directors and their interests, share schemes, pensions, premises, and arrangements for the offer; most importantly, statements regarding material contracts, litigation, sufficiency of working capital and documents available for inspection.

Terms and conditions for applying, and public application form.

4.2.6.5 What happens to the prospectus or listing particulars?

This section covers the procedure an issuer must go through with its prospectus or listing particulars and related documents to apply for listing. Most of what follows is derived from LR, ch. 7, and assumes that the company is not yet listed. If the company already has a listing, the application process is somewhat more relaxed.

There are a number of stages any applicant must go through:

(a) *10-day documents*

LR, para. 5.9, lists the documents which must be submitted to the UKLA at least 10 clear business days before the date of intended publication of the particulars (which will be the date the offer is actually launched). However, where a new applicant is seeking a listing or there are complex issues to be resolved, the draft prospectus should be submitted at least 20 clear business days before intended publication (LR, para. 5.10). The most important of these are:

(i) the draft prospectus or set of particulars;

(ii) letters from the reporting accountants that the company's accounts have been audited in accordance with international accounting standards or standards applied in the UK or the US, and that the comparative table (if relevant) is properly extracted from the audited accounts, and, if there is one, reporting on the profit forecast;

(iii) the derogation and 'non-applicables' letters (see **4.2.6.1**).

If, as is usually the case, revised drafts of the particulars are produced after the original draft has been lodged with the UKLA, the UKLA should be sent the new drafts, marked up to show the changes (LR, para. 5.11).

(b) *48-hour documents*

At least two business days before the company's application is heard by the UKLA, a number of documents should be sent to it. The most important are:

(i) the AFA form (application for admission to listing: LR, sch. 3A);

(ii) final copies of the prospectus or listing particulars (one copy signed and dated on behalf of the directors);

(iii) the form in which the prospectus or listing particulars is to be published in the press (see below).

The full list of 48-hour documents is at LR, para. 7.5. Paragraph 7.5(g) requires additional documents to be submitted by new applicants.

(c) *Approval*

The prospectus or particulars must be formally approved by the UKLA before publication. LR, para. 5.12, contains another list of documents which must be submitted to the UKLA in final form before formal approval will be given. They include a declaration by the sponsor in the form set out in LR, sch. 4A. In this, the sponsor is required to declare that the directors of the company have had their responsibilities explained to them (see LR, para. 2.9). In addition, in the case of a new applicant, the sponsor must declare (if relevant) that an accountants' report is not required (LR, para. 2.12) and that it has received written confirmation that the directors have established procedures which provide a reasonable basis for them to make proper judgments as to the financial position of the company (LR, para. 2.11).

At the hearing of the application for admission, permission for listing is granted and the UKLA stamps and dates the prospectus or listing particulars. As discussed in **4.2.3**, listing becomes effective (usually the next day) when admission is notified through the electronic systems used by the UKLA for communicating with the public (LR, para. 7.1).

(d) *Registration*

This is not required by the UKLA, but by s. 149 FS Act, which makes it a criminal offence not to have a prospectus or listing particulars registered by the Registrar of Companies on or before publication. Therefore, as soon as you have your UKLA approval, you race the prospectus or particulars to Companies House as they will be formally published the next day. Also note that the prospectus or particulars itself must say it is to be registered in this way.

(e) *Publication*

LR, para. 8.1, states that a prospectus or listing particulars must not be published until it has received the formal approval of the UKLA. Once approval has been given the publication requirements of The Listiing Rules must be observed (LR, para. 8.2). The prospectus or particulars must be made available to the public at the UKLA Document Viewing Facility and also at the registered office of the company for 14 days after admission of the securities to listing (LR, paras 8.4 and 8.5). Thereafter, the requirements depend on the type of offering which the company is making.

The basic requirement is that companies whose shares are not already listed must publish a formal notice in one national newspaper (LR, para. 8.7) A formal notice (known in practice as a 'box advertisement') contains brief details of the issue. LR, para. 8.10, details the required content of a formal notice.

If the company is not already listed and is marketing its securities by way of an *offer for sale* or an *offer for subscription*, it may elect instead to publish an offer notice, mini-prospectus or full listing particulars in a national newspaper (LR, para. 8.7). An offer notice (LR, para. 8.11) is a formal notice together with an application form attached. A mini-prospectus (LR, paras 8.12 and 8.13) is essentially a set of summary listing particulars which can be used in addition to a full prospectus or set of particulars. In practice, they have only been used in major offerings such as privatisations.

If the company is already listed, the publication requirements are as stated in the first paragraph above, save that, for offers to existing shareholders, the prospectus or listing particulars should be circulated to them (see LR, para. 8.14).

LR, paras 8.23 to 8.25 also requires an issuer to obtain the approval or authorisation of the UKLA for any other advertisements it produces as part of the offer.

(f) *Documents to be lodged later*

The UKLA also requires an issuer to follow up admission of its securities to listing with a final bundle of documents (LR, para. 7.8), principally a declaration from the company in the form of LR, sch. 6, that all legal requirements in connection with the issue have been satisfied.

The process is therefore this:

(a) 10-day documents or 20-day if a new applicant.

(b) 48-hour documents.

(c) Approval.

(d) Registration.

(e) Publication.

(f) Documents to be lodged later.

You should refer to the timetable in **3.7** to see how the whole process fits together. At the end of this long and arduous route through the maze of The Listing Rules, the prospectus or listing particulars will be in the hands of potential investors. The regulatory purpose is now over: the securities will have been admitted to listing and dealings will have commenced, and the marketing function – selling the shares to investors – now begins.

4.2.7 ADMISSION TO TRADING ON THE STOCK EXCHANGE

Whilst a company and its advisors are carrying out the processes detailed above to obtain admission to the Official List, they also need to take steps to obtain admission to trading on the Stock Exchange. The route to admission to trading is set out in the Stock Exchange's Admission and Disclosure Standards. Companies are encouraged to approach the Stock Exchange at the earliest possible stage to discuss their application and, in any event, no later than when they first contact the UKLA as regards their application for listing.

New applicants are required to provide the Stock Exchange with a company contact, a senior director or employee, and are encouraged to appoint a nominated representative from another organisation (this is likely to be the sponsor). These parties will liaise with the Stock Exchange throughout the process.

A timetable for admission must be agreed with the Exchange. This must operate such that admission to trading occurs at the same time as admission to the Official List.

The company must submit the following documents to the Stock Exchange no later than two business days prior to the day on which the application for admission to trading is to be considered:

(a) the application form for admission to trading signed by a company officer;

(b) two copies of the prospectus or listing particulars; and

(c) a copy of the board resolution allotting the securities or authorising the issue.

There is a fee payable in advance, calculated on a scale in accordance with the securities being issued. Following admission, the Stock Exchange must be provided with a statement of the number of securities issued.

The company is subject to a number of continuing requirements under the Stock Exchange's Standards, which are the equivalent to the continuing obligations in paras 9.1 to 9.9 of The Listing Rules (see **4.2.10**). Should a company fail to comply in any respect with the Standards, the Stock Exchange has powers of private and public censure, suspension of trading and cancellation of trading.

4.2.8 SHELF REGISTRATION

This is a new system, introduced in 1999. The detailed procedure for shelf registration is set out in paras 5.35–5.41 of The Listing Rules. Shelf registration allows a company that has been listed for at least 12 months to publish on an annual basis a shelf document, which contains much of the information required in listing particulars. If a company, during the next 12 months, wishes to issue and list further shares, all that is then required is the publication of a short issue note. The shelf document and the issue note together comprise the prospectus and listing particulars for the purpose of the new issue. The required respective content of the shelf document and issue note is set out in Table 1A in the appendix to ch. 5 of The Listing Rules. This table, as with the other tables in this appendix, makes reference to the relevant paragraphs of ch. 6 which describe the content of a prospectus or listing particulars.

Three copies of a shelf document must be submitted to the UKLA at least 10 clear business days before the relevant intended publication date (20 clear days if there are any complex issues to be resolved) (LR, para. 5.38). As with a prospectus or listing particulars, the draft must be annotated as required by LR, para. 5.11. The shelf document must be formally approved before publication. The UKLA publishes the document on its website for so long as the document remains current. A shelf document will remain current until the earlier of:

(a) the publication of the issuer's next annual report and accounts;

(b) 12 months from the date of publication on the website; or

(c) the date at which the issuer requests that the document be removed from the website.

When an issue of shares is to be made, the issue note must be submitted at least 10 clear business days before the intended publication date (LR, paras 5.40 and 5.9). It must also be annotated in accordance with LR, para. 5.11. Assuming it is approved by the UKLA, the issue note must then be published in accordance with ch. 8 of The Listing Rules, in the same way as a prospectus or listing particulars. Again, admission of the shares to trading will have to be sought from the Stock Exchange.

4.2.9 OVERSEAS COMPANIES AND THE LISTING REQUIREMENTS

The basic conditions required for listing (see **4.2.6.2**) apply equally to overseas companies (i.e., companies incorporated outside the UK), subject to the modifications contained in LR, ch. 17.

General conditions (described in LR, paras 17.2 to 17.4) are essentially that the company is listed overseas and that its accounts have been prepared in accordance with appropriate accounting standards. Its listing particulars may incorporate other documents by reference, such as the overseas equivalent of listing particulars, provided they are in English (LR, para. 17.5). The specific requirements thereafter depend on whether the listing in London for the overseas company will be its main (or primary) listing, or secondary to its overseas listing. For a company seeking its main or primary listing in London, the specific requirements are much as for other issuers. For companies whose main listing is overseas and which want a secondary listing in London, the specific listing requirements are modified (see LR, paras 17.14 to 17.21). The principal differences are that the sponsor does not have to report on the company's working capital position, and the subsequent continuing obligations are adjusted significantly (LR, paras 17.22 to 17.67). Any company (UK or foreign) with its primary listing overseas must additionally show that it is in compliance with the requirements of the relevant stock exchange (LR, para. 17.19) if it is seeking a listing in the UK as well.

The essential point to note is that, subject to these modifications, the general conditions and specific requirements for a prospectus or listing particulars otherwise apply as for UK companies. In addition, the overseas company's listed securities must be admitted to trading by the Stock Exchange.

4.2.9.1 Mutual recognition

Mutual recognition of prospectuses and listing particulars is now required throughout the EU. This means that listing particulars or a prospectus produced and approved in one EU Member

State for a securities offer must be accepted as listing particulars or a prospectus in any other EU Member State, provided they are translated and produced within three months of the listing in the first Member State. It is now possible to use the mutual recognition procedure even where no application for listing in the UK is intended, so that a UK-approved prospectus can be used in other Member States. The conditions for mutual recognition are set out in LR, para. 17.68.

Thus the Stock Exchange must accept as listing particulars or a prospectus a document in English for a Greek-registered company approved as such by the Paris Bourse, so long as the particulars or prospectus are not out of time. It is not then relevant how far the document complies with the specific requirements of ch. 6 of The Listing Rules: the fact of its approval as listing particulars or a prospectus in another Member State is generally enough. The only exception is where derogations obtained by the company in its first Member State (of which the UKLA must be informed) are not available in the UK.

Paragraphs 17.69 to 17.71 of The Listing Rules also set out the application procedure for companies taking advantage of entry to the market in this way. In essence they need to produce 10-day documents consisting of evidence of approval from the other EU Member State, and copies of the approved prospectus or listing particulars together with details of derogations obtained.

4.2.9.2 Exempt listing documents

Where securities have been listed in another Member State of the European Union for the past three years, or where the securities have been listed for less than three years but the relevant local stock exchange confirms the issuer has complied with its rules during that time, the Stock Exchange will grant a listing in London under LR, para. 5.23A(b) and ch. 5, app. 2, on production by the issuer of an exempt listing document in English.

The exempt listing document must include any equivalent to a prospectus or listing particulars produced by the issuer in the past year, the latest published accounts, together with information about the management structure, securities and capital, and major shareholders.

There can be no marketing of the securities through an exempt listing document – in other words, the listing works like an introduction (see **3.5.8**). The exempt listing document will need to be published in the same way as a prospectus or listing particulars (see **4.2.6.4**).

4.2.10 CONTINUING OBLIGATIONS

The Continuing Obligations are the obligations which a company listed on the Official List must observe. Failure to comply may lead to a suspension of listing. The obligations are contained in ch. 9 of The Listing Rules and equivalent provisions form part of the Stock Exchange's Admission and Disclosure Standards. One of their principal objects, as The Listing Rules make clear, is 'the maintenance of an orderly market in securities and to ensure that all users of the market have simultaneous access to the same information'.

4.2.10.1 Avoidance of a false market

In particular, this requires the prompt disclosure to the Company Announcements Office of the Stock Exchange of information necessary for the appraisal of the company's value (LR, para. 9.1). It is supported by a wide range of separate provisions requiring announcements on (for example) acquisitions and disposals, major new operational developments, board decisions changing the general character or nature of the company's business, dividends, annual profits, any changes in capital structure, and interests in the company's securities. LR, para. 9.2 imposes a requirement to make an announcement if there is a change in the company's financial condition or performance or in the company's expectation of its performance, and that change is likely to lead to a substantial movement in the company's share price.

The UKLA and the Stock Exchange can also require a company to issue an announcement where it is apparent that leaked information has resulted in sharp movements in its share price. The Stock Exchange can also halt trading in the shares and, if the company fails to make an announcement in good time, the Stock Exchange may make its own announcement or suspend the shares from trading altogether. Accordingly, it is good practice for a company to issue a holding announcement as soon as there appears to be a leak about a transaction or development relating to the company, even if the company is not ready to issue a full and detailed announcement.

In addition, the prevention of a false market in the company's securities requires equivalence of information about the company as between different exchanges on which the company is listed, and equality of treatment for holders of securities of the same class.

4.2.10.2 Informing the shareholders about the company and its securities

The company must communicate with its shareholders about, amongst other things, the allocation and payment of dividends and the issue of new securities. It should also notify the Company Announcements Office of the Stock Exchange of circulars and notices issued to shareholders and resolutions passed by them, of dates and decisions of board meetings, of any changes to the rights of securities and of the results of any new issue of securities.

4.2.10.3 Accounts

There are detailed provisions on information which the company's annual accounts, preliminary and interim results must contain. These are set out in LR, paras 12.40 to 12.59. These include explanations of material differences between published results and forecasts, explanations of any significant departures from applicable accounting standards (see **2.4.3**), and interests in the company or its securities held by any director or substantial shareholder (see **2.2.1**).

The company must publish half-yearly reports for the first six months of a financial year. These must contain, among financial details such as turnover, profits, dividends, tax and extraordinary items, information to enable investors to make an informed assessment of the trend of the group's activities and profits, and a reference to the group's prospects for the full financial year. The interim statement does not, however, need to be audited, though that fact must be stated.

4.2.10.4 The Model Code

This covers directors' dealings in the company's securities, and so has been covered in **2.2.2.1**. The Listing Rules require companies to adopt a dealing code for their directors at least as strict as the Model Code.

4.2.10.5 Overseas companies

The Continuing Obligations regime is modified for foreign companies whose primary listing is not in London. The detailed provisions are in LR, paras 17.22 to 17.67. They cover the same areas as for the ordinary obligations (for example, avoiding a false market, public announcements, accounts), except that they are adapted to fit in with the foreign company's domestic regulations – so, for instance, details of directors' and major shareholders' interests in shares are those required by the law of the company's country of incorporation (see LR, para. 17.33(a)).

4.2.10.6 Continuing Obligations as part of the seamless web

Although this sounds rather grandiose, the point is that the listed company cannot look just to the Continuing Obligations and believe this is where its obligations begin and end. There is the whole range of additional statutory and regulatory provisions to observe as well – the Companies Act 1985, the rest of The Listing Rules, the City Code and so on (see **chapter 1**). In particular, while The Listing Rules requirements regarding the avoidance of a false market are vital, they must be read alongside s. 47 Financial Services Act 1986, breach of which may give rise to much more serious problems for the company and/or its directors.

4.3 Offers of Unlisted Securities

All public offers of unlisted securities are now governed by the Public Offers of Securities Regulations 1995, which have replaced part III of and sch. 3 to the Companies Act 1985.

The Regulations apply to any investment which is not admitted to listing or the subject of an application for listing on the Official List. Accordingly, they apply to securities traded on the AIM or for which application is being made to admit to the AIM.

Over 300 companies were quoted on the AIM by the end of June 1999, with a total market capitalisation of £6.2 billion. For a new market, this is a successful beginning, enabling embryonic UK companies to find their money to expand from investors other than the commercial banks. Since AIM commenced, over 50 companies have now moved on to a listing and trading on the Stock Exchange.

4.3.1 OFFER TO THE PUBLIC

The Regulations require a prospectus to be issued whenever securities are offered to the public in the UK. 'The public' includes any section of the public, whether members of the company or institutional investors.

4.3.2 EXEMPTIONS

Paragraph 7 of the Regulations lists a series of exemptions from the need to publish a prospectus. Some of the most important are:

(a) Where shares are offered to no more than 50 persons.

(b) Where securities are offered to persons whose ordinary business activities involve them in buying, selling and managing investments.

(c) Where securities are offered to a restricted circle of persons who are sufficiently knowledgeable to understand the risks involved in accepting the offer (a 'professionals' exemption).

(d) Where securities are offered by a private company to its existing members or employees.

(e) Small issues of under 40,000 euros in total (currently about £25,500).

4.3.3 CONTENTS

What has to be included in the prospectus if the offer does fall within the Regulations? Schedule 1 to the Regulations sets out the contents requirements. These track in broad respects the requirements for listing particulars under Part IV of the FS Act. The prospectus requirements, in summary, are as follows:

(a) *General requirements*

These include the name of the issuer, the names and functions of the directors, and the date of publication of the prospectus.

(b) *The persons responsible for the prospectus and advisers*

This requires a declaration by the issuer's directors that 'to the best of their knowledge the information contained in the prospectus is in accordance with the facts and that the prospectus makes no omission likely to affect the import of such information'.

(c) *The securities to which the prospectus relates and the offer*

This should include a description of the securities being offered, including the rights attaching to them regarding voting and dividends. The prospectus must also state the number of securities being issued, the names of underwriters, and the expenses of the offer.

(d) *General information about the issuer and its capital*

This should include a summary of the memorandum of association, the structure of the issuer's share capital, the organisation of the group of companies of which the issuer is a member (if relevant), and any information about those who could or do exercise control over the issuer, including the percentage of share capital they hold.

(e) *The issuer's principal activities*

This should provide information about the issuer's corporate operations, and in particular any information on legal or arbitration proceedings which are having or may have a significant effect on the issuer's financial position.

(f) *The issuer's assets and liabilities, financial position and profits and losses*

The issuer will need to set out its annual accounts for the last three years. Where more than nine months has elapsed since the end of the last financial year, the prospectus should also include interim accounts since the end of the last financial year.

(g) *The issuer's administration, management and supervision*

This should include directors' service contracts, remuneration paid to directors and interests of directors in the share capital of the issuer.

(h) *Recent developments in the issuer's business and prospects*

This should identify significant recent trends concerning the development of the issuer's business since the end of the last financial year, and information on the issuer's prospects for the current financial year.

In addition, reg. 9 contains a general duty of disclosure in broadly similar terms to that set out in s. 146 of the FS Act. Thus, a prospectus must contain all such information as investors would reasonably require, and would reasonably expect to find there, for the purpose of making an 'informed assessment' of the assets and liabilities, financial position, profits and losses and prospects of the issuer, and the rights attached to the securities.

Regulation 10 requires a supplementary prospectus if there is a significant change affecting any matter contained in the prospectus after it has been issued and before the offer closes.

The Regulations permit exceptions for the contents and prospectuses for companies traded on the AIM, where the issuer is making a rights issue or the offer is for less than 10 per cent of the existing share capital. These are contained in the AIM Rules.

4.3.4 LIABILITY

The extent of liability for prospectuses is identical to that for listed securities set out in Part IV of the FS Act. Those responsible for the prospectus are liable to pay compensation to any person who has acquired the securities to which the prospectus relates if it is found to be untrue or misleading (reg. 14). *Possfund Custodian Trustee Ltd* v *Diamond* [1996] 2 All ER 774 indicates that this limits compensation to those who subscribe for the shares in the offer and rules out subsequent purchasers.

The persons responsible for the prospectus are set out in reg. 13. They include the issuer; the directors of the issuer; each person who accepts, and is stated in the prospectus as accepting, responsibility for, or for any part of, the prospectus; and each person who has authorised the contents of, or of any part of, the prospectus. They also make liable any person offering securities, where such person is not the issuer. On the face of it, this would extend responsibility for misleading statements in a prospectus to, for example, employees or other individual shareholders offering for sale their shares as part of a public offer. However, regulation 13(2A) (inserted by the Public Offer of Securities (Amendment) Regulations 1999) states that a person shall not be responsible where:

(a) the issuer is responsible for the prospectus . . . in accordance with this regulation; and

(b) the prospectus . . . was drawn up primarily by the issuer, or by one or more persons acting on behalf of the issuer; and

(c) the offeror is making the offer in association with the issuer.

Therefore, in the example above, employees would not be held responsible unless they had somehow otherwise accepted responsibility for or authorised some part of the particulars.

Penalties for contravening the Regulations are a fine or imprisonment, and the prospect of being sued by anyone who suffers loss as a result of the contravention.

An authorised person under the FS Act who either offers securities himself or assists another person who is offering securities, and fails to issue a prospectus when one is required, will have contravened its relevant SRO rules. Advisers to issuers (including the solicitors) will therefore be in breach of their rules if they wrongly advise that a prospectus is not needed.

4.3.5 AIM RULES

When an application is first made for a company's shares to be traded on the AIM, the AIM Rules require a document containing the information set out in sch. 1 to the Regulations to be issued. This would be the case even if the admission to the AIM were by way of an introduction. In the context of the AIM Rules, the prospectus is known as an admission document.

4.3.5.1 Conditions for admission to AIM

The conditions for admission to AIM are:

(a) Having a nominated adviser and a nominated broker. The nominated adviser is the substitute for the role of sponsor in an application for official listing. The adviser must be drawn from a register of approved advisers and could be a stockbroker, lawyer or accountant as well as a merchant bank. The nominated broker is a member of the Stock Exchange.

(b) The issuer must be a public company.

(c) The issuer's accounts must conform to UK or US accounting principles, or international accounting standards.

(d) The securities to be traded must be freely transferable.

(e) The issuer must have a model code for directors' dealings. There is a model code in the AIM Rules, which is similar to that set out in the Stock Exchange Listing Rules.

(f) If the company has been generating revenue for less than two years, the directors and all employees must agree not to sell their interests in the company's shares for at least one year from the date of joining the AIM.

There are no requirements or limits regarding the company's level of capitalisation or trading history or the number of shares in public hands.

4.3.5.2 Continuing obligations

These relate principally to disclosure obligations, particularly in relation to new developments or changes in the company's performance or financial condition. There are no rules requiring the consent of shareholders to particular types of transactions.

4.3.6 PRIVATE COMPANIES

Section 81 of the Companies Act 1985 is still in force. This makes it an offence for a private limited company to offer its shares or debentures to the public.

Therefore, when a private company is intending to make an offer to the public, its freedom to do so is governed by part III of the Companies Act 1985. Bizarrely, the Public Offers of Securities Regulations 1995 will determine whether a prospectus is required in relation to the private company's offer, but part III of the Companies Act 1985 will determine whether or not there is an offer to the public which is prohibited. It is important, for private companies, to have regard to both provisions. It is not safe to rely on the exemptions to the Public Offers of Securities Regulations 1995. You must also be safe under the definition of an offer to the public in s. 81.

FIVE

ACQUISITIONS

5.1 Introduction

The world of corporate finance uses the rather weighty term 'acquisitions' to describe anything from the humble sale of a small corner-shop business to the disposal of an international multimillion-pound supermarket chain. You will also come across the expression as a description of a takeover under the City Code (on which see **chapter 8**) – hence the phrase 'mergers and acquisitions'. In this chapter, however, the term refers to sales and purchases of assets or businesses, or shares *outside* the City Code (essentially, private companies). The term is therefore quite distinct from the 'takeovers' covered in **chapter 8**.

Acquiring things is the way of the capitalist world, and company strategy is no exception. Acquisition activity has been a feature of corporate finance work for many years. In 1995, there were 1,039 acquisitions of private companies with a total value of £18.1 billion. Why are acquisitions popular? There are some common factors which will help you to understand your client's particular motivation for making a specific acquisition or disposal. Without this understanding you cannot properly assess what is important to the client and what the client is seeking from the transaction.

When you look at these factors, do not assume that clients only fall into one of these categories: very often they fall into more than one at the same time or none at all. Nor should you assume that clients have always worked out what they are doing: often they are simply seizing an opportunity when it presents itself, whether or not it fits with whatever strategy they are developing.

We begin with the 'textbook' reasons for acquisition activity.

5.1.1 DIVERSIFICATION AND CONGLOMERATION

This was particularly fashionable as an aspect of corporate strategy in the 1960s and 1970s. For listed companies in particular, the ethos was that it made better business sense to hold a portfolio of assets or companies in different sectors of the market. For example, a tobacco company might own an insurance company and a paper and packaging business. The thinking was that if one sector was depressed, another was just as likely to be booming, so as jack of all trades a diversified company could ensure an overall picture of steady performance and reduce the shareholder's investment risk. There might also be benefits from integrating certain common operations despite the diversity of business base – for instance, product distribution.

5.1.2 CONSOLIDATION

This is, as you might guess, the reverse of diversification, and is driven by the philosophy that a company does better when it concentrates on what it really knows. It is particularly the case in difficult economic times that companies feel safer when they only have to worry about what they identify to be their 'core businesses'. Obviously a strategy of consolidation could lead to a planned programme of disposals, and possibly one which needs to be carried out relatively speedily (which may affect your negotiation strength).

5.1.3 VERTICAL AND HORIZONTAL INTEGRATION

These are rather technical terms for simple concepts.

Vertical integration takes place when a paper manufacturer decides to buy a forestry business and a chain of stationery shops which sell the paper products it makes. In other words, it is the process of integrating into the company both suppliers and buyers of its goods or services as a way of producing those goods and services more cheaply – it reduces the transaction costs.

Horizontal integration is the process of buying a similar business to your own at the equivalent point in the production cycle: to take our example above, a paper manufacturer buying a packaging business or another paper manufacturer. Where the businesses are different, this may help to integrate expertise in certain common areas such as marketing. Where the businesses are the same, there may be a number of motivating factors. The businesses may be complementary in that they have different customer bases or geographical penetration. Possibly the objective is simply to achieve economies of scale, or to create a single organisation of sufficient size to compete with the rest of the opposition.

Both vertical and horizontal integration assume a strategy of acquisitions. Both may possibly give rise to questions of merger control.

5.1.4 INTERNATIONAL EXPANSION

The rapid growth of international markets, particularly those throughout Europe, the ex-Soviet Union and the Far East, creates possibilities for business expansion. One of the best methods of penetrating an entirely new geographical market is to acquire a business which already operates in it. International acquisitions can be some of the most difficult as cross-border difficulties are added to what is already a fairly thick stew.

5.1.5 ACQUIRING WHAT YOU DO NOT HAVE OR DISPOSING OF WHAT YOU DO NOT WANT

This sounds too simple to be a serious corporate strategy, but simple ideas are often the best. If a company is suffering from a long-term cash-flow problem, acquiring a cash-rich business with a strong and regular cash inflow might be an attractive solution to its dilemma.

By the same token, a company weighed down by liabilities in one or two of its business areas may feel that the best course is to ditch them at the best price possible so that it is free from such difficulties and can concentrate on its profit-making operations.

The following are some unstated factors for acquisition activity.

5.1.6 RAPID EARNINGS GROWTH

Institutions, other shareholders and analysts often place significant emphasis on the growth of a company's earnings per share as a sign of corporate success. One way of achieving rapid increases in earnings per share is to boost profits artificially year-on-year by fresh acquisitions of successful companies, as the profits of the acquired companies then 'top up' the buyer's existing results. This may often obscure underlying weaknesses in existing underperforming businesses (which may be the intention).

5.1.7 ASSET-STRIPPING

Some acquirers have developed notoriety for their fondness in buying businesses which they identify as undervalued, then selling off their assets individually to the highest bidder to make sizeable profits on the whole deal. Some typical aspects of acquisition work decline in significance if this is the client's motivation: the client is less likely to worry about working with existing management or retaining employee goodwill.

5.1.8 MANAGEMENT IMAGE

This is an intangible factor but is often present. A lacklustre performance by a company will often be blamed on a management with no sense of direction or ambition. An acquisition or disposal may be one way of correcting that image by showing that the management has focused clearly on what in business terms it wants or does not want and how it is dealing actively with that objective.

5.1.9 FALLING IN LOVE

There are some acquisitions and disposals which are hard to understand at the time and later turn out to be dreadful mistakes. Often this is the consequence of the buyer falling in love with the prospect of a particular purchase, perhaps simply because of the target's reputation. In fact the acquirer is blinded by whichever feature it adores and later finds out that all is not what it seems: in these circumstances, advisers often despair as it is very difficult to make the acquirer see reason.

All these factors are also relevant in the takeover context (see **chapter 8**). Your first duty in these transactions is to take the trouble to find out what is really motivating your client.

5.2 Buying Companies or Businesses

In an acquisition, the buyer and seller have to agree on what is being transferred and, where there is a choice, to decide whether to transfer it as a company or a business. The choice may have quite different legal and tax effects for both buyer and seller, which it is the lawyer's job to understand and advise the client on. Let us look first, though, at what we mean by having a choice whether to transfer as a business or a company.

Assume P plc has several divisions, one of which is responsible for making televisions (others make radios, VCRs and stereo systems). P plc decides to sell off the TV side of its operation. It may do one of two things:

(a) Identify those assets which comprise the TV operation (for example, the factory, the employees, the machinery, the benefit of various supply contracts, the intellectual property, goodwill and debtors) and sell those off. This in turn could be done individually (for example, the factory could be sold off to a property investor while the intellectual property could be sold to an entrepreneur who wants to exploit a new invention). More usually it will be done on the basis of a going concern – in other words, the business is sold as a complete unit, lock, stock and barrel.

(b) Form a subsidiary company (M Ltd) which P wholly owns. P then makes M the owner of all the assets in the TV operation mentioned above. P retains control by means of the shares it holds in M, which it then sells, hence transferring control of M, and so the entire TV operation, to the buyer.

The asset or business sale involves selecting whatever is to be sold. The company or share sale involves a simple share transfer. There are a number of consequences of this difference. Let us look first at the legal or commercial reasons for picking one route rather than another.

5.2.1 LEGAL AND COMMERCIAL FACTORS

(a) With the company sale, everything that is in the company goes across on transfer. The entity before is the entity after. In this way, the seller gets rid of everything, including all liabilities. Does the buyer want all those liabilities?

(b) With the asset or business sale, it is possible to 'cherrypick' whatever is to be transferred. The buyer may choose to buy only the assets and leave the seller with the liabilities (e.g., creditors, outstanding loans). Does the seller want this?

(c) As a company sale only requires a share transfer, it has the potential for being a speedy and simple way to do the transaction. In contrast the asset or business sale requires identification of the assets (and liabilities?) and the buyer's agreement to purchase every one of them. This needs documentation, a careful analysis of the state of all the assets and separate transfer arrangements where appropriate (for example, the owner of the factory in our TV operation will change, which will necessitate a conveyance, and so an extra document, negotiation and inevitably more time and cost).

The client's chief concern is the commercial result of effecting the transfer as a business or a company sale. In particular, the client will want to know whether it makes a difference in terms of speed and cost. Any financial difference in going one route or the other will be highly influential, and tax will play a central role in these calculations.

5.2.2 TAX FACTORS

These are many and varied and only a brief mention of the salient factors is possible.

5.2.2.1 Asset or business sale

(a) *Capital gains tax*

CGT will be payable by the seller on the amount of any gain made on a disposal. The buyer will acquire the assets at a base cost equal to the price paid for them.

(b) *Capital allowances*

For the seller, there will be balancing adjustments on any outstanding capital allowances claimed for the assets sold. The buyer will be able to claim capital allowances for the assets bought.

(c) *VAT*

The assets need to be transferred as a going concern, otherwise VAT may be payable on the sale of assets as a supply of goods.

(d) *Stamp duty*

Stamp duty on a sale of assets (excepting those assets which pass by delivery) is:

(i) 1 per cent of the consideration where the value of the assets exceeds £60,000;.

(ii) 2.5 per cent where the value is more than £250,000 but does not exceed £500,000; and

(iii) 3.5 per cent where the price of the property exceeds £500,000.

(e) *Losses*

If the seller has trading losses at the time of sale, these will be lost as there is a cessation of trade.

(f) *Double charge*

Where the seller is a company, it may pay tax on the proceeds of sale of the assets (e.g., CGT). The shareholders may then pay tax again when they sell their shares in the company, which will have as part of their value the proceeds of the original assets sale – tax is effectively paid twice on this element. However, in practice the seller may be able to avoid this by stripping out the asset disposal proceeds from the company before the share sale, thereby reducing the value of the shares.

(g) *Hidden tax liabilities*

The buyer can 'pick and choose' whether to accept any of the tax liabilities held by the business.

5.2.2.2 Company or share sale

(a) *Capital gains tax*

CGT will be payable by the seller on the amount of any gain made on a disposal unless the gain can be rolled over into the buyer's securities as part of the consideration. As the buyer acquires the shares, the base cost of the underlying assets remains at their original value with the accompanying risk of a very high gain when they are finally stripped out.

(b) *Capital allowances*

There will usually be no balancing adjustments on outstanding capital allowances claimed by the company which has been sold. The buyer will not be able to qualify for capital allowances on the sum it pays for the shares it has bought, but the target company itself should continue to claim capital allowances on its own assets.

(c) *VAT*

No VAT consequences.

(d) *Stamp duty*

Stamp duty on a sale of shares (to be paid by the buyer) is 0.5 per cent of the value transferred rounded up to the nearest £5 (and subject to a minimum £5 duty).

(e) *Losses*

Losses in the company when it is sold can be carried forward if the trade continues and there is no major change in its nature or conduct.

(f) *Double charge*

The selling shareholders sell their shares only once and are subject only to the one tax 'hit' at point of sale – unlike the situation where a company sells an asset and then the shareholders later sell the shares in the company.

(g) *Hidden tax liabilities*

The seller is able to get rid of all the company's tax liabilities when it transfers to the buyer. The buyer accordingly will ask for tax warranties and usually a deed of indemnity.

The consequence of this analysis, as you can probably see, is that from the tax point of view (in general terms) the buyer tends to prefer to acquire assets or a business and the seller to sell a company or shares.

5.2.2.3 Tax restructuring

Because of some of the tax implications mentioned in these two lists, there are some common methods used in the run-up to an acquisition to save tax.

(a) *Dividend strip*

The seller pays itself a dividend out of the target company prior to sale and then reduces the sale price of the company. The advantage of this is that the shareholder is likely to pay less tax on its dividend than on the capital gain on which tax might otherwise be payable when the shares are sold, and the buyer pays less stamp duty as the shares are worth less. This is likely to make a company sale even more attractive to the seller.

(b) *Creating a company*

As we saw in the example above, the seller can turn a business into a company and then sell the shares in the company and so get the benefits mentioned in **5.2.2.2**.

If you should be asked to advise your client on the tax factors to be considered when deciding how to go about buying and selling, detailed tax advice is likely to be appropriate.

5.2.2.4 Tax clearances

There are a host of clearances which you may need to seek from the Inland Revenue and HM Customs and Excise, for instance:

(a) that HM Customs and Excise will regard a transfer of a particular business as a going concern, and so not assessable for VAT purposes, and

(b) that the Inland Revenue will not treat as subject to CGT the disposal of shares in a company where the consideration is securities in the buyer (s. 135 Taxation of Chargeable Gains Act 1992).

The important thing always to recall in these transactions is that clients' preferences and circumstances do vary. It may for instance be vital to the buyer to inherit the target's trading losses (to set off against the client's own rocketing profits), in which case the attractions of buying a business (with the possible consequential disappearance of trading losses) will be significantly reduced.

Sometimes the question of whether it is to be a company or an asset or business sale has been decided before instructions reach the lawyers, frequently by the company in consultation with its accountants or other tax advisers – so your scope for advice in this area may already be curtailed.

5.3 The Parties

The 'cast of thousands' is less likely to be in evidence for an acquisition than an issue of shares or a public takeover, though this does depend on the nature of the transaction. The reason is that acquisitions are more in the nature of 'private' transactions in character, between identified buyer and seller, rather than 'public' with the large volume of investors which this implies. The need for quite so many advisers is not felt to be so pressing. Acquisitions also tend to be transactions in which the lawyers play a larger role in directing events.

5.3.1 BUYER AND SELLER

Buyer and seller will often both be companies but of course may be individuals, unincorporated associations, partnerships and so on. Care should always be taken to ensure that appropriate constitutional authority exists for both to enter into the transaction.

As we will see in **5.5.1.6**, warranties are normally demanded by the buyer from the seller. Sometimes, the buyer will insist that the target directors, or the seller's directors or one of its substantial shareholders (where it is a company selling) should be a party to all, or some of, the warranties. This is because they may have as much knowledge or information about the company being sold as does the selling shareholder.

Because of some of the tax problems which arise from intra-group activity, some of the tax warranties which the buyer will ask for in a share sale will have to be given not just by the selling company but also other companies in the seller's group.

Of course, in view of the tax issues mentioned in **5.2.2**, the seller may need to reorganise itself prior to effecting the sale. Even if the entity to be sold is a separate company, some work is likely to be needed to ensure that what belongs to it is distinct from the property the seller wishes to retain: this is even more acute a problem where it is a business which is being sold.

5.3.2 TARGET COMPANY OR BUSINESS

In a sense, the target is entirely at the mercy of its seller. Nevertheless, it does of course have employees (though care will have to be taken to see they are not in fact employees of the seller). The directors of both the selling company (if there is one) and (if it is a share sale) the company being sold have a duty to have regard to the interests of the company's employees under s. 309 Companies Act 1985. As for the buyer, although extensive consultation in advance of an announcement about a sale is often difficult because of the need to keep such information confidential, as a practical matter, the support or at least neutrality of the employees to the sale is vital. The last thing a buyer wants to inherit is a hostile workforce, so time will need to be spent explaining to the staff of the company or business what the sale will mean for them. Additionally, the Collective Redundancies and Transfer of Undertakings (Protection of Employment) Regulations 1995 (known as the Worker Representative Regulations) apply to any business transfer. This gives the employees affected by such a transfer the right (unless it already exists, for instance under trade union arrangements) to elect representatives to consult with the employer about his proposals. Failure to comply may give rise to financial penalties.

In addition, the buyer will probably seek to secure the continued loyalty of key employees of the target and may negotiate revised contractual terms with them to this end (particularly new service agreements with directors of a target company who are to stay on the board after the sale). The buyer may also wish to change the standard terms of employment of the target employees. The Transfer of Undertakings Regulations and the Acquired Rights Directive do not permit such a change, even if agreed between employees and buyer, if the reason for it is the transfer of the company or business itself. It is therefore advisable only to set about such changes some time after the transfer is completed.

The buyer may insist that the directors of the company being sold (where it is a share sale) or the key employees of the business (where it is a business sale), should also be a party to all, or some of, the warranties in the sale and purchase agreement. This is because they may have as much knowledge or information about the company being sold as does the selling shareholder.

When the sale negotiations get underway, there will be an enormous amount of information required on the target's business operations and administrative arrangements (see **5.4.1.2**), and both the seller and the target will need to spend considerable time making this ready for the buyer to review.

5.3.3 MERCHANT BANKERS

Merchant banks typically play a less prominent role in an acquisition than in issues and takeovers. The banker's task is usually to set the deal up. Often buyer and seller have already identified each other through ordinary commercial channels and settled the outline terms of their deal in direct negotiation. In these circumstances, the banker's presence is otiose.

There are three specific cases where the banker can be expected to play a part:

(a) Where the seller is having or anticipates difficulty in locating a potential buyer for its business: a merchant banker will be able to use its existing contacts and clients to see whether it can solicit offers from any interested buyers.

(b) Where the seller wishes to sell its company or business off to the highest bidder, a merchant bank is often appointed to produce an information memorandum on the operation to be sold and then set up the mechanism for conducting an auction or contract race. This will involve sending each potential bidder a copy of the memorandum and soliciting sealed bids from each before handling the negotiations with the successful bidder.

(c) Where part or the whole of the buyer's consideration is its own securities, the bank is appointed to conduct a vendor consideration placing (with or without clawback) on behalf of the buyer and also the seller (see **3.6.5**): this will also require the appointment of a broker to identify potential placees.

5.3.4 ACCOUNTANTS

The accountants for both the buyer and seller are certain to be involved in a number of aspects of the transaction:

(a) The buyer will frequently instruct accountants (usually its own auditors) to carry out a thorough investigation of the entity it wants to buy, and the buyer generally places considerable reliance on the report the accountants produce, as it will contain a detailed analysis of the entity's operational and financial performance, and its prospects. Crucial to these accountants' success is adequate access to the financial records and management papers of the company or business being sold – hence often there will already be a preliminary, though provisional, agreement for the sale of the entity between the buyer and seller before the accountants start work (see **5.4.1.1**).

(b) Accounts or financial statements will often need to be prepared up to the agreed date of completion (as buyers will insist on current financial data on the target), and in practice these generally need to be reviewed and approved by accountants for both buyer and seller. This is also true of any other figures which are the subject of agreement by the parties – for instance, it is as well to instruct accountants to check any earn-out formula appearing as part of the agreed consideration (see **5.5.1.2**).

(c) If the buyer or seller needs to produce a circular to shareholders as part of the acquisition (see **5.6.4**), the accountants will need to check any figures it contains.

5.3.5 REGULATORS

The role of the regulators will be discussed in more detail in **5.6**. Of course, both the Inland Revenue and HM Customs and Excise may be involved if clearances and/or consents from one or both are required.

A particular company or business transfer may require the consent of regulatory authorities relevant to the commercial sector in which that business or company operates. Financial services businesses or companies will be authorised by their self-regulatory organisation, which will have to approve the change in ownership of the operation. Broadcasting companies or businesses obtain their licences from the Independent Broadcasting Authority if they broadcast on television, and from the Radio Authority if on radio. Approval from these organisations for the transfer of the licence will be required. Of course these are only illustrations of what might be needed: the possibilities are legion.

5.3.6 SPECIALISTS

This heading does not assume that the other professionals referred to in this section are not specialists: the term covers those experts who are called in to advise in special circumstances, bringing with them a degree of know-how in their field of specialism which the other professionals involved do not have. The types of advisers required will vary, depending on the peculiar nature of the target's business or problems. Particular examples are:

(a) *Actuaries*

One of the most common areas of difficulty in these transactions is the value of any pension funds which may be transferred as part of the acquisition (see **5.4.1.2**). Valuations of the target's pension fund by both the buyer's and seller's actuaries to determine whether it has been properly funded are a normal feature of these transactions, simply because of the huge liabilities a buyer might otherwise incur if not and the huge windfall otherwise accruing to the buyer if the pension scheme has been over-funded. Since actuaries can rarely agree on a valuation, they need to be involved from the outset.

(b) *Surveyors*

The sale of a company or business with a number of properties to its name will inevitably require the appointment of surveyors not only to verify the condition of the properties but also to value them as part of the process of agreeing the consideration.

(c) *Environmental consultants*

The potentially extensive nature of environmental liabilities and the difficulty of establishing exactly what they are in a given case often leads to the involvement of environmental consultants. Their task is usually to conduct an environmental 'audit' of the company or business and report to the buyer on any identified liabilities and the approximate cost of putting them right, so that these can be considered when negotiating the price for the sale. Not all companies and businesses merit this kind of approach: high-risk businesses are those in manufacturing, the generation and supply of power, the supply of fuels and water and waste management, though for just about any kind of business some consideration should be given to the use of environmental experts.

5.3.7 THIRD PARTIES

This refers to those parties with whom the target business or company has contracted for the supply or delivery of goods and services.

Where it is a company which is being sold, the company has entered into these contracts and the company will continue in existence after the sale as the same entity (only owned by different persons). Therefore these contractual relationships will continue automatically after the change in ownership. The only kind of contract which may be affected in these circumstances is one which can be terminated if there is a change of control of one of the parties to it. Joint venture agreements commonly have such provisions. The consent of the third party to the change of control in the company is then needed if the joint venture agreement is to stay in force.

With business sales, the contracts relevant to the business have been entered into by the legal entity which owns the business. In some cases, it will be open to the seller to assign its interest in the contract direct to the buyer (if, for example, there is an express contractual right to that effect). In others, the contract will not be assignable (if, for example, it is forbidden under the contract): this is something you will need to determine. In these cases, those contracts on which the business *depends* will need to be novated in favour of the buyer: but this cannot happen unless the third party agrees. The third party will therefore need to be cajoled into accepting the new owner of the business. Often business sales are made conditional on major contracts being novated, otherwise a buyer is at risk of inheriting valuable contracts which are unenforceable.

With less significant contracts, the objective is ultimately to substitute the seller for the buyer, though this will not be a condition of the agreement, simply an obligation the seller will continue to have after the sale completes. This is explained in more detail in **5.5.2.1**.

The point to remember is that third parties will play a role in the sale negotiations if their relationship with the entity being sold is important enough.

5.3.8 SOLICITORS

Last, but not least, are the legal advisers to the buyer and seller. As compared with equity offerings and public company takeovers, private company and business acquisitions offer greater opportunities to the solicitors to lead the transaction rather than playing second fiddle to others like the merchant bankers. In fact, it would be true to say that clients in this kind of work tend to rely on the lawyers, in conjunction with the accountants, to do the organising, thinking and negotiating for them. You are therefore much more likely to take on a management function in this kind of deal than in the others we have looked at. The solicitors' main tasks are these:

(a) Drafting: the agreement to buy the company or business (see **5.5.1** and **5.5.2**), the disclosure letter and all the other documents referred to below will be drafted by the solicitors.

(b) Negotiating these documents, particularly the agreement to buy and the disclosure letter, is largely the domain of the lawyer accompanied by the client.

(c) Due diligence: see **5.4.1.2**. Essentially this is a task for the buyer's solicitors and involves finding out as much information as possible about the target prior to signing the purchase agreement. The accountants' report is part of this process, though it tends to focus on the financial aspects of the target business or company. The lawyers are left with the task of unearthing and digesting all the documentary data which exists about the target so that the buyer gets as complete a picture as possible. The seller's solicitors will find a lot of their time is spent sorting out their client's documentary data for presentation to the buyer, and ensuring that the seller knows exactly what he is giving the buyer access to.

(d) Advising on the law: legal problems do arise on these transactions (it is not all practical issues!).

One thing that will characterise the approach of most firms to handling this kind of work is the team of specialists they are likely to draw on. It will already have become evident to you that these transactions throw up issues on tax, employment, pensions, property, the environment, and so on. Lawyers are rarely capable of a total command of all the relevant law in these areas, hence it is likely a number of solicitors will be involved in advising both clients on all the specialist aspects of the transaction. The skill for the solicitor is not only to keep the client happy but also to keep the rest of his team informed about what is going on and what problems the transaction has thrown up.

5.4 Timetable

It is difficult to provide an exact timetable for these transactions as so much depends on particular circumstances and what the parties agree between them. It is much easier to identify a standard series of events relevant to both company and business purchases. This is set out here. It should give you a reasonable idea of how these transactions proceed and who does what and when.

5.4.1 PRE-CONTRACT

This refers to the period leading up to signing of the purchase agreement.

5.4.1.1 Heads of agreement

The buyer and seller often agree to agree in the form of heads of agreement. These are usually denigrated by lawyers as worthless (as they have no legal effect), but they often help to focus the parties' commercial thinking much more effectively than any number of meetings.

They are usually expressed to be 'subject to contract' or 'not legally binding' to make it clear that they are a simple record of the main terms agreed between the parties in their preliminary commercial negotiations, rather than a formal and legally binding commitment. If you are advising on the drafting of the heads then you must ensure they are qualified in this way. If the parties want a legally binding contract then you may as well scrap the heads and move straight on to drafting and negotiating the sale agreement.

5.4.1.2 Due diligence

One of the most important activities in these transactions is the process of gathering as much information as possible about the target company or business. The buyer's warranties and indemnities offer it protection against the risk of unforeseen liabilities arising in the target after the sale is completed. However, it is not in the buyer's interest to have to take legal action to protect its investment. This uses up a lot of management time (it diverts attention from the real business of making money) and in any event may well take a lengthy period to resolve (leading to uncertainty).

Much the best solution is to take precautions to eliminate the risk of such liability arising or at least to identify and quantify it in advance. The due diligence process is designed to satisfy this demand. If the problems can be flushed out before they become the buyer's responsibility, then the buyer can use them as leverage in negotiations over the sale price rather than as the foundation of later, more expensive warranty claims.

Looking at this the other way around, it is in any event quite impossible for the buyer's solicitors to prepare appropriate warranties for the sale agreement until they understand better the protection the buyer will need. This in turn can only be discovered through the due diligence process.

What does due diligence actually involve? Usually, the parties will have agreed on the outline of the deal in their heads of agreement, and the seller will at the same time agree to the following:

(a) The buyer's accountants will be given access to the target's financial records to enable them to prepare a report on its financial history and performance and review its likely profitability in the future; this report will also require access to other information about the target, including material contracts, information about its existing assets (e.g., properties, investments) and liabilities (e.g., loans) and management history (including an appraisal of key staff). The buyer will rely on this report in making an informed assessment about whether to proceed with the purchase and, if so, at what price and on what terms. It is important to ensure that the accountants are clear about what exactly they are being asked to do, hence their instructions are often recorded in a letter.

(b) The buyer's solicitors will be given access to all the documentation relevant to an assessment of any legal difficulties which might be encountered in the transfer.

The buyer's solicitors will usually prepare a letter to the seller and/or its solicitors requesting the following information on the target:

(a) Material contracts: usually the seller or its solicitors will send copies of these to the buyer's solicitors to enable them to make a judgement about which contracts cannot be assigned to the buyer (if it is a business sale – see **5.3.7**), which contain 'change of control' provisions, and which of them contain terms which are unfavourable or onerous to the target and so might bring into question the value of that contract in the future.

(b) Licences and authorisations: the buyer will want to assess whether it can inherit the existing licence or should apply for a new one from the relevant authority, and to establish whether there have been any blemishes in the target's record of compliance with the terms of the licence.

(c) Pension scheme: there are two particular features in this area which need to be addressed early on:

  (i) The adequacy of the funding of the target's pension scheme. If it has been inadequately funded, the buyer will look to the seller to make up the deficit prior to transfer, or to adjust the purchase price proportionately. Alternatively, the fund may have a surplus, which will enable the buyer to take a 'pensions holiday' and suspend contributions to the fund after completion – but it will have to pay for the surplus in the purchase price. To this end, the first priority is to obtain the relevant data and send it to the buyer's actuaries or pensions consultants for immediate review and advice.

(ii) Establishing whose pension scheme the target employees belong to. Is it the target's own or the seller's? If it is the target's own scheme, is it to be preserved as a separate scheme following completion, or integrated into the buyer's existing pensions scheme? If the latter, a transfer payment representing the accrued benefits under the scheme will need to be made by seller to buyer. If the employees belong to the seller's own scheme, will they be allowed to join an entirely new scheme replicating the seller's existing one, or will they be integrated into the buyer's existing scheme (which will also generally require a transfer payment)? These questions can only begin to be answered if the information about the existing pensions arrangements is obtained speedily.

(d) Standard terms of employment and service agreements: this is to help the buyer assess what obligations will be involved in taking on the target employees.

(e) Material litigation: this can seriously affect the value of the target's business operation, and it is probably only the lawyers who can make an informed assessment about its likely success.

(f) Property, real and intellectual: these constitute some of the most important assets a business is likely to have, so it is important to establish what their status is.

With real property, the first step will be to carry out the appropriate Land Registry and Land Charges Registry searches to disclose any interests registered against the title. Is the property freehold or leasehold? If leasehold, the landlord's consent to assignment will be required. Is the plan to:

(i) get the seller to warrant good title to the property;

(ii) get the seller's solicitors to certify that the seller has good marketable title (i.e., *they* do an investigation of title), or

(iii) have the buyer's solicitors carry out their own investigation of title into the property?

The last is the most secure method open to the buyer, but it is the most expensive and time-consuming as the buyer's solicitors will need access to all title documents.

With intellectual property, the aim is to establish the nature of the target's existing intellectual property rights (be they patents, trade marks, copyright, registered designs and so on) and the state of their protection.

(g) Any other information of relevance, including insurance policies for the premises and contents, share schemes available for members of the target's staff, financial and trading arrangements between the target and the seller's corporate group (if, for instance, there are inter-group loans involving the target, these will have to be re-arranged on an arm's-length basis or paid off), and the company books and records (where it is a share sale).

In a share sale, the buyer's solicitors will conduct a company search against the target as an additional precaution.

5.4.1.3 Confidentiality agreement

In exchange for all this information, any well-advised seller will require the buyer and its advisers to treat the acquired information as confidential and only to be used for the purposes of the acquisition or otherwise with the seller's consent. The tricky part is defining the information: does it, for instance, extend to all information received by the buyer in connection with the acquisition (which might catch the buyer's own market research), and what about oral statements? Usually some compromise is arrived at whereby the buyer cannot disclose or use for other purposes *written* information obtained from the seller or its advisers *in the course of the acquisition negotiations and due diligence process*.

5.4.1.4 Tax clearances

It would be usual to apply for any necessary tax clearances at this stage (see **5.2.2.4**), and obtain them prior to signing the contract.

5.4.2 CONTRACT

This refers to the point at which the parties sign the sale agreement and so enter into a formal legal commitment to effect the acquisition. There are two documents you will always encounter at this stage, and one you may meet.

5.4.2.1 Share or business purchase agreement

This is discussed in detail in **5.5**. The agreement records all the principal elements of the acquisition and so is the key document in the transaction. Much of the lawyers' efforts will be devoted to drafting and negotiating this.

It is usual for the buyer to draft the agreement. Since the seller can hide behind the *caveat emptor* principle, the buyer has to make all the running in stating what he regards as appropriate protection in return for the price, so he will invariably draft his warranties and conditions first. The only circumstance where this is not the case is where the target is being sold in an auction. Here the seller does the initial drafting so as to use the competitive environment to obtain the most beneficial terms for the sale.

When the contract is signed and exchanged, the parties are committed to the acquisition. It is, however, quite typical for completion to be delayed following signing of the contracts, to allow time for any necessary consents and clearances (on which the contract will be conditional) to be obtained (see **5.5**). The signing will therefore be no more than that: no money will pass hands and, although in legal terms the beneficial ownership of the target will have passed to the buyer, the seller remains the legal owner until completion. Some transactions will be signed and completed on the same day if all conditions can be satisfied on signing the agreement.

If either or both the parties are corporate entities, it or they will need to produce evidence to the other party of due authorisation for the transaction in the form of board minutes and resolutions approving it. No party to a contract wants to take the risk that the company on the other side will later disown and seek to avoid the contract entered into by one of its directors on the grounds that he or she was acting without authority – hence this is simply prudent practice.

5.4.2.2 Disclosure letter

The disclosure letter is prepared by the sellers and their solicitors, and contains a list of all the facts already disclosed to the buyer which contravene the warranties contained in the agreement. The buyer agrees it cannot then sue for breach of the warranties caused by these disclosures, as they have already been notified before the contract is entered into. The buyer's remedy is, prior to signing, to negotiate a reduction in the price or to have the seller deal with and correct the disclosed problem. Since the disclosure letter limits the scope of the buyer's protection, it is the subject of fierce scrutiny and negotiation (as with the agreement itself). It will be signed by the seller at the same time as the contract is signed.

5.4.2.3 Vendor placing agreement

Where the buyer is using its own securities as consideration for the acquisition, it is usual for those securities to be placed with investors on behalf of the seller (and on the instructions of the buyer) to realise cash for the benefit of the seller. This arrangement is discussed in **3.6.5**. Particular care has to be taken to ensure that the conditions in the business or share purchase agreement and the vendor placing agreement do not result in circularity. The vendor placing agreement will be signed at the same time as the purchase agreement. If the securities are to be listed on the Stock Exchange, then listing particulars will be required (see **4.2**).

5.4.3 PRE-COMPLETION

This refers to the period between contract and completion. The parties will have stated a completion date in the contract, which they may agree to defer if further time is required to satisfy outstanding conditions. What needs to be done in this period is essentially the satisfaction of any conditions on which the contract depends. With the exception of tax clearances, which we have already seen should be sought as part of the pre-contract phase, pre-completion is the point at which all other necessary clearances should now be obtained.

Section **5.6** deals with the various regulatory regimes and licensing requirements likely to affect these transactions, and the pre-completion clearances needed are those which satisfy those regimes and requirements.

With business acquisitions, this is the point at which third parties who have contracted with the business will be asked to agree to the substitution of the buyer for the seller in those contracts. As discussed in **5.3.7**, the novation of major contracts will need to be a condition precedent. The treatment of a business's contractual obligations generally is discussed more fully in **5.5.2**.

5.4.4 COMPLETION

This is the point at which the acquisition is finalised. Completion takes place on the date specified in the business or share purchase agreement. What actually happens at completion?

5.4.4.1 Buyer's obligations

(a) To provide the consideration: if by way of cash, a banker's draft will be required; if the finance is through a vendor placing, then the buyer will need to show that all the placing's conditions are satisfied and that the cash which it has realised is available.

(b) To provide copies of the new service agreements which the buyer wants the target's key employees to sign.

5.4.4.2 Seller's obligations

(a) To produce the share transfers, any resignations of directors and company secretary which are required, certificate of incorporation, company seal and so on (if it is a share sale).

(b) To produce board minutes of the target approving the transfer of the shares for registration and the appointment of new directors (if it is a share sale). The buyer's solicitors will in fact draft these.

(c) To provide the deed of indemnity for tax liabilities (if it is a share sale).

(d) To provide evidence that all the conditions which it was the seller's obligation to seek (for example, the consent of third parties to the substitution of buyer for seller in the business's contracts) have been performed.

(e) If it is a business sale, to provide evidence that the buyers will have vacant possession of any property agreed to be sold under the business purchase agreement.

In essence then, the target is transferred legally into the name of the buyer, the seller gets its money and the transaction is wrapped up.

5.4.5 POST-COMPLETION

There will be a few minor details to attend to following completion; for example, if it is a share sale, stamping the share transfers for stamp duty and submitting notices of changes of directors and company secretary to Companies House. There will of course be a significant number of commercial changes to be made to the target's operations, particularly if new managers or new service agreements have been introduced. For the buyer's solicitors, there may be a significant amount of ongoing work as the target operation is restructured or integrated into the buyer's corporate group.

5.5 Purchase Agreement

The key document in any acquisition is the purchase agreement, whether it be a company or a business which is being bought. This will set out the agreed terms and conditions and apportion the risks as between the parties through the warranties. This section looks at the principal terms and warranties you can expect to find in any purchase agreement.

5.5.1 SHARE PURCHASE AGREEMENT

We start by looking at the standard main clauses in the agreement for a share sale. The later section on business purchase agreements (see **5.5.2**) concentrates only on the principal differences between a share and business purchase agreement, so much of what is said here applies equally to business purchases.

5.5.1.1 Agreement to sell

This is easily forgotten amidst the panoply of other provisions! The shares are sold free of all charges and encumbrances, subject possibly to a dividend strip to be paid to the sellers (see **5.2.2.3**).

5.5.1.2 Consideration

Will the consideration be cash or securities? If securities, it may be that the seller wants cash but the buyer has to issue its own securities into the market first to obtain that cash – hence a vendor placing will result (see **3.6.5**). Securities will also enable the seller to shelter a capital gain for the time being through roll-over relief. Securities in this context means shares or loan stock.

Should the consideration be provided now or in stages? Deferred consideration is sometimes used where the sellers are also key personnel in the future management of the business, and so are to remain employees of the target after the acquisition; in order to provide them with an incentive to maintain the profit levels of the company after the sale, part of their consideration is paid in future years on the basis of a percentage of profit. This is known as an 'earn out'. It is likely to give rise in addition to detailed provisions in the agreement fettering the discretion of the buyer to do as it pleases with the company after the sale: otherwise there would be an obvious incentive for it to run the company in such a way that its profits declined significantly.

How is the value of the company to be determined? The buyer will want to rely on the most up-to-date accounts of the company and the picture they give of its net asset value and profits record in arriving at an assessment of the consideration to be paid. There is a risk otherwise that the buyer will pay consideration in ignorance of recent financial difficulties which current accounts would reveal. Hence completion accounts are often prepared which state the financial position of the company up to completion. They are usually audited. There will usually be a clause in the agreement providing for an adjustment to the consideration depending on what the completion accounts reveal.

5.5.1.3 Conditions

Typical conditions are described at **5.6.7**. If the conditions are not satisfied, the agreement may provide either that it lapses, or that the buyer has the option to terminate, or complete the acquisition in spite of the failure to satisfy the condition, or agree a new date for eventual completion which will allow enough time for the condition to be satisfied. Usually the parties will agree, whichever option is selected, not to bring claims against each other for an outstanding condition unless one of them is at fault for not bringing it about.

5.5.1.4 Completion

This records the events described at **5.4.4**: the primary purpose of this clause is to state when and where completion will take place and remind all parties that this is the point at which the money is paid over. The buyer will preserve a right to terminate under the contract if any of the completion requirements are not satisfied and a right to claim damages (though this will be subject to the point about damages for non-satisfaction of conditions mentioned above).

One point covered later in the clause about warranties, but relevant to completion, is the restatement of the warranties at completion: in other words, the buyer will usually want the warranties repeated at completion (which will mean updating the disclosure letter accordingly). The buyer will insist on this because he is not taking over the running of the company until completion – and it is only when he is managing the operation that he can reasonably be expected to assume responsibility for its liabilities. If warranties are updated to completion, and between exchange and completion it then becomes apparent that a further disclosure against the warranties will need to be made, the buyer will usually insist on the right to terminate and claim damages if the identified problem is material.

5.5.1.5 Action pending completion

The purpose of this is to place restrictions on what the seller can and cannot do with the company between exchange and completion. The buyer's fear is always that the seller's incentive for running the operation in a business-like fashion will decline significantly following signing and exchange of contracts. Hence the agreement will usually constrain the seller between exchange and completion from entering into material contracts, or dismissing employees, or buying and selling material assets, or issuing further shares in the company (and a host of other things) without the buyer's consent.

5.5.1.6 Warranties

Put simply, these are promises made by the seller to the buyer regarding the state of all aspects of the company's operations. They are needed because, in these transactions, it is not even possible for the buyer to presume that the seller owns what it is proposing to sell, as would be the case with a sale of goods by virtue of the implied warranty as to title under the Sale of Goods Act 1979. As a result, warranties are the centrepiece of any negotiation on a share purchase agreement. The warranties will always vary, depending on the nature of the company's business, but there are some relatively standard provisions you would expect to see in all cases, of which these are the most important:

(a) Accounts: that the latest accounts have been prepared in a way which is consistent with the company's previous accounts (and so provide an accurate comparison), and that they give a true and fair view (as defined by the Companies Act 1985 (see **2.4.3**)) of the company's financial affairs at the time they were prepared.

(b) Title: that the sellers have full and unfettered title to sell the shares.

(c) Material contracts: that the sellers have not entered into any material or unusual contracts (for example, over a certain value, or of an unusually long term, or of a loss-making nature, or which contain particularly onerous obligations for the company to satisfy). This will usually give rise to an extensive set of disclosures in the disclosure letter, and in many ways the principal purpose of this warranty is to flush out copies of all the company's significant contracts as part of the due diligence exercise.

(d) Assets: that the company has full and unencumbered title to its assets.

(e) Litigation: that the company has no ongoing, threatened or pending litigation claims, and has conducted its operations in accordance with all legal requirements including relevant licences and consents.

(f) Borrowings: that the company has no undisclosed borrowings. Once again, this will inevitably force a series of disclosures.

(g) Information: that the information supplied by the sellers in the course of the due diligence exercise is true, complete and accurate in all material respects and no information has been omitted which might render the information given untrue, inaccurate or misleading in any material respect. Given the reliance which the buyer will place on the information which emerges from the due diligence process (see **5.4.1.2**), it is vital to have some protection against the risk of the seller concocting a tissue of lies – hence this warranty is of great importance.

(h) Disclosure letter: in connection with the information warranty, it will be of equal importance to ensure that the accuracy and completeness of the disclosure letter is warranted by the seller.

(i) Employees: that the company is not in breach of any of the contractual or statutory obligations it owes to its employees.

(j) Real property: the inclusion of this warranty assumes that the other possible methods of dealing with the company's real property interests in the acquisition (see **5.4.1.2**) are not being used. The seller will be warranting that the company has good marketable title to its real properties and they are not subject to any undisclosed mortgages or charges.

(k) Environment: that the company is in full compliance with all relevant environmental legislation. This often gives rise to difficult negotiations in view of the latent, long-term and very costly nature of many environmental liabilities, and the toughening legislative regime in the UK and EU.

(l) Taxation: that the company has complied with all relevant tax legislation. In addition to this, the seller will normally be asked to indemnify the buyer against any tax liabilities for the period up to completion. The indemnity will be a separate document attached to and to be read in conjunction with the agreement.

In addition to the warranties, the seller is likely to be asked to give indemnities to the buyer, particularly for tax liabilities and possibly for other liabilities such as those arising in connection with the company's environmental history. It is important to understand how the seller's liability under warranties and indemnities differs.

Where there is a breach of warranty, the seller is liable for any reduction in the value of the shares resulting from the breach (to put the buyer into the position the buyer would have been in had the warranty been true). Where there is an indemnity (or a similar so-called 'pound-for-pound' clause), the seller is liable for any increase in the company's liabilities or reduction in the value of the underlying assets, irrespective of the effect on the value of the shares. For example, the breach of a warranty about the value of book debts will only permit recovery if this affects the value of the shares; if the seller has indemnified the buyer against the risk of book debts becoming irrecoverable, and then one is indeed lost, all the buyer has to prove is the size of the lost book debt and the buyer can recover automatically – the effect the loss will have on the shares is quite irrelevant. Indemnities are therefore generally resisted by sellers except in the context of tax liabilities where they are standard.

The warranties will always be given by the seller. The buyer may also require directors of the company, or a parent company or directors or key shareholders of the seller, to join in the warranties where they have played a significant role in the management and direction of the target company. In this case, the buyer will usually make the warrantors jointly and severally liable for a breach of any of the warranties.

It is usual for warrantors to seek to qualify the warranties they give by reference to their knowledge at the time that they gave them: thus, wording is used such as 'to the best of the seller's knowledge, information and belief, there is no outstanding litigation' etc. Otherwise the seller will be concerned that the warranty is really a guarantee. Obviously the buyer will be keen to resist this kind of limitation to the scope of the warranties, which will depend largely on the comparative negotiating strength of the parties. A buyer who has to concede the qualification will usually insist that the phrase 'to the best of the seller's knowledge, information and belief' is itself qualified by the words 'having made all reasonable enquiries', so that at least the buyer is not relying on the seller's inadequately researched information.

5.5.1.7 Limitations on the warranties

The seller will only accept the raft of warranties and tax indemnity in return for some restrictions under the agreement as to the following:

(a) The maximum amount for which claims can be made (usually settled at the total consideration payable).

(b) The minimum monetary amount per claim (to deter frivolous claims).

(c) The time-limits within which claims must be brought: these will override the Limitation Act 1980, and usually parties settle on anything between 18 months and three years. This is on the basis that after this any undisclosed problems with the company will have become apparent and it is therefore pointless to keep the warranties open for longer. Sometimes an exception may be negotiated by the buyer for the environmental warranty. Six years for the tax deed of indemnity is common, because of the threat of Inland Revenue investigations into the tax affairs of a company that far back.

5.5.1.8 Pensions

Appropriate arrangements will need to be made for the continuing provision of a pension scheme to the company's employees following completion, and the various alternatives are described in **5.4.1.2**.

5.5.1.9 Restrictive covenants

The buyer will usually seek restrictive covenants from the seller to prevent the seller soliciting the company's customers or setting up an identical operation next door within a fortnight of completion. The covenants will need to be specific about the kind of business which is being restricted and reasonable in terms of geographical and temporal limitations.

5.5.1.10 Assignment

Unless the seller is happy to be sued by future buyers of the company, it will be necessary to prevent the buyer from assigning the benefit of the agreement, so there is usually a provision in the agreement requiring the seller's consent before this can be done.

5.5.1.11 Retention fund

The buyer may seek to have the seller's obligations under the agreement supported by a retention fund. Part of the buyer's consideration is paid into a retention fund until the claims period for the warranties (see **5.5.1.7**) is at an end. If the seller becomes liable under any of the warranties during that period, the buyer's claim (if proven) is paid out of the retention fund. Any outstanding amount in the fund is paid over to the seller when the claims period has concluded. This gives the buyer some assurance that his warranty claims will be met out of ready cash. Retention fund arrangements are usually resisted fiercely by sellers as they are kept out of a proportion of their consideration for some time.

5.5.1.12 Costs

Who will bear the legal and accountancy fees to which the transaction will give rise? Usually each party bears its own.

5.5.1.13 Interest

Any sum not paid over in accordance with the agreement will attract interest.

5.5.1.14 Arbitration

Do the parties want to refer disputes to arbitration rather than rely on the courts and normal litigation procedures? Arbitration may be costly, though it may also be quick and efficient. It may in fact be most appropriate to have an expert arbitrator appointed to resolve any differences arising on the more technical parts of the agreement, for instance, the drawing up of the completion accounts (see **5.5.1.2**), whilst relying on the courts to sort out differences arising elsewhere.

5.5.1.15 Governing law

If any of the parties to the agreement are foreign, it is prudent to state that English law is the governing law of the contract and require the foreign party to submit to English jurisdiction for legal proceedings: where there is no doubt that the *situs* of the contract is the UK, this clause is redundant.

5.5.2 BUSINESS PURCHASE AGREEMENT

This section concentrates on the differences between share and business purchase agreements. Much of what was mentioned in **5.5.1** will be relevant for business purchase agreements as well. The following paragraphs discuss the clauses which will be different.

5.5.2.1 Agreement to sell

Obviously with the share purchase agreement, the agreement is to sell the shares. With the business purchase agreement, the agreement is to sell the business, which is in turn comprised of a collection of assets fused into a going concern. Hence the business purchase agreement will need to describe these assets and the fact that they are being sold as a going concern.

The assets to be sold obviously depend on the nature of the business which is being sold. Commonly, though, the following will figure in the list (and all of these will be listed individually in the agreement and defined):

(a) Property: freehold property will need to be sold free of encumbrances and mortgages. Leasehold property will need to be sold with the landlord's written consent. It is often not possible to obtain this in time for completion. Unless the property is absolutely fundamental to the business, it is not usual to make the landlord's consent a condition of the contract. More often, the seller agrees to use its best endeavours to obtain the consent within a reasonable period. Although there are risks associated with this (clearly the landlord may refuse consent and it may be reasonable for the landlord to do so), the agreement will often provide a fallback – namely that the buyer finds alternative premises and the seller funds the difference (or agrees to take less consideration).

(b) Stock: stock or work in progress of the business will need to have been recently valued. Since stamp duty is not payable on assets passing by delivery and stock is such an asset, it is helpful from the buyer's point of view to attach as high a value to stock as possible, as it saves stamp duty (which is imposed at rates of either 1, 2.5 or 3.5 per cent in business sales, rather than the effective $\frac{1}{2}$ per cent in share sales (see **5.2.2**));

(c) Chattels: this includes plant and machinery, cars, vans, fittings, office equipment and the like – it may be appropriate to draw up an inventory of everything included as a chattel and attach it as a schedule. As with stock, there is a considerable advantage to the buyer in having as much of the asset value being bought identified as chattels since that will save stamp duty.

(d) Intellectual property: this includes trade marks, copyright, registered designs, patents and know-how.

(e) Investments: for instance, shares held in other companies.

(f) Contracts: normally the parties will agree that the buyer takes over the business's ongoing contracts, whether they be for the supply of goods and services, joint ventures or other arrangements. Major contracts which the buyer regards as fundamental to the business will need to be novated prior to completion and so this will need to be a condition to the agreement. Less important contracts will need to be checked to ensure they can be assigned. If so, the seller will undertake to get this done. If contracts cannot be assigned, the parties will generally agree that the seller will hold the contracts for the benefit of the buyer and the buyer will function *de facto* as the contracting party. In this event, the seller will want to be indemnified against the risk of liability arising through the buyer's non-performance, and the buyer will seek an assurance that any moneys paid to the seller by the contracting third party are held by the seller for the buyer's benefit.

(g) Debtors: there are a number of options available.

The first is to assign debts to the buyer: notice of assignment will then need to be issued to each debtor. There may be two reasons for avoiding this: first, the time it takes up, and second, if debts are excluded from the sale, no stamp duty is payable on them, which is tax-efficient from the buyer's point of view.

The parties may therefore agree instead that the seller legally retains title to the debts and the buyer collects them on the seller's behalf for a fee. The consideration payable is reduced accordingly. The buyer will want an assurance that the seller will not issue writs against outstanding debtors who continue to be customers of the business following completion. Alternatively, the seller retains and collects the debts itself and so any money it receives for them, and the buyer agrees to pay the seller any money it should accidentally receive in respect of them.

(h) Creditors: as far as creditors are concerned, there are also a number of options.

The buyer may agree to assume the obligation to pay the creditors. Legally, unless the third party agrees to the buyer replacing the seller, it is still the seller which is responsible for paying the outstanding debts of the business, hence the seller should obtain an indemnity from the buyer against any liability which the seller incurs because the buyer fails to pay up.

Alternatively, to save the buyer stamp duty (which is payable on the assumption of liabilities), the seller hangs on to the creditors and agrees with the buyer that it will pay its debts promptly, and indemnifies the buyer against any losses it may suffer if the seller does not.

A final option is for the buyer to agree to pay off the creditors as agent for the seller in return for a reduction in the consideration price. The seller will want the buyer to agree to do so promptly and to indemnify the seller if the creditors sue the seller for non-payment.

(i) Cash on deposit: this is often excluded from the sale as otherwise stamp duty is paid on it.

(j) Goodwill and transfer of the business as a going concern: goodwill covers the intangible benefits which the buyer will inherit with the business (for instance, reputation and the value which recognised brand names carry). The value of those benefits is represented by the amount which the buyer is willing to pay in addition to the net asset value of the business. If the goodwill is excluded from the assets to be transferred, this may cause difficulty in showing that the business is being transferred as a going concern. This would give difficulties with VAT and the transfer of employees.

VAT is payable on the sale of a business by the seller if the business is not sold as a going concern and the buyer is not registered for VAT. This means that the seller will have to pay VAT at 17.5 per cent out of the purchase price received, as the purchase price will be deemed to be VAT-inclusive. Obviously this reduces the net amount of consideration the seller expects to receive.

To counteract this, the transaction can be structured so that the business is sold as a going concern, and advance clearance obtained from HM Customs and Excise to confirm this.

If clearance is not forthcoming, the parties will generally agree (assuming the buyer is registered for VAT) that the buyer will pay the purchase price plus 17.5 per cent VAT, and the seller will give the buyer an invoice which will enable this output VAT to be set off against the buyer's input VAT – though sometimes, the parties may agree to split the cost of the extra VAT.

As for the employees, under the Transfer of Undertakings (Protection of Employment) Regulations 1981 (SI 1981/1794), employees working in the business immediately before the point at which the business is transferred (completion) will continue by automatic operation of law to be treated as employed by the business after transfer (and therefore as not dismissed), *provided* the business is transferred as a going concern. Despite the automatic application of the regulations, the agreement will usually identify the employees and state that they will be transferred as one of the business's assets.

In view of the importance of both these points, the agreement will usually state that the parties agree the business is sold as a going concern.

5.5.2.2 Warranties

Since the process of buying a business permits the buyer to select the assets it wants to buy and the liabilities it does not want to inherit (for example, creditors or outstanding tax liabilities), the warranties in a business purchase agreement are less wide-ranging and demanding than would be the case with a typical share purchase agreement. It is unlikely that the buyer will extract an indemnity from the seller for outstanding tax liabilities which the buyer chooses to take on, though there will probably be warranties that the liabilities do not exceed what has already been identified – hence there is usually no deed of indemnity in the purchase of a business. The warranties will cover similar ground to those sought in the purchase of a company. Their focus will be to seek assurance from the seller that the value of the individual assets is as stated and that there are no material undisclosed liabilities relevant to particular assets or in general which might affect the value of the business.

5.6 Regulation of Acquisitions

5.6.1 THE BASIC PRINCIPLE: FREEDOM OF CONTRACT

We start from the position that parties are free to buy and sell businesses, assets and companies under contract on terms they choose. The acquisition or disposal is governed by the private treaty which the parties freely enter into. This has a number of important consequences:

(a) The regulatory constraints considered in this section are very important. Your client, though, will not thank you for a masterful exposition of them if you cannot draft or negotiate a contract. It is in the contract that almost all of the issues arising in the acquisition will be settled or provided for. You have to know both the law of contract and be capable of drafting and negotiating a contract to advise properly in this area.

(b) Unlike a takeover, where regulation has defined quite closely the way in which the transaction may be conducted (see **chapter 8**), acquisitions are inherently flexible transactions which can be moulded to suit the individual idiosyncrasies of clients. Regulation may interfere with this flexibility to some extent, but the starting-point is what the clients want rather than what the rule books say you can do. The lawyer needs therefore to be prepared to draft and negotiate creatively.

However, there are a number of rules which will contribute to the way the transaction is moulded. These regulations turn the transaction from one governed by purely private considerations to one with a public dimension.

5.6.2 CITY CODE ON TAKEOVERS AND MERGERS

This is covered in detail in **chapter 8**. Subject to some exceptions, the Code will apply if it is a *public company* which is being acquired. In these circumstances, an offer must be made to the target's shareholders to acquire their shares. The Code governs the nature, timing and content of that offer. You should refer to **chapter 8** for detailed information.

5.6.3 FINANCIAL SERVICES ACT 1986

This bites on acquisitions in a number of ways.

5.6.3.1 Acquiring and disposing of investment businesses

The FS Act regulates the conduct of an investment business by requiring it to be authorised. Authorisation is granted to the owners of that business. If those owners change because the business is being transferred, then either the new owners need to make an application of their own for authorisation, or approval for the transfer may be needed from the authority which granted the original authorisation. The background to the regulatory structure introduced by the FS Act has been explained more fully in **1.5**.

There is sometimes a concern that the buying and selling of a business or a company *per se* will amount to the conduct of investment business. This can never be the case with the sale of a business as a business is not an investment under sch. 1 FS Act (unless it has interests in shares or other securities). Company sales, which are trades in shares and so technically caught by the definition of investments under the FS Act, are in fact exempted by virtue of para. 21 of sch. 1.

Advisers in company sales (merchant banks, accountants and lawyers) must think about the need for authorisation if they can be described as arranging a deal in investments (sch. 1, para. 13) or giving investment advice (sch. 1, para. 15).

5.6.3.2 Section 47

This has been discussed in **1.5.1.4**. Section 47 creates specific problems in the context of acquisitions which might not at first sight appear obvious.

(a) Investments for the purposes of the FS Act include shares but *not* assets or a business – hence s. 47 is never of relevance to a business sale (unless the business owns investments such as shares), but does catch a company or share sale.

(b) One of the consequences of applying the basic principles of contract to acquisition work is the rule *'caveat emptor'* – let the buyer beware. At common law, the seller is under no duty to disclose information about the business or shares it is selling. Section 47(2) FS Act makes it an offence to do any act or engage in any *course of conduct* which creates, and is intended to create, a false or misleading impression as to the market, price or value in investments. Although at common law the seller is obliged to disclose nothing to the buyer, any failure to disclose a fact about the target company which might otherwise affect the price the buyer is prepared to pay will be creating a false impression and, if it is designed to have that effect, it will amount to a course of conduct caught by the section. If the facts are material and are concealed dishonestly, this will also be a breach of s. 47(1). To be safe, sellers of companies should disclose to buyers anything which might have an effect on the value of the target.

(c) Any representations expressly made to potential buyers of companies (whether orally or in writing) to encourage them to acquire will fall foul of s. 47(1) if they create a false or misleading impression and the makers of the representations know that or are reckless about it.

5.6.3.3 Investment advertisements

These are covered in detail in **1.5.1.4**.

In view of the FS Act's definition of 'investments', a business purchase agreement should not constitute an investment advertisement.

A share purchase agreement may be an investment advertisement if, for example, the seller is auctioning the company off to the highest bidder and so sends the draft agreement to several possible buyers, in effect 'advertising' it for sale, or where the seller distributes an information memorandum about the company. In normal cases, however, the need to have an authorised person issue the investment advertisement under s. 57 FS Act can be avoided through relying on one of the exemptions described in **1.5.1.4**.

5.6.4 LISTING RULES REGULATION

This may have an impact on the acquisition of a private company or business in two ways: the definition of transactions and the issue of listing particulars.

5.6.4.1 Transactions

The Listing Rules oblige listed companies to observe certain requirements when involved in 'transactions'. The first general point to note is the breadth of this term 'transactions'. It covers all transactions, exempting specifically only transactions in the ordinary course of business and issues of equity finance (provided they are not related to an acquisition). Nevertheless, what it will principally catch are acquisitions or disposals.

The purpose of these controls is to keep shareholders of these companies informed of purchases and sales their companies are making and to give them a veto over particularly large or sensitive transactions. The requirements which the companies must observe depend on how the relevant transaction is classified. They are set out in The Listing Rules, chs 10 and 11.

5.6.4.2 Classification of transactions

(a) *Class 1* transactions must be notified to the Stock Exchange Company Announcements Office and to the company's shareholders in a circular, and also require approval of the company's shareholders in general meeting.

(b) *Class 2* transactions must be notified to the Stock Exchange and require a press announcement.

(c) *Class 3* transactions only require notification to the Stock Exchange if the consideration for the acquisition includes securities which are to be listed (or dealt with in the AIM if it is an AIM company).

(d) *Transactions with related parties* must be notified to the Stock Exchange and will generally require a circular and the approval of shareholders in general meeting.

Reverse takeovers must be approved by shareholders in general meeting: they are dealt with in **8.10**.

What makes a transaction Class 1, Class 2 etc? This depends on the size of the transaction, which in turn is gauged by comparing the value of the company making the acquisition or disposal with the value of the company or business being acquired or disposed of. There are five methods by which value must be compared:

(a) gross assets;

(b) profits;

(c) turnover;

(d) consideration paid compared with the market capitalisation of the buyer;

(e) gross capital.

If the comparison *in any one of the five categories* equals or exceeds the percentages set out in the table below (which is based on LR, para. 10.4), then the transaction falls within the relevant classification and the appropriate requirements apply. The exception is Class 3: *all* the figures must be below 5 per cent for a transaction to be in Class 3. If one of those five methods of comparison produces an anomalous result, the UKLA may disregard the result it produces (see LR, para. 10.6). The UKLA may aggregate separate transactions for the purposes of these classifications if they are connected, or there have been multiple transactions in the last year.

Classification	*Size of transaction*
Class 1	25 per cent
Class 2	5 per cent
Class 3	less than 5 per cent
Related party transaction	see below
Reverse takeover	100 per cent or change of control in buyer

A related party transaction is one between the company and one or more of its directors or substantial shareholders, irrespective of the size of the transaction. The UKLA is anxious to control these to prevent possible abuses by directors of their powers. The term 'transaction' is again very broadly construed, including not just sales and purchases. However, LR, paras 11.7 to 11.9, exempts certain related party transactions which would otherwise be caught, for example, giving an indemnity to a director or granting options to directors under share schemes, or 'small transactions' (below 0.25 per cent in the table of comparisons above).

A reverse takeover is one where the target is at least as big as the buyer, with the possible result (where the buyer's securities are the whole or part of the consideration for the purchase) that the target shareholders end up controlling the buyer. The Listing Rules and AIM Rules require the consent of the buyer's shareholders to such a transaction.

5.6.4.3 Examples

Let us look at some examples. Assume for these that Yellow plc (Y) is listed on the Official List. Y has gross assets of £100 million and profits of £10 million.

(a) *Y wants to buy G, an independent plc with profits of £3 million*

This is a public company takeover governed by the City Code on Takeovers and Mergers – refer to **chapter 8** for further details. In addition, though, the transaction will be a Class 1 for Y on the profits comparison and so will require shareholder approval.

(b) *Y wants to buy B, a business with assets of £5 million and profits of £1.1 million*

The transaction is a Class 2 acquisition for Y on the profits and assets comparisons, requiring notification to the Stock Exchange and a press announcement.

(c) *Y wants to acquire 2 per cent of G's shares, and one of Y's directors already owns 0.1 per cent of the shares in G*

G is not a related party of Y, despite the director's shareholding. The director would need to control at least 30 per cent of G's votes or have a majority of votes on the board under his control for G to count as his 'associate' and so be caught by the terms of YB, ch. 11, as a related party of Y.

5.6.4.4 Definitions of figures to be used

To assist in calculating the percentage ratios, The Listing Rules provide definitions of the figures to be used. These are set out in paras 10.7–10.19.

5.6.4.5 Notifications

Notification to the Stock Exchange must contain particulars of the transaction, details of whatever is being acquired or disposed of, the value of the consideration, other relevant financial information and the benefits resulting from the transaction. What shareholders need to be told depends on the classification of the transaction. All circulars should comply with the general requirements of LR, ch. 14 (including giving clear explanations).

(a) *Class 1 Circular*

The specific contents requirements for these are set out in LR, ch. 10, app. They are more relaxed than the requirements we have seen for the contents of a prospectus or listing particulars (see **4.2.6.3**). They include the need for statements about working capital and changes in the financial position of the company since its last financial statement. A Class 1 Circular needs to contain details of the company's litigation, material contracts, current indebtedness and trading prospects. It also requires a directors' responsibility statement (see LR, para. 10.38(e)) and a recommendation paragraph stating that the proposed transaction is in the best interests of the shareholders as a whole (see LR, para. 14.1(d)). Like a prospectus or listing particulars, a Class 1 circular needs to be approved by the UKLA first before it can be distributed to shareholders.

(b) *Related party transaction circular*

The contents requirements for listed companies sending out these circulars are set out in LR, para. 11.10. The two most important requirements are for statements about material contracts and significant changes in the financial position of the company since its last financial statement. In addition, the circular must have a statement from an independent adviser describing why the transaction is reasonable and fair so far as the shareholders are concerned. The related party must not be allowed to vote on the transaction at the general meeting.

Consultation with the UKLA on a related party transaction and the contents of the relevant circular will be needed at an early stage.

5.6.4.6 Listing particulars and prospectuses

This is the second way in which The Listing Rules can impact an acquisition. If the consideration to be provided by the buyer consists (at least in part) of the issue of new securities, and the buyer is listed or dealt in on the AIM, then the issue will require listing particulars or a prospectus (as appropriate). You should refer to **chapter 4** for further details about these documents.

If the transaction requires listing particulars or a prospectus, the company is likely to combine such a document with any circular it needs to send shareholders to satisfy the requirements of The Listing Rules (see LR, para. 10.43).

5.6.5 MERGER CONTROL

The statutory and regulatory provisions intended to prevent undue restrictions in the competitive environment in the UK and EC are considered in detail in the context of public company takeovers in **8.16**, though they are of equal relevance to private acquisitions or disposals. A decision by the Office of Fair Trading not to refer a merger for consideration by the Competition Commission (see **8.16**) will usually be a condition of the acquisition. Any reference will therefore lapse the purchase agreement.

5.6.6 OTHER REGULATORY RESTRICTIONS

The range of other possible regulatory constraints which may catch a specific acquisition is limitless, and the lists above and below contain only the most obvious and routine snags you are likely to encounter. You must never disregard any licensing requirements particular to the industries in which the acquired entity operates. We have already mentioned the Financial Services Act 1986, but in addition other financial concerns will be subject to regulatory controls. The transfer of a banking business will need the approval of the Bank of England; the transfer of an insurance business that of the Department of Trade and Industry. There are a number of other industry-specific restrictions which are of special importance:

5.6.6.1 Industry Act 1975

The President of the Board of Trade may prevent the transfer to a non-UK resident of 30 per cent or more of a manufacturing business if he considers it to be specially important. Exercise of this discretion is rare.

5.6.6.2 Inland Revenue

Tax consents, rulings or clearances are often needed, as we have seen (see **5.2.2.4**).

5.6.6.3 Companies Act 1985

In all the excitement of assorted regulations, it is easy to forget the standard Companies Act 1985 requirements which need to be observed.

If the consideration for the acquisition includes the issue of the company's own securities, do bear in mind the possible need for a s. 80 authority to allot or a s. 89 disapplication.

The Stock Exchange may require related party transactions to be approved by the shareholders in general meeting but, in the event that it does not, is the transaction caught by s. 320 (substantial property transaction involving directors)? If so, it will in any event need approval from the shareholders in general meeting.

5.6.6.4 Corporate regulation

Any acquisition or disposal by a company must comply with a company's memorandum and articles of association. The transaction must fall within its objects, and special requirements in the articles regarding shareholder approvals need to be observed (as do borrowing restrictions if the buying company is borrowing to fund an acquisition).

5.6.7 CONDITIONS

Most of these regulatory controls will not inhibit a transaction proceeding (the merger control provisions are the most obvious exception). It is essential though to ensure they are complied with in case sanctions should follow: failure to observe the Yellow Book requirements could lead to de-listing. Hence it will always be a condition of the acquisition proceeding that relevant regulatory requirements are observed and fulfilled. You need to ensure therefore not only that your client is properly advised about the application and effect of any relevant regulations but also that the contract has been adequately drafted to deal with their impact on the transaction.

5.7 Checklists

The following checklists summarise the issues which you will need to address in structuring an acquisition, advising your client on the due diligence exercise on the target, drafting the agreement and ensuring you have all the documents the transaction requires.

5.7.1 STRUCTURING THE TRANSACTION

(a) What is the business or commercial background to the transaction?

(b) Has any decision been made as to whether this is to be a company or business sale? If not, see **5.2**.

(c) Are either of the entities listed on the Official List or dealt in on the AIM? This will help determine whether there are any UKLA and Stock Exchange requirements to observe regarding notification of the transaction.

(d) Is there any overseas element involved in the transaction? Consider the impact of overseas regulators and the need for overseas advice.

(e) What is the expected value of the transaction? This will determine whether:

  (i) the class requirements of The Listing Rules come into play, possibly requiring shareholder's approval – see **5.6.4**;

  (ii) there are any merger control implications – see **8.16**.

(f) What is the nature of the business to be acquired? This will help determine whether there are likely to be any special approvals or consents needed for the transaction – see **5.6.6**.

(g) What form will the consideration take? Securities may also require a vendor placing. Will it be deferred? Will there be an earn-out element? (See **5.5.1.2**.)

(h) What tax clearances will be required? (See **5.2.2.4**.)

5.7.2 GETTING TO GRIPS WITH THE TARGET

Information and documents are needed on the following:

(a) the memorandum and articles of association of the target if it is a share sale, and the seller if it is a business sale;

(b) accounts relevant to the company or the business (and accountants' report);

(c) material contracts;

(d) employment contracts, and any materials relevant to the benefits enjoyed by those working for the target, e.g., pension rights, share schemes etc.;

(e) loan documents, mortgages, charges, debentures relevant to the company or the business;

(f) title deeds relevant to the property belonging to the company or business;

(g) the target's intellectual property rights.

5.7.3 DRAFTING THE AGREEMENT

You should expect your agreement to cover the following points:

(a) agreement to sell;

(b) consideration;

(c) conditions;

(d) completion and action up to completion;

(e) assignment;

(f) costs and interest;

(g) restrictive covenants regarding non-solicitation of customers or non-competition;

(h) warranties and limitations thereto. Warranties should cover:

  (i) capacity and title of the sellers;

  (ii) information supplied;

  (iii) accounts;

  (iv) borrowings and liabilities;

  (v) material contracts;

  (vi) compliance with laws and litigation;

  (vii) employees and pensions;

  (viii) assets;

  (ix) real and intellectual property (if relevant);

  (x) environment.

Do not forget the tax deed of indemnity!

5.7.4 ADDITIONAL CONSIDERATIONS FOR PURCHASES OF BUSINESSES

These are the assets the agreement and its warranties will need to deal with:

(a) property (freehold and leasehold);

(b) stock;

(c) intellectual property;

(d) contracts;

(e) investments;

(f) chattels, plant, machinery;

(g) cash;

(h) goodwill;

(i) possibly debts;

(j) possibly liabilities.

5.7.5 DOCUMENTS LIST

This is a summary of the key documents you are likely to require in a typical acquisition:

(a) heads of agreement;

(b) confidentiality agreement;

(c) instructions to accountants;

(d) request for information from the seller;

(e) due diligence documents;

(f) share or business purchase agreement and deed of indemnity;

(g) disclosure letter;

(h) vendor placing agreement;

(i) completion documents (share transfers, conveyances, satisfaction of conditions, shareholder and board resolutions to show corporate approval for the transaction);

(j) circular to shareholders and, if necessary, listing particulars or prospectus.

SIX

JOINT VENTURES

So far we have concentrated on the acquisitive side of corporate finance activity. There is of course a cooperative side as well, and this is epitomised by the joint venture.

6.1 What is a Joint Venture?

The idea is simple, though the number of forms it may take are legion (see **6.3**). In essence, a joint venture is a cooperative enterprise between two or more persons pursuing an agreed commercial goal or set of goals and in which the joint venturers share in agreed proportions the financing and control of the enterprise and the profits and losses it makes. The parties to such a venture can just as easily be individuals as companies.

It is perhaps easier to define a joint venture by reference to what it is not:

(a) *A franchise arrangement*

The nature of a franchise is that the franchisee is much more free than under a joint venture to pursue a personal business aim and the franchisor does not share in the profits in a true sense as usually only a premium or fixed fee is taken.

(b) *A collaboration agreement*

This will usually involve an agreement to share information and work on a specific area, often intellectual property, but not to form a joint enterprise in the process.

(c) *A service contract*

This term is not used in its more normal context of a director's employment contract. An example is a management services agreement in which one party agrees to provide the management services for a project or manufacturing facility owned by the other in return for a fee. Other examples are marketing or distributorship arrangements. There is no sharing of profits or risks (as there would be in a joint venture), simply a contractual deal in which one party supplies its expertise to the other at a price.

6.2 Why a Joint Venture?

It may seem perplexing that two parties would agree to establish a joint venture as opposed to pursuing a business goal for their own individual benefit. Are the commercial rewards forsaken not greater than those gained? This of course is always a difficult matter of judgment, and the parties to a joint venture clearly judge not. There are a number of reasons why a joint venture may suggest itself as the natural vehicle for a business venture:

(a) In a new venture, particularly one where the initial investment required is very large, or the potential losses very substantial, sharing the costs and liabilities with someone else may be the only viable way to launch the operation. In a sense, the joint venture here is a way of spreading cost and risk where both are difficult to quantify: no one wants too much of either.

(b) A joint venture may be a genuine sharing of different capacities and expertise. One party may have an outstanding business idea and the expertise to make it work, but no resources. Whilst a loan may be one solution, another is to find someone who has resources and is looking for a good idea to fund on the basis of taking a slice of the profits if the idea comes to fruition. A joint venture has been formed.

(c) Sometimes joint ventures are designed to create a virtual monopoly in a market. Life becomes much more comfortable for two competitors, each holding 40 per cent of a particular market and therefore close rivals, if they agree to pool resources and efforts: then they hold a combined market share, are not undercutting each other's margins and can cooperate gradually to squeeze out their smaller competitors. Of course this sort of conduct is anticompetitive and subject to regulatory restraint (see **8.16**), but it may still be a strong driving force behind a joint venture.

(d) We look at public company takeovers in **chapter 8**. One of the longer term defensive strategies for a company which fears it may be the target of a takeover bid is to lock some of its assets or resources away in a joint venture. The joint venture will usually provide that if either party to it experiences a change of control (such as would obviously be induced by a successful takeover offer for one of them) then the other party has a pre-emptive right to take over the entire joint venture. This is likely to be a significant deterrent to a would-be predator as the predator may forfeit the most coveted assets in the target.

Joint ventures therefore present a number of attractions. Of course, they are only one possible solution to the sort of problems described above. Certain business cultures have arguably proved more fertile for the sort of cooperative exercise which the joint venture entails than others (such as the US and the UK) which put a premium on acquisitions as the preferred business development method. Certain business areas, such as property investment and development and technology, attract a significant number of joint ventures, primarily because of the investment needed.

6.3 What is Needed for a Joint Venture?

One commodity which is absolutely essential at the start and indeed all the way through, and over which the lawyer can have a significant influence, is goodwill. The joint venture is a cooperative enterprise. It depends on a spirit of mutual trust. This is not to say that the parties to it will not disagree or negotiate fiercely for what they want. But without some mutuality of understanding the venture will not get started. The lawyer can do great damage to perfectly amicable relationships by approaching the transaction in a confrontational style. This will not enhance your client's prospects nor endear you to the client in the long run.

Let us look at the sort of questions you will need to ask:

(a) How will the joint venture be constituted? The assumption here is that the enterprise is to be conducted through a body or entity jointly owned – so a new body of some sort will need to be created. What alternatives exist?

(i) Company. The parties can become shareholders in a company. This is likely to be private and limited. Will it become a subsidiary of either or both of the parties (see **9.2**)? The articles of association will regulate the parties' management and shareholding rights, though they will enter into a shareholders' agreement as well to govern other aspects such as the funding of the venture (see **6.4.1**).

(ii) Partnership. A partnership may arise if the conditions of the Partnership Act 1890 are satisfied. If the parties choose a partnership as their preferred vehicle, they will want to draft a partnership agreement rather than rely on the Act.

A looser arrangement such as an unincorporated association is not appropriate given the doubt in law about the use of such a structure for business purposes; in any event, your clients would be well-advised that this kind of informal approach is not ideal in offering suitable legal safeguards.

If the joint venture is to operate overseas, or the parties are prepared or want (perhaps for tax reasons) to site the joint venture offshore, some jurisdictions offer the potential for a limited partnership which combines the benefits of the more flexible and less regulated partnership with limited liability status.

The principal attraction of selecting a corporate entity is limited liability status, and this is the more typical route for joint venturers to choose. The rest of this chapter will assume this is the entity preferred.

(b) Have the parties agreed in principle on the structure and operation of the joint venture in heads of agreement? If not, do they wish to sign these to form the basis for further discussion? Heads of agreement in this context need to be treated with the same sort of care as for those signed in business and company acquisitions (see **5.4.1.1**).

(c) Joint ventures often involve the parties sharing, or giving access to, information about each other which is confidential. Have the parties considered the need for a confidentiality agreement to deal with this?

(d) What is the joint venture's business aim? Apart from anything else, some objects for the memorandum of association will need to be drafted.

(e) How will the parties set the joint venture in motion? Will they provide premises, staff and equipment, or will the joint venture arrange this from the funds it inherits?

(f) How is the venture to be financed? Simply through the money put in when the shareholders subscribe for their shares? If so, will they contribute in equal measure? Will there be any debt financing? If so, from whom and how will it be secured? Who will provide future financing? If from the shareholders, will it be in equal shares?

(g) Will the joint venturers take equal profit shares? If it is a company, will the profits be paid by way of dividend?

(h) How will the management of the venture be organised? Will it be 50–50? What if there is a deadlock? Will the managers have the right to decide everything in relation to the venture's affairs or will some of the more important decisions be referred to the venturers themselves?

(i) How is termination of the venture to be governed? Will breach of the shareholders' agreement be a termination event? If one party wants to get out of the joint venture, will the other party or parties have the right to buy the departing party's interest?

There will always be a host of other issues to address: this list is only of the most obvious and important. The rest of the chapter is devoted to a closer look at the physical and documentary structure you would seek to give a corporate joint venture.

6.4 Joint Venture Companies: the Lawyer's Role

You will need to begin with the questions above and refine them further (see below). What you are aiming to do is to gather the necessary information to prepare the two crucial governing documents for the joint venture, the shareholders' agreement and the articles of association.

6.4.1 THE SHAREHOLDERS' AGREEMENT

Why are the articles of association not sufficient to bind the joint venturers together? The articles in a joint venture company regulate the affairs of the joint venturers as shareholders and managers. Some other document will have to record the arrangements regarding provision of staff, premises and facilities for the venture, the provision of finance, and termination, amongst other things. This is the role of the shareholders' agreement. The shareholders' agreement, as a private contract, is not subject to the disclosure requirement of the articles, and so is a perfect vehicle for any confidential or sensitive material.

However, the normal procedure is for the parties to agree on their respective shareholding interests and structure, and the powers of the managers, in the shareholders' agreement and make it one of the terms of the agreement that the articles will be drafted (they are usually attached to the shareholders' agreement as an appendix) in accordance with its provisions. Since it is easier to amend articles (by 75 per cent of the shareholders) than the shareholders' agreement (all parties will need to consent), usually the shareholders' agreement will state that it will be a breach of the shareholders' agreement for the articles to be amended without the consent of all the joint venture parties. The shareholders' agreement will invariably state that it takes precedence over the articles if there is any conflict between them: obviously the technique is to ensure this does not arise in the first place.

So, what does the shareholders' agreement consist of? The answer is that it depends entirely on the nature of the particular joint venture in question. The following are the most important of the subjects you would expect the agreement to tackle, and some have already been raised in the checklist of questions above:

(a) *Termination*

Usually mutual consent, a material breach of the agreement or insolvency, administration or receivership procedures against any of the parties will be a termination event, but there will generally be others, including possibly *force majeure*.

The agreement will need to address what happens to the venture on termination. Does it dissolve, with the assets returning to the contributing venturers? It will depend on the event of termination. If the event is a breach of the agreement, the transfer provisions described below in (b) are likely to be invoked. If the parties have agreed to terminate, dissolution would be the normal procedure.

(b) *Transfer of an interest*

If one of the venturers would like to pull out, what will happen to that party's interest? Will it be an event of termination in itself? More usual would be a pre-emptive right for the other joint venturer(s) to buy that interest out. Often this will be on the basis that the transferor's shares in the venture will be offered to the other parties at a price per share which they can accept or reject. If they reject, then, under the terms of the agreement, the party who intended to depart must buy the other shares in the venture at the same price. This is known as the 'Russian roulette' procedure, for obvious reasons. It concentrates the mind on calculating a fair value for the shares. The articles will need to reflect this pre-emption arrangement. These provisions will often apply both to voluntary transfers and forced transfers (for example if there is deadlock or an event of termination – see (a) and (c)).

(c) *Deadlock*

If the management of the venture is unable to decide an issue, it is wise for the parties to consider in advance how this will be dealt with. If the agreement simply says the parties will talk about it, this does not take you very far. Consider the following solutions:

(i) Referring the issue to an independent third party or an arbitrator.

(ii) Giving a casting vote to the chairman of the venture, whichever of the two parties he or she happens to represent.

(iii) Deadlock is an event of termination (see (a)).

(iv) Deadlock forces the pre-emption procedure into play (see (b)).

(d) *Management of the company*

How will the board of directors be constituted (i.e., how many directors will be appointed by each of the venturers)? What is the quorum for their meetings (one director from each of the venturers would be normal)? Can the venturers appoint whoever they choose to the board or is there a process of mutual consultation or consent? Will the directors have unreserved managerial powers or will certain decisions be reserved to the shareholders? Often the shareholders reserve to themselves decisions requiring expenditure over a certain value, or relating to activities such as further issues of shares, indebtedness, acquisitions and disposals and so on. Once again, the articles will need to reflect the terms of the agreement on these points.

(e) *Financing, both initial and subsequent investment*

Is all the initial investment to be by way of cash? Will payments in kind, for example, assets or know-how, be acceptable in lieu? If the parties are to match each other's initial contributions, is this to be repeated for future contributions? What happens if one of the parties cannot find the money for subsequent investment – is this a breach which forces a transfer of that party's shares or an event of termination leading to dissolution? Is any of the financing by way of debt? Will there be any security arrangements, for example, charges over the venture's assets?

(f) *Restrictive covenants*

It will be in the interests of each of the parties to ensure that the other joint venturers cannot compete with the joint venture or solicit any of its customers for their own business. Such activities will undermine the viability of the venture. There may also sometimes be an obligation on the joint venture parties to refer business relating to the venture's own activities (for example, new customers) to the venture on a pre-emptive basis.

These provisions are at the core of the agreement.

6.4.2 THE ARTICLES OF ASSOCIATION

Some of the provisions of the shareholders' agreement described above will find their way into the articles, in particular the terms about management, share transfers and pre-emption, and voting deadlock. In addition, there are a number of other elements which you would not normally expect to find in standard articles:

(a) *Share capital*

Will there be different classes of share capital for different parties to the joint venture? Sometimes this is done so that a shareholders' meeting is only quorate if holders of each class of share are present, and to confer the right to appoint a certain number of directors on the holders of each class (so that each venturer has its own director(s) on the board).

(b) *Members' meetings*

What will the quorum be? A representative from each class of shareholder would be normal. Will there be a chairman and, if so, will he or she have a casting vote? Often the role of chairman alternates between the parties and no casting vote is allowed (see also **6.4.1**). Will it be possible to pass resolutions in writing?

(c) *Managers or directors*

The articles will need to deal with the quorum, appointment and their powers. How are they to be removed? Only with the consent of the shareholders who appointed them? Normally this would be the case, subject to automatic vacation of a position on the board for failure to attend board meetings and so on. Will the directors be allowed to appoint alternates?

(d) *Dividends*

The shareholders will receive their profits on their investment in the joint venture company largely by way of dividend. The articles will need to specify what the policy on dividend payments is and how often dividends will be paid out.

6.5 Other Issues

Some of the issues mentioned so far, for instance, the issue of classes of shares, have company law implications which need to be thought through carefully. Any joint venture will have to consider a number of other issues, most of which we have come across before:

(a) The potentially anticompetitive effect of joint ventures was noted earlier. Advice will be needed on the application of the following to the joint venture: the Fair Trading Act 1973, the EC Merger Regulation and arts 81 and 82 of the Treaty of Rome (see **8.16**). Clearance from the Office of Fair Trading may be required as a condition of the shareholders' agreement. Depending on the nature of the business the venture will be entering into and which its joint venturarties are involved in, consider also the need for regulatory approvals from other sources.

(b) If any of the joint venturers are listed companies, their participation in the joint venture may amount to a transaction for the purposes of the Stock Exchange Yellow Book, ch. 10, in which case, depending on the size of the transaction in comparison with the company's own assets, the company may need approval from its own shareholders (see **5.6.4** for a more detailed analysis of the application and operation of these provisions). This will also need to be a condition to the shareholders' agreement.

(c) There is likely to be some need for agreements accompanying the other documents described so far. In particular, the joint venture may well be dependent on information, know-how or technology developed to date by the joint venturers, who will want to ensure that their rights over such property are protected. Thus there would usually be a licence from the joint venturers to the joint venture company to use such property only for the venture's purposes and, if the venture terminates, it reverts to the licensor.

(d) It will be important for corporate joint venture parties to decide whether the joint venture company of which it is a member is a subsidiary undertaking under the Companies Act 1985. If so, it will qualify as a subsidiary for accounting purposes and so will require disclosure in the parent's annual accounts, a result the parent may find undesirable (see **9.2**).

(e) As with other corporate finance transactions, joint ventures have tax implications. These will depend largely on whether it is an incorporated or unincorporated structure which is used. It is advisable to bring the tax experts into the planning for the transaction at an early stage.

This is only a very broad overview of this type of transaction and the typical areas in which the lawyers are called upon to advise. Each joint venture is different and different issues will inevitably arise.

SEVEN

MANAGEMENT BUY-OUTS

Management buy-outs ('MBOs') are acquisitions and disposals by another name. Often the most appropriate buyer of a company or a business will be its existing management, who understand the business better than anyone else and are likely to be ready buyers – after all, they have a vested interest in securing its future. The MBO is nothing more nor less than an acquisition of assets, a business or shares by the incumbent management from the existing owners of the relevant enterprise. This type of transaction does, though, have a number of distinct features.

7.1 Typical Structure

7.1.1 WHO IS THE BUYER?

The directors and/or managers (supported by their financing arrangement – see below) will usually become shareholders in a company as the vehicle with which to acquire the target enterprise.

7.1.2 WHAT IS BEING SOLD?

The same issues arise in this context as with ordinary acquisitions. The managers are likely to prefer an asset purchase as they can select what to buy and leave the liabilities with the seller. Furthermore, problems with s. 151 Companies Act 1985 are often encountered in MBOs (see **7.2.4**), and these can be avoided entirely with an asset purchase as there is no acquisition of shares involved. It would, though, be normal for the purchase to be of an existing company, or of a new company set up by the seller as a sale vehicle, and to which the assets or business to be sold are transferred prior to the disposal (this is sometimes known as a 'hive-down'). The rest of this chapter assumes this structure.

7.1.3 FINANCING

The single biggest practical problem the managers will have is financing the acquisition. After all, it is very unlikely that they will personally have the resources to fund a multimillion-pound acquisition. Normally, they will therefore need external investment from venture capitalists and lending institutions.

The arrangement is usually that the corporate vehicle set up by the managers to make the acquisition buys the whole of the target's issued share capital: this will be the only asset held by the acquiring company which is purely a holding company. The managers subscribe a significant proportion of the shares in the acquiring company out of their own resources, and this money goes towards the acquisition price. The majority of the finance for the acquisition, though, comes from borrowings from investing institutions. The lenders will secure this debt on the assets and shares of the target company. They may also purchase a slice of the equity in the acquiring company in their own names so they can benefit from any improved performance which the managers are able to reap from the target.

There may be separate institutions prepared to buy up some of the shares in the acquiring company to help the managers out, without providing any debt financing. These are the venture capitalists. Sometimes they may prefer the securities they buy to be preference shares, convertible loan stock or some sort of debt instrument which carries either a guaranteed entitlement to a dividend or interest: this sort of finance is known as 'mezzanine' as it is somewhere between secured debt and pure equity or risk capital. It offers them more protection for their investment than ordinary shares.

The extent of borrowing which is normally needed in this sort of transaction means they are often said to be highly 'leveraged' – in other words, the proportion of debt to equity is very high. This also creates possible problems for the managers after they have completed the purchase. All available cash generated by the company is likely to be needed to pay off the interest and principal on the debt, which makes it difficult for the management to generate adequate amounts of working capital for ordinary business needs. The consequence has been that the MBO company often finds it very difficult to survive: this has been true of a number of MBOs in recession-hit industries such as retailing. It is usually only 'mature' businesses, where there is a reliable profits stream founded on a well-established customer base, which can produce the cash supply needed to pay off the heavy debt financing in these transactions.

7.1.4 AGREEMENTS

There will of course be the sale agreement between the acquiring company on the one hand and the selling shareholders on the other. This will generally follow the familiar form already seen (see **5.5.1**). There will be a number of differences from the typical sale agreement, though:

(a) The acquiring company will not secure the standard warranties a purchaser would seek – after all, the management team will know the business better than the selling shareholders.

(b) The sellers will often wish to be paid part of their consideration on a deferred basis related to future profits of the target: they are keen to ensure they do not lose out completely if the company makes good in the future.

In addition, there will be a subscription or shareholders' agreement between the directors/managers and their backers who are taking shares in the acquiring company. This will govern the management of the company and the board, future financing of the company and other issues such as the company's dividend policy. A much more detailed picture of what you can expect to see in this kind of document will be found in **6.4.1**. Accompanying the shareholders' agreement there will of course also need to be articles of association for the acquiring company, which will reflect the provisions of the shareholders' agreement (see also **6.4.2**).

The last of the most important documents will be the loan agreement between the lenders and the acquiring company. The terms will include restrictions on disposals of the target's assets (in addition to security in the form of a charge), restrictions on any change in the nature of the acquiring or target company's business, warranties by the managers and events of default under which the lenders may terminate the loan agreement.

7.2 Issues to Watch

There are a number of areas to be particularly cautious of with MBOs.

7.2.1 TAX

As with other acquisitions, tax considerations can be critical, and the issues addressed in **5.2.2.2** are equally relevant here. Additional factors to be conscious of are:

(a) If the sellers need to create a new company first as a target vehicle for the sale (the process referred to earlier as a 'hive-down'), it is vital for the seller to ensure that the creation of this new company and the transfer of assets to it do not discontinue the trade, otherwise there will be a danger of the loss of capital allowances and tax losses. The managers will be particularly keen to retain these as they will help significantly to reduce the size of the target company's tax bill following completion of the acquisition, provided its trade is not subject to a major change in the period after the sale.

(b) One of the disadvantages of the hive-down is that, at the point when the new target company leaves the seller's group (when sold to the managers), the target company is subject to CGT on the gain in value of the assets transferred to it while a member of the seller's group. The managers usually seek an indemnity from the seller against the costs of such a tax charge.

(c) The sale of the target is a disposal by the seller which is subject to CGT. One way of minimising any chargeable gain is, where possible, for the seller to ensure that the gain arises in a vehicle (say, another group company) where there are tax losses against which the gain can be offset.

(d) As far as the managers are concerned, it will be vital to ensure that the interest costs on the loan financing after the sale can be set off against taxable profits.

7.2.2 DIRECTORS' RESPONSIBILITIES

The usual problem with MBOs is that some members of the board of the selling company are also involved in the MBO team. Special care should be taken to minimise the resulting problems arising from this potential conflict of interest.

As a practical matter, and also in conformity with Investment Committee guidelines, it is therefore normal for a committee of independent, non-executive directors on the selling company's board to be established to consider the commercial merits of the MBO offer for the target in comparison with other possible offers. Should they choose not to recommend the MBO offer, institutional shareholders will almost certainly not back it and it is therefore unlikely to get off the ground.

Another issue is the advisers used by the MBO team. These must clearly be different from those used by the selling company.

If the seller is a company which is disposing of net assets worth more than £100,000 or more than 10 per cent of its net assets, and one of its directors is involved in the buy-out team, s. 320 Companies Act 1985 needs to be watched carefully and may require shareholder approval for the transaction (see *LPC Guide: Business Law*).

If the seller is a company listed on the Stock Exchange, and one of its directors is involved in the buy-out team, this will be classified as a related party transaction under ch. 10 of The Listing Rules (see **5.6.4**), which may require a circular to shareholders and their approval.

7.2.3 TAKEOVER

The City Code will apply as much to an MBO as any other transaction. If the MBO team is acquiring a UK public company, the provisions of the City Code on Takeovers and Mergers and the jurisdiction of the Takeover Panel will be relevant (see **chapter 8**).

7.2.4 FINANCIAL ASSISTANCE

Section 151 Companies Act 1985 (see **8.12** for more details) will effectively prevent the target company from contributing to the MBO team's costs, or providing guarantees, security (including a charge over its shares or assets) or indemnities to the lenders or equity investors unless:

(a) the buyers acquire assets rather than shares, or

(b) you use the s. 153 exemption, that the principal purpose of the assistance is not to acquire shares but as an incidental part of some larger purpose of the target company (such as facilitating the MBO), or

(c) you use the so-called 'whitewash' procedure under ss. 155 to 158 Companies Act 1985 (see **8.12**), which is only available for private companies and so would only apply if the target company were a private company.

EIGHT

TAKEOVERS

8.1 What is a Takeover?

You have now encountered 'acquisitions', and have probably heard of 'mergers' as well as 'takeovers'. So what is the difference?

There is no simple definition of these terms by which everyone abides. They are often used interchangeably: the same transaction may be referred to as a merger, a takeover and an acquisition.

An acquisition is in fact *any* transaction in which something is acquired. Since a takeover involves the acquisition of shares, takeovers are also acquisitions, though for the purposes of this book 'acquisition' means sales and purchases of assets or businesses *or* shares falling *outside* the City Code on Takeovers and Mergers (essentially, private companies). A takeover implies the acquisition of control over assets, a business or a company. We use the term 'takeover' in this chapter in the sense of a purchase of *shares* falling *inside* the City Code on Takeovers and Mergers. These transactions are also often referred to as public company takeovers. In short, a person (an individual or a company) takes over a public company by writing to its shareholders and offering to buy their shares in return for cash or, in many cases, securities such as shares or debt instruments.

The term 'merger' has no precise definition, but is often used in preference to 'takeover' where the takeover is intended as a fusion of two companies and not a submergence of one within another. Some takeovers are what is known as 'recommended', which is explained in **8.5.3.1**. Recommended takeovers are often characterised as mergers as they usually imply a meeting of minds between the company taking over and the one being taken over.

Before we take this chapter any further, there are two other terms you need to understand. Any takeover, as with the acquisitions we saw in **chapter 5**, will involve a buyer and a seller. However, the terms used when referring to buyers and sellers in the takeover context are slightly different. The buyer will offer to acquire the shares it wants, hence it is referred to as the 'offeror' or the 'bidder'. The company whose shares the offeror wants to buy, as it is on the receiving end of the offer, is referred to as the 'offeree' or the 'target'. In a sense, this is slightly misleading. Those who sell their shares to the bidder are in fact the target company's *shareholders*, so the proper legal analysis is that they are the offerees: but the term 'offeree' in this chapter conforms with its practical use and means the target.

8.2 Why Launch a Takeover?

We saw in **5.1** some of the main reasons for acquisitions taking place. Exactly the same factors are relevant in takeover activity.

One additional factor in takeovers is opportunism. Takeovers are public transactions and the City Code sets out certain unassailable limitations on the timetable which applies to them. Unlike an acquisition by private treaty or contract, this means it is not possible simply to announce to the world that a takeover has taken place. Under the rules, as we will see, it has to happen under the full gaze of the world at large, and any takeover offer made has to be held open for a fixed period of time. Consequently, there is every opportunity for a potential rival offeror to hear of the bid, and have time to prepare and ultimately make an alternative offer to the target shareholders, even though no such thought was in its mind before the first bid was announced. In other words, once a target is put 'in play' by an offer, there is nothing to prevent the quick and the wily from joining the game – and they often do, recognising it may be their best chance to snap up a good buy. There have been numerous examples of this in practice. The infamous takeover of Distillers by Guinness in 1986 (which led to a series of criminal prosecutions in the late 1980s and early 1990s) was just such a piece of opportunism, since it was preceded by an initial bid from Argyll which eventually failed.

8.3 The Takeover 'Market'

Much as there is an equity market which companies tap when seeking capital investment (see **chapters 3** and **4**), so there is a distinct market in the UK for takeovers.

Since the Takeover Panel began work in 1968, there has been on average 225 announced takeover proposals in the UK every year. Approximately three-quarters of all public takeover offers in the EC occur in the UK. Takeover activity is therefore, in absolute and relative terms, an important 'industry' in this country.

There is a well-established body of precedent and rules governing the form and conduct of takeover offers in the UK. In large part, this is because of the work of the Takeover Panel (see **8.8.5**) and the corpus of regulation in the City Code on Takeovers and Mergers for which it is responsible.

There has developed, on the back of the emergence of takeovers as a significant feature of City life from the 1950s onwards, considerable expertise among City professionals and business people in advising on and handling takeover transactions. This expertise has grown to a point where a company interested in expanding its operations through an acquisition, but without a clear idea as to who, what or where to acquire, can approach a merchant bank in the City and obtain advice on potential suitable targets and an appropriate takeover and marketing strategy. By the same token, a company which fears a potential bid can approach a merchant bank for advice and assistance in preparing a pre-emptive defence strategy for use in the event that the company's fears are realised: many UK companies hold so-called 'defence manuals' at the ready for precisely such an eventuality (see **8.6.7**). Merchant banks can and do make substantial profits out of their takeover advice. Another feature of this expertise is the assortment of professional so-called asset-stripping individuals and companies who have built their reputations and their wealth entirely through acquiring companies and then making them profitable or selling them off at a profit. For these, takeovers is their trade.

8.4 Parties to a Takeover

A first step in understanding the structure and mechanics of a takeover is clarifying who is involved and their contribution to the transaction.

8.4.1 BIDDER

Typically the offer is made by a single bidder but occasionally an offer is made by a consortium of individuals or companies, sometimes to spread the cost. The separate members of the consortium will almost certainly be treated for the purposes of the Code as if they were one bidder (see **8.5.3.2**).

Where listing particulars are required in connection with a takeover offer, the bidder will be a person responsible for those particulars under s. 150 Financial Services Act 1986 (see **4.2.5.7**).

The bidder's shareholders may have to approve or be informed of the takeover under ch. 10 of The Listing Rules (see **5.6.4**), or consent to the issue of new shares under ss. 80 and 89 Companies Act 1985 (see **3.3.1.3**) or for other Companies Act 1985 purposes such as an increase in authorised capital. Target companies may also on occasion write to the bidder's shareholders and try to persuade them that the bid is not in *their* best interests: this is quite permissible though usually ineffective.

8.4.2 TARGET

The target shareholders are the recipients of the offer and its success lies in their hands. If those holding a majority of the shares choose to accept the bidder's offer, control of the target will pass to the bidder.

One exception to this is that very few UK companies have provisions in their articles of association which effectively prevent a change of control without the consent of the UK government. These are usually companies which have been recently privatised – particularly utilities such as water and electricity companies. Articles may provide for the government to have a so-called 'golden share' giving it special voting rights or veto powers. Alternatively or additionally, there may be restrictions on shareholders holding more than a 15 per cent interest in the company. The restrictions generally have a limited life: the 'golden shares' in the electricity industry expired in March 1995.

The target board of directors may often prefer, for whatever reason (and this is considered in more detail in **8.5.3.1**), to recommend the bidder's offer to the target shareholders. In these circumstances, the offer document from the bidder will contain the target board's recommendation and some information about the target for which the target will be a person responsible if the offer requires listing particulars.

8.4.3 DIRECTORS

Rule 19.2 of the City Code makes the respective directors of the offeror and offeree companies responsible for the documents issued by their companies in the course of the takeover and requires them all, individually, to take responsibility expressly for all such documents save for some advertisements. If listing particulars are required by the transaction, the bidder's directors will be persons responsible under s. 150 Financial Services Act 1986, and if the takeover is recommended, the target board will be persons responsible for those parts of the particulars describing the target.

Therefore, whether advising the bidder or the target, ensure early on in a transaction that all the members of the board will be available to approve documents to be issued during the takeover or that they have appointed an attorney (preferably another member of the board) to do so on their behalf. Standard practice is for the main board to convene at the very early stages of the bid to appoint a committee of directors to take all decisions on behalf of the main board in relation to the takeover, including the approval of documents. Many decisions in takeovers have to be taken at short notice when it is often difficult to pull together the entire board.

Directors will of course also need to be advised of their responsibilities and the potential liabilities which may result.

The target board is obliged to obtain and communicate to its shareholders competent independent advice by r. 3 of the City Code. The offeror board must also do this where the directors have a conflict of interest, the most obvious example of which is where a target director is also a director of the bidder.

8.4.4 MERCHANT BANKERS

Both bidder and target will appoint their own merchant banks (in some cases, joint banks may be appointed). Much as we saw for equity offerings, the merchant bank takes on the role of 'manager' of the transaction, in the sense that it coordinates the activities of the other parties and is the client's main sounding-board when devising and planning strategy and tactics in the course of the bid. In connection with this, the merchant bankers are chiefly responsible for communicating with the Takeover Panel on issues of interpretation of the City Code and obtaining guidance or rulings where necessary, with the lawyers assisting when needed (see **8.8.5**).

The merchant bank to the bidder issues the offer document on behalf of the bidder, for purely traditional rather than legal reasons. This means it is a person responsible under s. 150 Financial Services Act 1986 if listing particulars are also required for the transaction (as it will have authorised the issue of the document). The bank will also have to approve any documents which as investment advertisements require an authorised person's imprimatur under s. 57 Financial Services Act 1986. In relation to this, and indeed all aspects of the conduct of the takeover, the merchant bank will need to comply with any relevant rules of its SRO, usually for merchant banks the Securities and Futures Authority.

One other aspect of the bidder's merchant bank's role will be to arrange and underwrite a cash-underwritten alternative where this is to take place (see **8.6.3.1**): it will negotiate and agree the form of the underwriting agreement with the offeror and appoint a broker to arrange the sub-underwriting on its behalf.

For its services, the merchant bank will usually negotiate a fee structure which will be substantially success-related but guarantees it something in the event of failure. These fees are in addition to anything received by way of commission for any underwriting which takes place.

8.4.5 BROKERS

The bidder and the target will each have a firm of brokers to their names who will be responsible for observing and reporting back on movements in and the inclination of the market towards the takeover offer. This is vital for the offeror properly to gauge whether the value and nature of its existing offer are satisfactory, and for the target to determine its strategy. For example, if the market is generally perceived to favour the offer, will the issue of an optimistic profit forecast by the target be enough to mollify investors?

It is also important for both sides to track significant share purchases: once a target is 'in play', there is the danger to the offeror of a rival bidder emerging. The tell-tale signs of this will be significant levels of share purchases by an unknown buyer. Obviously the target needs at all times to know how many shares a bidder holds to ascertain whether it is winning or losing the battle.

The bidder's brokers will also handle any purchases of the target's shares which the bidder makes and will arrange the sub-underwriting for any cash-underwritten alternative (see **8.6.3.1**). Where the offer includes securities to be listed, the brokers will, as with ordinary listing arrangements (see **3.3.4**), liaise with the UKLA and the Stock Exchange, prepare a derogation letter and ensure that the UKLA is satisfied that its requirements for the contents of offer documents (see **8.5.5.1**) have been met.

8.4.6 ACCOUNTANTS

Both sides to the bid will appoint accountants.

The bidder's accountants will need to consider (where the offer includes securities to be listed) The Listing Rules requirements in ch. 6 and ch.12 (see **4.2.6.3**). However, r. 24 of the City Code requires the offer document to contain a significant amount of financial information on the offeror and the offeree company. This needs to be extracted from the company's most recent financial statements. As a matter of practice, the bidder's accountants will be asked to confirm, in the form of a comfort letter, that they are satisfied that the information produced is correct and accurately set out. They will also need to report to the directors that any profit forecast for the bidder has been compiled with the care and objectivity which r. 28 demands. This rule also imposes a duty on the accountants to discuss the assumptions underlying any profit forecast with their client. They must also satisfy themselves that the forecast has been properly made and is based on the stated assumptions.

The same requirement regarding profit forecasts will extend to the target's accountants.

Accountants to the bidder and target are in practice also asked to review the figures and statistics produced by their opposite numbers to help in constructing their respective clients' arguments in the bid.

8.4.7 PUBLIC RELATIONS CONSULTANTS AND PARLIAMENTARY LOBBYISTS

Public relations consultants are frequently hired to improve the presentation of the case of both sides to the bid, both in the formal documents and through advertising campaigns. Parliamentary lobbyists assist in the process of influencing the President of the Board of Trade's decision should the Office of Fair Trading recommend he refers a merger to the Competition Commission (see **8.16**); they will do the same should the European Commission be involved or the consent of any other regulatory bodies to the merger be required.

8.4.8 SOLICITORS

Both parties to the bid will appoint solicitors and it is possible that other advisers will appoint their own legal advisers (often a merchant bank will seek advice independent from that taken by the company it represents, particularly in hostile offers). What do the solicitors do?

Much of their work is concerned with checking the accuracy of documents produced in the course of the bid, which will generally demand a verification exercise akin to that for equity offerings (see **3.3.7**).

Of course they also spend much of their time advising on the legalities of a transaction, which requires consideration of all the legal and regulatory issues, partly to ensure that any action proposed is legal, decent, honest and truthful and partly to help in the formulation of the most effective strategy for their client.

The role of proffering legal advice extends to the City Code, though the Introduction to the City Code makes it absolutely clear that 'to take legal, or other professional, advice on the interpretation or application of the Code is not an appropriate alternative to obtaining a view or ruling from the [Panel] Executive' (see **8.8.5**) for further analysis of this). This is not to say that the lawyers have *no* role in relation to interpretation of the Code, simply that their view is not of itself sufficient.

There is to some extent a tension between the merchant bankers and the lawyers. The merchant bankers often see it as their role to deal with the Takeover Panel, and the lawyers, quite legitimately, feel that they are probably better placed to offer an informed view on what the City Code means, given it is now a detailed set of rules which runs in totality to just over 150 pages. Lawyers accordingly need to be sensitive to other advisers and particularly the role of the Takeover Panel when they set about advising on the City Code.

8.5 Outline of a Takeover

The easiest way to understand how a takeover fits together is to look at a skeleton timetable and examine each phase of the transaction.

In the timing of a takeover, there are certain things which are laid down by the Code and immutable (or pretty much so, unless the Panel otherwise decides). There are also certain things which are optional. This timetable indicates the points in the timetable fixed by the rules of the Code.

As every takeover is unique, this timetable only sketches what you are likely to find in a typical or ordinary transaction: more complex deals, involving, for instance, the intervention of overseas regulatory bodies (such as the US Securities and Exchange Commission) will alter the timetable in some respects.

The timetable here assumes the bid is contested: where a bid is recommended, only those references marked * are relevant. The rest can be discounted. The rules cited are those in the City Code, of which more later.

Some of the terms mentioned here may strike you as gobbledegook: they are explained in **8.5.2**.

8.5.1 TIMETABLE OF A TAKEOVER

Day	*Activity*
Before announcement	In the period leading up to the announcement, the bidder prepares its strategy (see **8.6.6**): this may take days, weeks or months; * for a recommended bid, this is the period in which negotiations between bidder and target boards will take place.
1	Target board informed of bid (r. 2.5). Bid announced publicly.* Offer period begins.*
3	Target posts announcement of bid to its shareholders (r. 2.6).*
28	Last day to post offer document (r. 30.1), though this is often in practice done earlier. *The rest of the timetable takes its lead from the day the offer document is posted (whenever that actually happens). This day is referred to from now on as day 0.**
0 + 14	Target posts first defence circular to its shareholders (r. 30.2).
0 + 21	First closing date for offer (r. 31.1).*
0 + 39	Last date target can announce profit forecast or other significant financial information (r. 31.9).
0 + 46	Last date for bidder to revise its offer (r. 32.1).
0 + 60	Last date on which offer can be declared unconditional as to acceptances (r. 31.6).*

0 + 81	Last date to declare offer wholly unconditional (r. 31.7).
0 + 95	Last date for money or other consideration to be provided to target shareholders (r. 31.8).*
Thereafter	Section 429 Companies Act 1985 notices dispatched (see **8.13**).*

Before we move on, let us pause to understand what some of these terms mean.

8.5.2 DEFINITIONS

8.5.2.1 'Closing date'

This is the date on which the offer will lapse unless the bidder extends it. The first closing date cannot be less than 21 days after the posting of the offer document. At that point, the bidder can choose to call the whole offer off. Alternatively, the bidder can announce that the offer has gone unconditional as to acceptances (see below). In practice, this only happens with a recommended offer (see **8.5.3.1**), so the bidder normally announces it will extend the offer. The extension cannot last beyond 0 + 60, which is the final date by which the offer must either have succeeded or lapsed.

8.5.2.2 'Unconditional as to acceptances'

The bidder must obtain at least 50 per cent of the target's shares and have that as a condition to the offer (r. 10). An offer is unconditional as to acceptances where the bidder has got the 50 per cent. The bidder may declare the bid unconditional as to acceptances whenever the 50 per cent target is reached. If the bidder does not get the 50 per cent by the final closing date (0 + 60), the offer must lapse.

8.5.2.3 'Wholly unconditional'

This means that all the conditions of the offer have been satisfied, the condition about 50 per cent acceptances, the condition that the offer not be referred to the Competition Commission and any others set out.

Do bear in mind that some of the dates here are dependent on the occurrence of earlier events in the timetable, which may in fact happen earlier than the date required by the rules. Therefore treat these dates in practice with care.

Let us look now in more detail at the activity taking place around this timetable.

8.5.3 BEFORE THE ANNOUNCEMENT

This is the stage at which the bidder prepares strategy, and decides how to finance the bid and what sort of a bid to make (see **8.6.2**). A lot of analysis will be needed to assess the strengths and weaknesses of the target for the forthcoming battle.

8.5.3.1 Recommended offers

Of course, it may be that the target board is interested in the idea of a takeover, so an initial approach to its directors may prove fruitful and lead to a negotiated merger which the target board is prepared to recommend to its shareholders. Although it seems perverse for directors effectively to sign away their company, there may be all sorts of reasons for them taking this action: they may feel their company has no real prospect of survival as an independent entity, or they may feel it is simply in their shareholders' and employees' best interests.

Target boards should, however, be cautious about the information they give away to a potential bidder. Rule 20.2 of the Code requires the target to give equality of information to any other genuine potential bidder, even if the other bidder is not to the target board's taste. In a 1992 bid, Midland Bank (the target) sought to resist giving Lloyds Bank, a competitor bidder, the same information as Midland had given Hongkong and Shanghai Bank, but the Takeover Panel required it to do so.

Should the bidder attempt to persuade the target directors of the value of a merger only for them to turn the idea down, there is nothing then to prevent the bidder from launching a hostile bid for the target, though on average some 30–40 per cent of hostile offers do fail. If the bidder has any inside information about the target as a result of the discussions which have taken place, the Criminal Justice Act 1993 may prevent the bidder from making market purchases of the target's shares (see **8.14**).

8.5.3.2 Share purchases

If the bid is to be contested, the bidder may build up a stake in the target to facilitate reaching the ultimate target of 50 per cent of the target's shares. When doing this the bidder needs to take account of the consequences of buying stakes of a certain size:

Stake	*Result*
3 per cent	Notification of bidder's interest to the company under Part VI of the Companies Act 1985 (see **8.11**).
10 per cent	If 10 per cent of the target shares are acquired in the year leading up to the offer or during the offer period, the bidder must offer all the target shareholders *cash* at the highest price the bidder has paid for those shares in that time (r. 11).
15 per cent	The Substantial Acquisitions Rules (SARs – see **8.9**) prevent the bidder (or indeed, anyone) from acquiring 10 per cent or more of the target's shares in any seven-day period if that gives the bidder between 15 per cent and 30 per cent of the target in total. Either the bidder buys less than 15 per cent in total, or spreads the 10 per cent acquisition out over more than a week.
30 per cent	Rule 5 of the Code places an absolute prohibition on the bidder acquiring 30 per cent or more of the target. The prohibition does not apply where the offer is recommended by the target. Acceptances of the offer are not counted in determining whether 30 per cent of the target has been acquired, only purchases in the market. As soon as the bidder does go through the 30 per cent limit, it must make a takeover offer for all the target's shares in accordance with r. 9 (unless the bidder intends to make a partial offer – see **8.6.2.4**). This is the case *even if he has already made an offer*. The real problem about a mandatory offer under r. 9 is that it must be in cash at a price equal to the highest price paid by the bidder for target shares in the past year. Therefore, if he has already made an offer, he may at this stage have to increase it. Furthermore, apart from the 50 per cent acceptance condition, virtually no other conditions are permitted, which may not suit the bidder.

In addition to these restrictions, the bidder should also consider, when making share purchases:

(a) The Criminal Justice Act 1993 on insider dealing (see **8.14**), which may prevent any purchases if the bidder has acquired price-sensitive information about the target, perhaps through discussions with the target itself.

(b) Rule 6, which obliges the bidder to pitch its offer at a *price* at least equal to the highest price it has paid for the shares in the past three months (r. 9 applies to mandatory offers only).

(c) The restrictions mentioned above apply to the bidder acting alone or in concert with others, so there is no point in believing that the bidder can appoint several friends to buy shares on its behalf and thus escape the trap set by the various percentages mentioned above. In fact, the City Code presumes the bidder's subsidiaries, directors and professional advisers amongst others to be acting in concert with the bidder, though these presumptions are rebuttable.

The target, unless an offer takes it completely by surprise, will have gleaned from purchases of its shares or rumours on the stock market that a bid is in the offing and so will have begun to plan its defence. This involves instructing its advisers and discussing with them strategic alternatives (for example, what submissions to make to the Office of Fair Trading to have any proposed merger referred, whether the company's performance can in any way be improved before a bid emerges, launching an advertising campaign, and so on – see **8.6.7** for a discussion of the target's strategic alternatives). Most listed companies have so-called 'defence manuals' on the shelf with a ready-made 'action list' to put into effect in the event of a sudden bid announcement: the list will detail the sort of activities mentioned above.

8.5.4 THE ANNOUNCEMENT AND AFTER

In a hostile bid, the target board is informed of the bid and the bidder immediately circulates a press announcement describing the terms of its offer. The target will need to communicate this to its own shareholders as soon as possible. A fairly hectic process of campaigning by the opposite sides begins almost immediately through the financial pages of the newspapers. Both sides will also prepare their submissions to the Office of Fair Trading as quickly as they can and start to use the lobbyists to influence the decisions of any of the regulators involved.

The bidder's main focus at this stage will be to prepare its offer document within 28 days of the announcement. Usually the bidder will seek to move much faster than this to keep the pressure on the target.

8.5.4.1 Rule 6

The bidder will continue to buy shares in the market but must beware of all the issues raised above. In addition, if the bidder or anyone acting in concert with it buys shares at a price above the current value of the offer, then r. 6.2 requires the bidder to raise the value of its offer to match that price – so bidders need to take precautions not to buy shares if the market price is currently above the offer price.

8.5.4.2 Irrevocable undertakings

To assist the bidder in obtaining the 50 per cent acceptance needed, it may also approach certain institutional shareholders in the target to see if they will be prepared to oblige themselves irrevocably to accept the offer. In a recommended offer, the target directors generally sign themselves up to such an undertaking. Usually the party giving the undertaking agrees to accept the offer and agrees not to do anything which might prejudice it. This is perfectly proper practice. Care has to be taken with the law regarding unsolicited calls (see **1.5.1.4**) and insider dealing (see **8.14**) in this context. These 'irrevocable undertakings' also count when counting up the shares which the bidder holds for the purposes of the restrictions mentioned above in **8.5.3.2** (including the SARs).

With a recommended bid, the same process of announcement and preparation of the offer document is required, though here of course the bidder will receive the target's cooperation.

8.5.5 POSTING OF THE OFFER DOCUMENT AND AFTER

The bidder's offer document will need to be posted within 28 days of the announcement of the bid. This is a time-limit the Panel rarely relaxes.

8.5.5.1 The offer document

For a start, though the offer is made by the bidder, the document is usually issued on behalf of the bidder by its merchant bank, for reasons of convention only.

The document is a contractual offer and so will need to set out the terms on which the offer is made, provide an acceptance form and stipulate how the contract between the bidder and target shareholder is effected.

The document must 'sell' the bidder to the target shareholders, so it will contain a fair amount of 'marketing copy' on the qualities of the bidder and what it can offer the shareholders. It is also likely to detail the existing weaknesses of the target's management or its strategy. Aside from the legal risks associated with this (see **8.17.4**), the Takeover Panel has made it clear (in a statement regarding the Enterprise bid for Lasmo) that 'tendentious and excessive claims and allegations should be avoided'.

The document must comply with the City Code's own requirements (which incorporate requirements of the UKLA in relation to takeovers) and are set out in r. 24. These are very detailed. In essence, it should contain:

(a) A responsibility statement from the bidder's directors in which they say they take responsibility for it and reasonably believe it to be accurate and not misleading. All the directors need to be a party to this. In a recommended offer, parts of the offer document will describe the target and the directors of the target will take responsibility for those parts of the document which relate to it.

(b) What the bidder intends to do about the target and its employees – this is usually confined to something reasonably positive about its and their future but nothing expansive or which might tie the bidder's hands in future.

(c) Financial information about the bidder and the target, including the figures for the two companies' net profits and dividends for the past three financial years and a statement of the assets and liabilities of the bidder in its last accounts.

(d) Disclosures as to shareholdings of the bidder and persons acting in concert with it in the target.

(e) Directors' pay and benefits.

(f) Where the bidder is using cash as consideration for the offer, the merchant bankers or accountants must confirm that the resources to finance the cash element of the offer are available.

(g) Sufficient information to enable the shareholders to reach a properly informed decision about the merits of the offer (r. 23).

(h) The terms of the offer, including the consideration offered, how it will be paid and the method of acceptance of the offer.

(i) The nature of the offeror's business, its financial and trading prospects and borrowings.

(j) References to both bidder's and target's material contracts, which include constitutional documents, two years of audited accounts and directors' service agreements, as well as all contracts outside the ordinary course of business entered into in the past two years.

In a recommended offer, the offer document will set out how the merger will work (for example, how the two businesses will be fused; whether all the target directors will remain on the board), its commercial rationale and a description of the two businesses.

8.5.5.2 Layout of a typical offer document

You have seen what an offer document should contain to comply with the City Code's requirements. How will it actually be set out?

There are no formal obligations regarding this, nor does the Takeover Panel pre-vet documents in any way. Offer documents, therefore, do not need to follow a set pattern, though in practice (often through the influence of precedent) they do. This is broadly what you could expect to find.

Front page

Advice to shareholders to obtain independent financial advice (which r. 24(2)(b)(ii) requires as a 'heading').

If the bidder is offering its own securities as consideration, the offer document may also constitute listing particulars and so the points mentioned in **4.2.6.4** should be included.

A statement that the offer is being made by the merchant bank on behalf of the bidder (the usual arrangement).

Any provisions to deal with US securities regulations.

Any provisions needed under SFA rules to protect the merchant bank from the risk that target shareholders can treat themselves as its customers.

Following pages

Letter from bidder's chairman describing the rationale of the bid, the bidder's intentions, information regarding the bid (for instance, the consideration offered) and how the offer is to be financed.

Business statistics illustrating the comparative performance of bidder and target, and showing what the bidder will do for target performance and strategy.

Offer letter from merchant bank to target shareholders setting out the terms of the offer, its value, financial information relating to bidder and target, statement regarding bidder's intentions towards target employees, any offers for other classes of target securities, and the procedure for acceptance.

Conditions to the offers (for example, obtaining 50 per cent acceptances) and further terms of the offers (much of this is required by r. 24), including rights of target shareholders to withdraw their acceptances, and whether the bidder leaves open the possibility of a revised offer.

Rights of overseas shareholders.

Forms of acceptance: there may be two separate forms of acceptance, one for CREST members (see **1.6.2**) and one for non-CREST members. Alternatively, there may be one acceptance form which combines to serve both types of shareholder.

Additional information: this will include the directors' responsibility statement pursuant to r. 19.2, disclosures of bidder's interests in target shares, and documents available for inspection (as required by r. 26).

Definitions: these usually conclude the document.

8.5.5.3 The defence document

Once the document has been posted to the target shareholders, the target board gets to work preparing its first response. Needless to say, this is not the case with a recommended offer.

The defence document must be ready within 14 days of the offer document being posted, though the Panel will sometimes be prepared to grant a limited extension to this where the offeror has attempted to spring a surprise and left the target very little time to prepare.

The defence document, like the offer document, is also a selling document and so needs to contain all the arguments which refute the bidder's assertions and persuade shareholders to hold on to their shares.

It also is subject to detailed requirements from the City Code, and, in particular, r. 25. In outline, the defence document should contain:

(a) A responsibility statement from the directors of the offeree. Only in rare cases where, for instance, a director suffers a conflict of interest, will he be relieved of the need to take responsibility.

(b) Sufficient information to enable the shareholders to reach a properly informed decision about the merits of the offer (r. 23).

(c) The views of the board on the offer, and the views of its merchant bankers. The verbal formula typically used is something like, 'The board, which has been so advised by [its merchant bank], considers the offer to be inadequate, etc.'. The idea is that the shareholders receive a considered and objective view and not one which just represents the potentially prejudiced judgement of the directors.

(d) A reaction to the bidder's plans for the target and its employees.

(e) Shares in the bidder held by the target, shares in both held by the target's directors and associates, and whether the target directors will be accepting or rejecting the offer in respect of their own holdings in the target.

(f) Details of target directors' service contracts.

In addition to all this work on the preparation and dispatch of documents, both sides will continue with their campaigning and lobbying, and the bidder will progress (subject to the restrictions mentioned earlier) any share-buying programme it has initiated.

8.5.6 THE FIRST CLOSING DATE AND AFTER

Rule 31.1 dictates that the first closing date of the offer can be no earlier than 21 days after the offer document has been posted. At this point, if the bidder has not yet received 50 per cent acceptances, it must decide whether to allow the offer to lapse or extend it. The bidder must also announce the level of acceptances from target shareholders immediately after the closing date.

In a recommended offer, normally a bidder can announce it has 50 per cent acceptances by this time, because target shareholders tend to follow their board's recommendation and accept quite quickly. In a contested offer, however, very few shareholders will have accepted by the first closing date. They tend to wait as long as possible in case a revised offer emerges, another bidder appears, or the target announces better than expected prospects. As a result, the bidder in this kind of offer does not expect to win by 0 + 21 and will therefore usually anticipate extending the offer. This extension cannot be beyond 0 + 60, what you might call the final closing date for the offer (r. 31.6).

The other thing for the bidder to watch is r. 31.5 which prevents a bidder from going back on its word. If, at some stage during the offer, the bidder tells the world that it is not prepared to extend its offer beyond a certain time, then it will be held to that even if it later changes its mind – so make sure there is no implication in press announcements or offer documents or television interviews to this effect.

Assuming it is a contested bid and the offer has been extended, the target will prepare further arguments in its defence. It must release any new information (such as profit forecasts, announcements about restructuring its operations, asset revaluations and so on) by 0 + 39. This is usually treated fairly inflexibly by the Panel. In normal practice, therefore, the target makes every effort to release a circular to its shareholders just before 0 + 39 containing encouraging news which will entice them to hold on to their shares. Any profit forecasts must comply with the standards of care stipulated in r. 28 and have a series of assumptions stated and effectively reported on by the accountants. One word of warning: it is very easy to make statements about future prospects which are not intended to be profit forecasts, but which do in fact amount to the same thing. They will need to comply in exactly the same way as an express profit forecast with r. 28.

Meanwhile, in the contested bid, both sides will continue with their campaigning and the bidder with its share-buying. The restrictions under r. 5 (the cap at buying more than 30 per cent of the target) disappear after the first closing date provided there is to be no reference to the Competition Commission or the European Commission and the bidder does not mind complying with the requirements for a r. 9 bid (see **8.5.3.2**).

When the bidder sees the target's new information, it has seven days (up to 0 + 46) within which to decide whether to revise the offer. Much as with extensions to the offer, r. 32.2 prevents a bidder increasing the value of its offer if such a move has already been ruled out in a statement, even if there is a later change of mind.

Whether or not the bidder chooses to revise the offer (if that option is open), it is likely to issue a further document in reply to the target's new information.

8.5.7 METHODS OF ACCEPTANCE

Those members of the target who hold share certificates will be required to send in the form of acceptance and share certificate. Those who hold their shares in uncertificated, dematerialised form (see **1.6.3**) will be required to complete a form of acceptance and to arrange for the input of instructions to CREST to transfer their shares to an 'escrow account', under the control of the bidder's receiving agent. The latter (a member of CREST (see **1.6.3**)) will transfer the shares from this account to the bidder on the offer becoming unconditional. Should the offer lapse or the shareholder withdraw acceptance, then the receiving agent will be required to transfer the shares back into the shareholder's main CREST account.

For the purpose of declaring an offer unconditional as to acceptances (see **8.5.2.2**) before the final closing date, the bidder's receiving agent can take into account shares standing in the escrow account.

8.5.8 THE CONCLUSION OF THE OFFER

The offer will conclude in one of the following ways:

(a) The bidder will have obtained its 50 per cent acceptances by 0 + 60 and can declare the offer unconditional as to acceptances. The offer must go wholly unconditional (that is, satisying all other outstanding conditions) within 21 days of the offer being declared unconditional as to acceptances. Sometimes this is difficult to fulfil because of the delay in obtaining a definitive ruling from the OFT as to whether the merger is to be referred. The Takeover Panel is usually prepared to oblige with a relaxation.

The Takeover Panel is very unlikely to relax the final date in the offer timetable – 14 days after the offer is declared unconditional in all respects – because this is the point by which the target shareholders must be paid their money.

There is likely to be a minority left in place and so the bidder will activate the s. 429 Companies Act 1985 procedure if it holds over 90 per cent of the target shares (see **8.13**).

What if the bidder does not have the requisite 90 per cent? This is rarely a problem. Once the offer has gone wholly unconditional, the target board will usually recommend its shareholders to accept the offer (if it is still open) or sell their shares in the market as there is little to be gained from holding on. If it is a problem, then the bidder is simply left with a minority shareholding which it will hope to be able to buy out at a later date by negotiation.

(b) The bidder does not attain 50 per cent by 0 + 60 and so its offer must lapse. The bidder now has, perhaps, a sizeable stake in the target. Why does it not use this as a platform for an immediate fresh bid? The Code restricts this under r. 35 by preventing the bidder from making a new offer for a year and from buying any shares in the target in that time if that would take the bidder over 30 per cent.

Both of these possibilities apply equally to a recommended offer.

Let us look now at some of the strategic decisions which will figure in the planning of both bidder and target in the bid.

8.6 Strategic Planning in Takeovers

Both the bidder and the target need to undertake a significant amount of planning to ensure they decide on the most appropriate strategies, and to avoid potential pitfalls. This section will look at some of the most prominent issues you will need to think about to advise properly on strategy, or, at least, to make an informed contribution to the debate.

8.6.1 TAX ISSUES

Before we look at the alternatives open to the bidder, we need briefly to address the most important of the tax questions and the effect they will have on the nature of the takeover offer.

(a) Will the offer give rise to a tax charge for the target shareholders? If so, what can be done to minimise this? This is considered in **8.6.3.9**.

(b) If the acquisition is to be financed by debt, the bidder will want to deduct its interest costs from its taxable profits to reduce the size of its tax bill. How can this be achieved?

The simplest method is for the bidder to make its offer through a vehicle resident for tax purposes in the UK. Then, once the bid is complete and the UK target is merged with the offering vehicle, the offering vehicle's financing costs can be set off against the target's profits. Given the UK is a relatively high-tax jurisdiction, this is a tax-efficient way of keeping the new merged company's tax bill low. Where the bidder is an overseas company, this may suggest the need for a UK-resident subsidiary to be established through which to make the bid.

(c) If the bid is unsuccessful, and the bidder has acquired some target shares, what is its exposure to tax if it chooses to sell those shares?

This is a real issue because (i) there is always a chance the bid will fail, (ii) the value of the stake acquired could be very high and the capital gains charge for an immediate disposal could be substantial, given that target shares usually appreciate in value significantly during the course of a bid, and (iii) if the offering vehicle is in the UK, the shares will be held in the UK and so will be subject to tax in a high-tax jurisdiction if sold.

One way around this is to establish the offering vehicle initially in a non-tax-paying jurisdiction. If the bid fails and the offeror has to sell the target shares it has acquired, it keeps its tax charge to zero on that disposal. If the bid is successful, the offering vehicle can later migrate to a jurisdiction where the bidder has a high tax bill, for example, the UK. The offering vehicle will generally have incurred significant costs (including possible ongoing financing costs), which can be set off against profits elsewhere in the bidder's group.

There are of course a host of other tax issues which will need to be addressed. It is vital to involve tax specialists to deal with these from the earliest point.

8.6.2 THE NATURE OF THE OFFER

What sort of offer should the bidder seek to make? A number of possibilities are canvassed below.

8.6.2.1 General offer

This is the sort of takeover offer this chapter has hitherto been concerned with, namely an offer to acquire all the securities of a company which falls within the City Code's jurisdiction. We have seen that with this type of offer, either the target directors will recommend it to their shareholders, or else the bidder will have to make a hostile offer leading to a contested bid.

Some of the factors behind the target board's decision to recommend a bid have already been discussed (see **8.5.3.1**). The reason the bidder may particularly want to explore the possibility of a recommended bid is that it will generally be a quicker route than a hostile bid.

As we saw when looking at the timetable earlier (see **8.5.6**), you can generally assume that target shareholders will respond quickly to a recommendation from their board that they should accept an offer. There is usually every chance that such an offer can be declared unconditional as to acceptances by 0 + 21, whereas most contested bids will not be settled until the eve of 0 + 60.

In terms of cost, any cash underwriting required goes unconditional much sooner if the timetable is shorter, hence working out cheaper for the bidder on a recommended offer (see **8.6.3.1**). Furthermore, the expense of lobbying and advertising campaigns will be substantially reduced.

There is also an argument that a bidder will have a better chance of making a takeover work if it has secured the cooperation and goodwill of the incumbent management before the offer. A hostile bid is likely to create significant tensions and frictions for the bidder's management when it comes in to assume the reins of power, both from existing managers and employees. It may therefore be significantly to the bidder's advantage to exploit any opportunity that exists to persuade the target's board to contemplate a recommended bid.

8.6.2.2 Scheme of arrangement

This is a method of corporate restructuring not confined to takeover activity but one which is quite often used in this context. A scheme of arrangement is a procedure provided for by s. 425 Companies Act 1985. Put very simply, a scheme enables a company to restructure itself provided it obtains a special resolution of shareholders or any class of shareholders affected by the reconstruction, and has the whole process approved by the court, upon which the scheme is binding on all shareholders.

Typical reconstructions in the context of a merger follow one of two paths. Either the existing shares in the target are cancelled, or transferred to the bidder, and cash, or new shares in the bidder, are issued to the target shareholders in return. The transfer of shares attracts stamp duty whereas cancelling them saves this cost.

The benefit of pursuing this route is that the bidder needs only a majority in number of shareholders representing 75 per cent in value of the target shares voting at a general meeting to obtain absolute control of the target. With a general offer, to guarantee absolute control, the bidder needs a minimum of 90 per cent of the shareholders to accept the offer (see **8.13**).

The main difficulty with the scheme is that in a general offer only 50 per cent of the target shares are needed to obtain effective control: there may still be a minority outstanding, but at least the bidder is thereafter steering the ship. The scheme in contrast must get 75 per cent of the target's shares supporting it to get it through.

A scheme can also be rather slow, depending on how quickly it will take to get a hearing set down with the court.

You might think that one of the advantages of using a scheme rather than a general offer was that it took you outside the City Code's jurisdiction and all the complications which ensue. The City Code, however, regards a scheme used to effect a takeover as a transaction which falls within the ambit of its review. The timetable laid down by the City Code, however, is subject to the timetable which the court determines for the scheme to be approved. Nevertheless, as an alternative method for a recommended rather than hostile offer, it is an idea worth considering.

8.6.2.3 New holding company

A third option is to set up a new company ('Newco') which is to acquire the shares of both bidder and target, so the two existing companies disappear into a new entity. Two routes for the acquisition of the shares of bidder and target exist: either Newco makes a general offer for all the securities in both bidder and target, or both companies enter into a scheme of arrangement under which their shareholders agree either to transfer their existing shares to Newco or to have their shares cancelled, and take Newco shares or cash instead.

Why do this rather than pursue one of the other options? The likeliest reason is the desire to effect a genuine merger of two equals.

There are some disadvantages. To use a general offer to acquire both bidder and target requires the appropriate percentage of acceptances from each of the companies, so there is twice the risk of failure. Stamp duty is payable on two lots of shares to be transferred (unless the scheme of arrangement is used which enables the shares to be cancelled). It is nevertheless a route which the parties sometimes find it to their advantage to utilise.

8.6.2.4 Partial or tender offer

These are both methods for securing less than 100 per cent control of the target.

(a) *Partial offer*

A partial offer is like a general offer save that the bidder is bidding only for a proportion of the voting share capital of the target. Each target shareholder may accept the offer in respect of an equivalent proportion of his shareholding. Thus if a bidder wants to acquire 25 per cent of a target, a shareholder with 100 shares may accept in respect of 25 of his 100 shares.

The main benefit to the bidder is the prospect of acquiring either significant influence or negative control (i.e., the ability to vote down anything requiring a special resolution) over the company for much less than it would cost to make an outright bid.

If the bidder wishes to acquire more than 30 per cent of the target, this requires the preliminary approval of shareholders with more than 50 per cent of the voting rights (excluding the bidder and those acting in concert with it). This is a material disincentive.

Partial offers are in practice therefore rare in the UK as they present significant practical problems. Rule 36 governs them and it requires the Takeover Panel's consent in advance of any such offer.

(b) *Tender offer*

A tender offer is governed by r. 4 of the Substantial Acquisition Rules. It is specifically the procedure whereby a bidder seeks to acquire less than 30 per cent of the target (a partial offer may be made for larger stakes).

The offer must be made by means of an advertisement placed in two national newspapers which should state the terms of the offer. The offer must be open for at least seven days. The bidder cannot send the equivalent of an offer document to target shareholders persuading them to take up the offer, but the target is entitled to circulate a document detailing why they should reject the offer. The offer must also be made for a specified proportion of the target shares and only cash is permitted by way of consideration.

Mechanically, the bidder may fix the price at which it is bidding for target shares, or it may set up an auction in reverse, so that it states the maximum price it is prepared to pay and shareholders state the minimum price they will accept and the bidder then sets a striking price once all the tenders are in from shareholders. All bids at or below that price will qualify under the tender.

Once again, given the strictness of the rules, tender offers are not popular mechanisms in UK takeover practice.

8.6.2.5 Reverse takeover

A reverse takeover is simply a takeover by a smaller company of a larger company, the effect of which is that the target company's shareholders become the majority shareholders in the bidder. Usually the target company board also becomes the controlling interest on the bidder's board. This type of bid is treated exactly like an ordinary general offer. The Stock Exchange requires the bidder in such a bid (obviously if listed) to obtain its shareholders' approval in general meeting, as the effect of the transaction will be loss of control over their company.

8.6.3 THE NATURE OF THE CONSIDERATION

The consideration for the offer is essentially a matter of commercial judgment of what looks most attractive from both the bidder's and target shareholders' points of view. In very general commercial terms, the kind of consideration most likely to appeal to target shareholders is cash. If there are competing bids, one cash and one not, and the value of the two bids is equivalent, the cash offer is likely to be the most attractive. It is for that reason that many non-cash bids offer a cash alternative (see below).

We will look at various types of consideration in turn and consider their respective advantages and disadvantages.

8.6.3.1 Cash

As we have seen already, the bidder may in fact have no choice about offering cash. The City Code requires it in two circumstances:

(a) Rule 11, which requires a cash alternative where the bidder has bought at least 10 per cent of the target's shares in the year leading up to the offer or during the offer period. The value must be the equivalent of the highest price paid for the shares bought in that time. The basic thinking behind this is to ensure that, if the bidder has paid a significant number of shareholders (which the Takeover Panel deems to be 10 per cent) cash for their shares, then all the shareholders should be entitled to participate in this.

(b) A mandatory bid under r. 9 (where the bidder acquires more than 30 per cent of the target's shares) must have a cash alternative at the same price as the highest the bidder has paid for the target's shares in the past year.

The principal difficulty for the bidder, even if it wants voluntarily to offer cash, is that it may be in short supply. How can this be resolved?

The common method is through a cash-underwritten alternative. This is very much like a vendor placing (see **3.6.5**) and exists to solve the same basic commercial problem, namely the mismatch between the need for cash and the availability of non-cash assets in the form of securities. The bidder offers target shareholders its securities with an express cash alternative. In respect of any securities for which the cash alternative is chosen, the bidder's merchant bank is instructed to procure subscribers for those securities by placing them in the market. The cash paid by the placees in consideration for the securities is then passed on to the target shareholders. As with a vendor placing, the merchant bank agrees to underwrite the placing if it does not attract investors, and it will also instruct the brokers to arrange a sub-underwriting on its behalf. The terms of the underwriting agreement are similar to the agreement we saw in **3.5.4.1**.

The other way of obtaining cash is through a loan. The main technical issue this raises for the company is whether it is able under its articles of association to borrow at the required levels. Commercially, of course, borrowing always brings with it an interest cost, and the real issue here is whether that can be set off against profits to reduce tax (see **8.6.1**).

8.6.3.2 The bidder's own securities

The bidder will think about using its own securities as consideration for any number of reasons. It may have no or insufficient cash resources available and be close to the limits on the borrowing restrictions in its articles of association. It may simply be that it regards its gearing ratio as too high.

8.6.3.3 What type of securities?

The securities can, in commercial terms, cover the whole spectrum of financial instruments from ordinary shares to bonds. There is no restriction in the Code on what can be offered, which allows for maximum flexibility.

Commercial considerations usually play the critical role in determining the nature of the securities to be issued. One such is that the cost of debt to the company is generally cheaper than that of equity, provided the interest payable on the debt instruments can be set off against tax. Another key factor in this choice is the effect it has on the bidder's accounts.

8.6.3.4 Accounting treatment

There is no getting away from the fact that this is a complex subject! Although the accountants will of course have prime responsibility for dealing with this question, the lawyers involved also need to grasp the issues as they will have a significant impact on the structure of the offer. A takeover brings two entities and hence two sets of accounts together. The question arises how the merger of those accounts is to be achieved. The methods are described below, together with their relative attractions and limitations.

8.6.3.5 Merger accounting

The target's assets and liabilities are merged into the bidder's at the value stated in the target's accounts, and the appearance is as if the two entities have always been one.

Merger accounting can only be used in rare cases. The requirements are currently set out in the Companies Act 1985, sch. 4A, para. 10 and FRS 6. Essentially, the bidder must acquire 90 per cent of the target's equity securities (shares with unrestricted rights to income and capital) with its own equivalent securities. Other criteria set by FRS 6 relevant in determining whether the transaction is a merger or an acquisition include the management of the combined entity (is it truly merged?) and the parties' relative sizes (if the acquirer is much larger, this makes it less likely to be a genuine merger).

Thus, if the bidder wants to be able to use the merger accounting method, it will need to issue equity securities or, at least, securities which carry such rights. This will restrict the nature of the securities it can offer.

8.6.3.6 Acquisition accounting

The target's assets and liabilities are accounted for in the merged accounts at a 'fair value' (not necessarily the same as the value stated in the target's accounts but the price at which the asset or liability could be exchanged in an arm's length transaction). In addition, the profits and losses of the target can only start to appear in the merged accounts as from the date of the acquisition, and not as if the two entities have aways been one and the same. Any excess of the price paid by the bidder over the total fair value of the assets and liabilities is treated as 'goodwill'.

This method of accounting has to be used where merger accounting is not available, though may also be used instead of merger accounting. It is subject to the requirements set out in

FRS 7: the underlying thrust of this is that the target should be accounted for as it actually stands at the time of the acquisition, not as the acquirer intends to organise it. Post-acquisition reorganisation costs are not therefore part of the cost of the acquisition. It is an attractive method from one point of view, in that the addition of the target's profits from the date of acquisition can give the impression of a sudden increase in the merged entity's earnings. With merger accounting, profits are restated as if the two entities have always been together and so the rate of profits increase will seem flatter.

Its disadvantage is the creation of goodwill. Goodwill may be treated in two ways. The first is as an asset, and the Companies Act 1985 requires that it be written off over a number of years (sch. 4, para. 21). This will have an adverse impact on the merged entity's reported profits as an element of these is being accounted for in writing off the goodwill.

The alternative (in fact preferred by SSAP 22) is to write goodwill off straight away against reserves. Obviously this may have a significant impact on the available distributable reserves of the merged entity. There are two ways around this:

(a) The first is a reduction of capital, either of the company's share capital or share premium account (see **9.7**). This creates a reserve against which goodwill can be written off.

(b) The second is to create a merger reserve as a result of obtaining merger relief (see **8.6.3.7**). Goodwill can then be written off against this.

The accountancy profession is currently debating the best approach to dealing with goodwill when the acquisition accounting method is used, as the technique of immediately writing goodwill off against reserves tends to emasculate balance sheets and has resulted in other 'creative' accounting measures to restore their appearance.

8.6.3.7 Merger relief

As mentioned above, the availability of merger relief may facilitate the use of the acquisition accounting method. When a company issues shares, the difference between the nominal value of the shares and the value of the target shares acquired (the premium) must be paid into the share premium account. This is then treated as capital and is subject to the restrictions in s. 130 Companies Act 1985.

Under s. 131 Companies Act 1985, if the bidder obains a 90 per cent holding of the equity securities of the target in exchange for equity securities of its own, merger relief is available. This allows the bidder to create a merger reserve with the premium which would otherwise have been transferred to the share premium account. As discussed above, goodwill can then be written off against that reserve.

8.6.3.8 Summary of accounting treatments

(a) Both merger relief and merger accounting depend crucially on structuring the bidder's consideration as equity securities (that is, shares with unrestricted rights to income and capital) and planning to do what will effectively be a straight share-for-share exchange with the target shareholders.

(b) The requirements for using the merger accounting method are stricter than those for obtaining merger relief.

(c) If the issue of equity securities is either not possible or not desired, the bidder will have to acquisition account, and then some careful thought will need to be given to the appropriate method for writing off the arising goodwill.

(d) Of course, it is possible for the bid to be structured in such a way that the bidder obtains merger relief and still chooses the acquisition accounting method.

The lesson is: consult the accountants early on and consider carefully the impact on the accounting position of the use of certain types of securities as consideration.

8.6.3.9 Tax treatment

The securities offered to the target shareholders are largely chosen for the commercial or accounting reasons already considered. Another factor in the choice is tax.

A target shareholder resident in the UK who accepts an offer of cash for his shares will be treated as having disposed of those shares and so will be subject to capital gains tax on the gain arising. The charge to CGT can be deferred if the shareholder accepts securities as consideration. The advantage of deferral to the shareholder is that he can then choose to realise the gain (i.e., sell the securities he has accepted) at a time when available reliefs can help significantly to reduce the extent of the chargeable gain. This is therefore one more favourable factor suggesting the use of securities as consideration, and it is also why, even with an all-cash offer, bidders will usually offer a 'loan note alternative'. Those shareholders with a particular CGT problem can then consider taking up the loan note option. A loan note in these circumstances is usually denominated in sterling, carries interest at a rate slightly below LIBOR, is unsecured, unlisted and repayable at the option of the holder every six months or so over something like a five-year term.

8.6.4 WHAT IS BEING BID FOR?

This may seem a strange question, but remember that the City Code itself states that it does not apply to offers for non-voting, non-equity capital. The exception to this is mentioned later. Where there is more than one class of equity share capital, r. 14 requires that a comparable offer be made for each class whether such capital carries voting rights or not.

A comparable offer is one that compares in terms of value (though it need not be identical) and is made simultaneously with the 'main' offer. It does not have to be the same type of consideration: it may be possible to offer one type of security to one class and another type to a different class.

The exception to the principle that offers for non-voting and non-equity capital are irrelevant under the Code is r. 15. If a target's equity share capital is the subject of a bid, any securities with conversion rights, subscription rights or options over that equity share capital must be the subject of an 'appropriate offer'. This should be appropriate in terms of value and type of consideration. As far as timing is concerned, it is quite normal to await the outcome of the 'main' offer before implementing a r. 15 offer: then if the 'main' offer fails, the r. 15 offer need never arise.

8.6.5 DEALS WITH THIRD PARTIES

The bidder may identify before it announces its offer that it will have difficulties satisfying the requirements of the Office of Fair Trading and Competition Commission because of the potential anticompetitive effects of its bid. A preventive measure to ease the path of the bid is to agree a sale of part of the target's operations to a third party before the bid begins. There are, though, a number of issues to watch here:

(a) There is always the risk that this will amount to the giving of unlawful financial assistance by the target for the acquisition of its own shares (remember s. 151 Companies Act 1985 catches indirect financial assistance as well).

(b) If the third party is already a shareholder in the target, this sort of deal will probably fall foul of r. 16 of the Code as it is an arrangement with a shareholder with favourable conditions attached which are not being extended to all shareholders: this is a rule which will strike at other possible bid tactics which may suggest themselves.

8.6.6 BIDDER'S TACTICS

All the issues set out so far in **8.6** are of course strategic questions for the bidder to decide. There are also tactical questions to consider about the conduct of the bid. Some of these have already been discussed. The list below is no more than a summary of some of the key tactics which may be considered and some of the limitations on them which will need to be observed.

(a) The bidder may attempt to build up a stake in the target through share purchases in the market to help it towards its goal of acquiring 50 per cent: we have already looked at some of the restrictions to be considered when doing this (see **8.5.3.2**).

(b) The bidder will also attempt to secure support from existing shareholders in the target by getting them to pledge their shares irrevocably to the offer: we have looked at irrevocable undertakings and some of the issues to think about when seeking them (see **8.5.4.2**).

(c) The other crucial issue for the bidder to focus on is price. Remember that 0 + 46 is the last date on which the bidder can revise its offer. Most institutional and other shareholders will be swayed ultimately by an attractive price for their shares. If the first offer was not compelling, a revised offer may be a 'knock-out' blow.

8.6.7 DEFENCE STRATEGY AND TACTICS

To a great extent this is necessarily reactive – it depends on the nature and circumstances of the offer. All that this section therefore does is offer some general guidance on ideas for defence which the target will usually want at least to consider.

As a prelude to this, it is important to dwell for a moment on the legal responsibilities of the target board, who, after all, will be in charge of the direction of the target's response. Some case law exists (*Dawson International plc* v *Coats Patons plc* [1989] BCLC 233 and *Heron International Ltd* v *Lord Grade* [1983] BCLC 244) which indicates that where the target directors are faced with two competing bids and certain defeat, their duty is to act in the best interests of the existing shareholders. This may not be simply to recommend the higher bid. The lower bid may be in the best interests of the company where, as happened recently, the target board judged it was less likely to be the subject of a Competition Commission reference and so more likely to proceed successfully (the target was UAPT–Infolink). Where the future of the company is open to doubt, the target directors will need to judge what is in the company's longer term commercial interests as well as in the immediate interests of current shareholders, and justify their conduct by reference to that standard. It is also important always to recall that the directors can exercise their powers of management only for proper corporate purposes and not simply to protect their own positions as either directors or shareholders (*Hogg* v *Cramphorn Ltd* [1967] Ch 254). Nor should the managers forget their responsibility to have regard to the interests of employees under s. 309 Companies Act 1985.

The Code (r. 3) stipulates that the board should obtain competent independent advice on any offer and communicate the substance of that advice to its shareholders.

Now to turn to some of the possible strategies available.

(a) The temptation for a target under threat is to secure its position by making a takeover bid effectively impossible or practically unwinnable. One method which suggests itself is to increase the shareholding interest of 'friendly' shareholders by issuing further shares to them so that majority control cannot be obtained without acquiring these shares. In the United States, some companies have provisions in their articles of association which are automatically activated in the event of a takeover offer being made and which bring about circumstances which block any chance of such an offer succeeding, such as enhanced voting rights for certain shares. This is a strategy known as the 'poison pill' because of its effect on those who swallow it!

These strategies may not work in the United Kingdom. The City Code states in General Principle 7 that:

> At no time after a bona fide offer has been communicated to the board of the offeree company, or after the board of the offeree company has reason to believe that a bona fide offer might be imminent, may any action be taken by the board of the offeree company in relation to the affairs of the company, without the approval of the shareholders in general meeting, which could effectively result in any bona fide offer being frustrated or in the shareholders being denied an opportunity to decide on its merits.

Rule 21 develops this by stipulating certain types of prohibited frustrating action, including issuing further shares and selling or agreeing to sell assets of a material amount. Remember, though, these are all subject to shareholder approval. Furthermore, defensive measures can be built in, provided this is done well in advance of any possible offer: of course, any listed company will have difficulties in amending its articles of association in the ways described given The Listing Rules' provisions.

(b) One thing which neither General Principle 7 nor r. 21 prevents, and which is a defensive strategy regularly employed by targets, is the lobbying of public authorities such as the Office of Fair Trading and the Competition Commission in an effort to persuade them to prevent the bid proceeding. In many cases, this is the method most likely to succeed in thwarting a bid. References to the MMC are the commonest form of regulatory intervention sought by targets.

Related to this is the use of tactical litigation to hold up a bid. This is very uncommon and difficult to mount in the UK following the Court of Appeal's ruling in *R* v *Panel on Takeovers and Mergers, ex parte Datafin plc* [1987] QB 815 regarding the justiciability of the Takeover Panel's decisions (see **8.8.7**). Such litigation is much more widespread in the USA. In the UK, it will be subject to r. 21.

(c) A target may recognise that the game is up, that it cannot survive as an independent entity and that its only strategy is to find the best way to lose which is in the interests of the target shareholders. The target board may therefore recommend the bid to its shareholders. Alternatively, it may not trust the bidder or feel that its plans for the target are unsuitable or that the price it is offering is inadequate. One solution would be to seek an alternative bidder prepared to offer more money and with plans more in keeping with the existing management's own ideas – a so-called 'white knight'.

A competing offer may be announced at any time in the course of an existing bid. If this happens, the timetable for the first bid is adjusted so that it corresponds exactly with that for the second (i.e., giving the first bidder time to react to the 'white knight').

(d) Of course the only way the target will lose the takeover battle is if its shareholders sell out to the bidder. This they will only do if either the price they are given is one they believe they cannot refuse or if they believe the bidder can offer a better future in terms of direction for the company and quality of management. The target's best form of defence therefore must be to show its shareholders that (i) the price offered undervalues the worth of the company, and (ii) the target management and its strategy are clearly better. This is of course what the defence documents will seek to do. The target needs, however, to ensure that its case is presented well in the press and is understood by investors. Someone will therefore need to work hard on the company's public relations image and its communications with shareholders.

By the same token, effort expended in producing an encouraging profit forecast for the target (if that is possible) is likely to be well rewarded with loyal support as this is tangible evidence of a future pay-off for shareholders.

As well as working on the profit forecast, a target may try to show that the offer undervalues the company's worth because it attaches too low a figure to the company's assets: a revaluation reported to the shareholders will strengthen the target's case. It will be subject to the same timing restrictions as for a profit forecast: the last date on which either could be announced is 0 + 39.

(e) Particularly where the substance of the bidder's case is that the target needs to restructure its business, the target's best response may be to adopt the bidder's idea and to effect a reconstruction of its operations. Once the bid is announced or in the offing, this will fall foul of r. 21 unless the shareholders approve. If a bid is likely but not imminent, this may be a useful pre-emptive strike.

In some cases, companies on the receiving end of a bid are far-sighted enough to have produced a 'defence manual', an internal and obviously highly confidential document, which will describe its proposed defence strategies, contain draft documents such as the outline of relevant press announcements and set out how the defence of the bid will be managed (for example, who from the target will work on the defence team and what support and information they will require). This is then kept in readiness (and updated as appropriate) for any possible bid – otherwise, a bid will catch the target completely napping and give the bidder a significant head start.

Let us now return to look in detail at the legal and regulatory provisions relevant to takeover practice.

8.7 Law and Regulation in Takeovers

There are a number of areas of law and regulation relevant in takeover work:

(a) the City Code on Takeovers and Mergers and the jurisdiction of the Takeover Panel (see **8.8**);

(b) the Substantial Acquisitions Rules (see **8.9**);

(c) the UKLA and its requirements under The Listing Rules (see **8.10**);

(d) the continuing requirements under the Stock Exchange's Admission and Disclosure Standards;

(e) the Companies Act 1985, and in particular those sections dealing with:

   (i) notification of interests in shares (Part VI of the Act, ss. 198–220, see **8.11**);

   (ii) financial assistance for the acquisition of shares (ss. 151–8, see **8.12**);

   (iii) acquisition of minority interests under ss. 428–30 (see **8.13**);

(f) the Criminal Justice Act 1993 on insider dealing (see **8.14**);

(g) the Financial Services Act 1986, particularly ss. 47, 56 and 57 (see **8.15**);

(h) the merger control regime in the UK and the EC (see **8.16**);

(i) the application of the common law and, in particular, the law of defamation, which rears its head quite frequently in takeovers (see **8.17**).

Of these areas, the City Code is clearly the most important. It is the foundation of takeover regulation.

8.8 The City Code on Takeovers and Mergers and the Takeover Panel

We have already heard much of the rules of the City Code. When do we have to worry about them? How does the Panel work?

8.8.1 WHEN DOES THE CITY CODE ON TAKEOVERS AND MERGERS APPLY?

The answer to this is set out in para. 4 of the Introduction to the City Code (sometimes referred to as the 'Blue Book' by practitioners, to distinguish it from the Stock Exchange's Yellow Book). Basically, you need to look at two things, the nature of the target company and the nature of the transaction.

8.8.1.1 The nature of the target company

If the target company is a UK incorporated *public* company, and is resident in the UK, the Isle of Man or the Channel Islands, the City Code applies to the takeover offer made for it. The company does *not* have to be listed. A private company which has been listed in the past 10 years but is no longer listed will also be caught, as are some statutory companies (like water companies), and Isle of Man and Channel Islands listed companies. It makes no difference in determining whether the City Code applies where the offeror comes from. It may be a company registered in the Cayman Islands and conducting most of its business in the USA – but if it is acquiring a UK public company resident in the UK, the City Code bites.

8.8.1.2 The nature of the transaction

The City Code catches a takeover transaction however it arises, whether via the normal route of a takeover offer made to all target shareholders, or through some other route such as a scheme of arrangement (see **8.6.2.2**). Basically, the Takeover Panel will look through the substance of a transaction and, if it looks like a takeover, it will regard the City Code as applying (provided the target company is covered by the City Code).

8.8.2 WHAT IS THE CITY CODE ON TAKEOVERS AND MERGERS?

This was explained in **1.6.4**. Essentially it is a set of principles of best practice in these transactions, now regularly updated and refined by the Takeover Panel as the organ designated for this purpose by an assortment of City bodies. Though the system of regulation can best be described as voluntary, because there is no formal legal sanction for ignoring the City Code, this is fundamentally to misconstrue how it works.

8.8.3 WHAT HAPPENS IF THE CITY CODE IS IGNORED OR BREACHED?

There are a series of sanctions, described in more detail below, which may be visited on a party in breach of the City Code.

The point of most of these sanctions, and what has made them so effective in practice, is the risk they carry that a party on the receiving end (or associated with that party, including advisers) will have its reputation tarnished or, worse, be shunned or excluded from the takeovers market or the securities market as a whole. All parties therefore take the risk of any of these sanctions being applied very seriously indeed: they may have highly damaging commercial consequences.

(a) The Takeover Panel may make a public announcement to the effect that a party has failed to comply with the City Code's provisions. This would be highly damaging to the chances of a takeover's success.

(b) The Takeover Panel may issue a censure or reprimand. Companies and advisers fight very hard to avoid this. Self-regulatory organisations in the City, like the Securities and Futures Authority, will not authorise a party to carry out investment business under the Financial Services Act 1986 if they have been formally reprimanded by the Panel, as they see it as evidence of unfitness.

(c) The Takeover Panel will bring pressure to bear on merchant banks to bring the companies they are advising into line, and may, simply through the threat of censure or worse, force the merchant bank to take drastic action and resign from acting for the company in question. In terms of strategic direction for the takeover and public relations, this would be disastrous for the company.

(d) The Takeover Panel may ask City institutions not to act for a particular individual or company in any takeover or similar transaction, so that he or it is unable to carry on that sort of business in the City. This is known as 'cold-shouldering' and has only happened once in the Panel's history. Once again, the self-regulatory organisations support the Panel in this by including in their rules a requirement that member firms will not act for a party which has been 'cold-shouldered' in this way.

It is true to say, though, that it is unusual for these sanctions to be invoked. The reason is not so much that everyone lives in dread of a thunderbolt from the Takeover Panel, but that the Takeover Panel itself prefers to seek a remedy for a breach of the City Code than to punish the offending party. The following are illustrations of what in practice the Takeover Panel may require where the City Code has been breached. The basic philosophy under which the Takeover Panel operates is not to be hidebound by fixed rules about available remedies, but rather to identify and apply a remedy appropriate to the circumstances.

(e) The Takeover Panel may require a company to amend a document issued in the course of the takeover, for instance, the offer document. This will be to correct a misleading statement. It would be easy for the Takeover Panel publicly to castigate the party for getting the document wrong, but its preferred approach is to ensure that everyone knows what the document should have said.

(f) The Takeover Panel may require that a party which has bought shares in the market in the course of a takeover has to sell them. This would be the case where the purchase was in breach of the City Code.

(g) The Securities and Investment Board (now the FSA) endorsed the City Code as part of its Statement of Principles. This means that compliance with the City Code by authorised persons may be enforced in the same way that the FSA enforces the Principles themselves. The FSA will only do this at the request of the Takeover Panel. This enables rulings of the Takeover Panel to be directly enforceable by the FSA, SROs and RPBs. This does therefore strengthen the potential consequences arising from failure to observe the City Code.

There are other remedies which the Takeover Panel has used in particular cases, for example, preventing a potential bidder from launching a bid at all because of its conduct leading up to that point. The point is that the Takeover Panel has the flexibility to devise solutions to fit the bill.

Let us look now at the way in which the City Code is interpreted, as this is central to the entire regulatory system for takeovers.

8.8.4 THE NATURE AND INTERPRETATION OF THE CITY CODE

To understand the methodology of interpreting the City Code, we need to see first how it is set out. It comes in two parts, the general principles and the rules. We will focus for now on the general principles, as this is where the City Code starts and it is from them that the rules themselves are derived.

8.8.4.1 The general principles: what are they?

There are 10 of them and they are, to quote the City Code, 'essentially statements of good standards of commercial behaviour'. This may sound pretty meaningless, but in fact, they play an integral part in defining the nature and interpretation of the City Code. They play two principal roles:

(a) The first has already been mentioned: they form the basis of the more specific rules, and are an aid to their interpretation. If, for example, a question arises as to the specific application of one of the rules to a particular takeover, the first question the Takeover Panel will ask itself will be, Does this case come within the principle underlying the rule? If so, the Takeover Panel is very unlikely to entertain any arguments that the rule be disregarded.

(b) They are binding on the parties to a takeover offer, and so may prevent conduct which might otherwise appear, from an analysis of the rules, to be permissible.

8.8.4.2 The general principles: the basic themes

The general principles have five basic themes:

(a) *Equality of treatment and opportunity for shareholders*

Any aspect of an offer which treats target shareholders of the same class differently is unacceptable.

All shareholders should receive the same information and get new information at the same time. The appropriate method of releasing information is either through a general press announcement or a circular to all shareholders.

(b) *Adequacy of information and advice*

The highest standards of care and accuracy should be applied in the preparation of documents or advertisements during an offer.

Directors, in advising their shareholders, should act independently and therefore without reference to any conflicting or personal interests. The principle extends to the directors' own advisers, namely, the merchant bank and other advisers like accountants and solicitors. The Takeover Panel will prevent an adviser from acting if its independence is in any way in doubt.

(c) *Prohibition on frustrating action*

We have already seen that general principle 7 prevents the target from doing anything (after it becomes aware that a bid is looming) which frustrates an offer or denies the shareholders the opportunity to decide it on its merits, *unless* the shareholders have consented to this in general meeting. The principle is that the shareholders, as owners of the target, should be free to make up their own minds on what they want. Rule 21 expands on this by stipulating some situations which are considered frustrating action.

(d) *Maintenance of an orderly market*

An offer should be announced only after careful and responsible consideration. This is designed to prevent a 'stop-go' policy on the part of a potential offeror which creates a highly volatile market in the target's shares, which is not in its or its shareholders' interests.

(e) *The 'siege' principle*

Although this is not embodied as such in a general principle, the Takeover Panel takes into account a fifth general theme in practice, which is that the target company should not be laid siege to from an unwanted offeror beyond a reasonable length of time. This explains the timing restrictions placed on a bid (see **8.5.1**), and r. 35, which prevents a failed bidder from trying again for another year.

8.8.4.3 The general principles: limitations

The general principles are not to be taken as the last word on what is or is not acceptable. There are a series of unwritten limitations which apply. It is not possible in the space here to be comprehensive about the extent of these, but a number of examples will illustrate that exceptions to the application of these principles do exist, and that they should not therefore necessarily be taken as gospel.

First, the principle of equality of treatment ought to mean that the same offer and information are made available to all shareholders, *wherever they live*. In general terms, that is true. Regulatory complications in the United States and Canada mean, however, that it is often not possible to extend offers to those jurisdictions, because compliance with the relevant regulations is wholly impracticable. The Takeover Panel understands and accepts this and so some offers are simply not made available to North Americans.

Secondly, as we have seen (**8.6.7**), the principle prohibiting frustrating action does not prevent the target from seeking to persuade the Office of Fair Trading that the bid should be referred to the Competition Commission, even though such a referral would effectively kill the bid.

8.8.4.4 The general principles: how are they interpreted?

The general principles are not like statutory provisions: there is a woolliness about them which makes a lawyer feel uncomfortable. But this is central to the interpretation of the general principles and the entire City Code. The thinking behind them is set out in para. 3(a) of the Introduction to the Code. This is fundamental to a proper understanding of the City Code and so to any advice to be given in relation to it:

> These general principles . . . are . . . expressed in broad general terms and the Code does not define the precise extent of, or the limitations on, their application. They are applied by the Panel *in accordance with their spirit to achieve their underlying purpose*; the Panel may modify or relax the effect of their precise wording accordingly. [Emphasis added.]

There are two things to note about this:

(a) The general principles are not capable of strict legalistic analysis: this approach will get you nowhere. Normal principles of interpretation must give way to what might be called a purposive approach – what is the spirit of the provision? This will govern the Takeover Panel's view. Lawyers must therefore not treat the principles or, indeed, the rest of the City Code as if they were a statute.

(b) The Takeover Panel is the arbiter of the application and operation of the general principles, hence an understanding of how it works is vital to an adequate appreciation of the Code. Moreover, a point in the general principles which is unclear cannot be resolved by the lawyers giving an opinion – the Panel has to be consulted (see below and **8.4.8**).

In conclusion on the general subject of the interpretation of the City Code, the general principles can in general terms be regarded as a distillation of basic principles of commercial morality and fairness as applied to takeovers. It is in this spirit that the Takeover Panel adjudges conduct in the course of a bid, whatever the specific wording of the City Code, and the advice of the lawyers must be tailored accordingly.

We have already seen what the Takeover Panel is (see **1.6.4**); what is its role?

8.8.5 WHAT IS THE TAKEOVER PANEL'S JOB?

When referring to the Takeover Panel in this section, you should take this to mean not just the full Panel but the Panel Executive too. The Takeover Panel's job is the regulation of the takeovers market. It does this in a number of ways.

(a) It updates and revises the City Code.

(b) It responds to enquiries from parties to a takeover (or, more likely, their financial and legal advisers) about the interpretation and application of the Code. The Panel Executive never gives advice in writing and confines itself to oral statements over the telephone or in meetings. The full Panel will issue written decisions. It is possible to obtain guidance from the Panel Executive on a 'no-names' basis, though this can never be categorical. Firm rulings are only possible when the Panel Executive knows who the parties involved actually are.

(c) It monitors developments in the takeovers market through regular checking of share price movements and reports in newspapers and journals. The object of this is to ensure that the Takeover Panel is fully apprised of all information of significance in relation to current or potential takeovers.

The Takeover Panel sees its primary and overall objective as being the protection of equity shareholders and what might be called the maintenance of an orderly takeovers market. Its concern is, put very simply, that the holder of equity, and particularly the individual shareholders as opposed to the institutions, does not have legal or economic rights prejudiced or oppressed in the course of a takeover.

We have already seen what the general principles have to say, and you will have begun to appreciate that underlying much of the Takeover Panel's *raison d'être* is a desire to ensure that takeovers are governed by basic principles of commercial morality and fairness.

There are two common misconceptions about the Takeover Panel's role.

The first is that the Takeover Panel's approval for documents issued in the course of takeover offers is required as a precondition of their issue: this is not the case. In other words, the

Takeover Panel does not operate like a clearing house for these documents in the way in which the Stock Exchange does for listing particulars. If documents are incorrect when issued in the course of a bid then, as we have seen in **8.8.3**, the Panel will take steps to ensure errors are subsequently remedied.

The second is that the Takeover Panel considers the commercial benefits or viability of a proposed offer: once again, this is not the case. It is concerned solely to ensure that the correct procedures are complied with. It simply ignores the question of whether an offer is a good thing or not, though this does not of course prevent it from ruling on whether the offeror has been behaving badly in the course of its bid.

8.8.6 HOW DOES THE TAKEOVER PANEL FUNCTION?

The first point of contact with the Takeover Panel on a particular takeover is likely to be a telephone call to the Panel Executive from one of the advisers involved, either checking on a point of interpretation or informing the Takeover Panel that a bid is on its way. Thereafter, the Takeover Panel acts primarily as a reactive body, responding to requests for guidance on interpretation of the City Code or what the parties should do as the bid proceeds. On a day-to-day basis, it will act through a case officer appointed to oversee a particular bid.

In the event that the parties or advisers to a takeover are unhappy with the ruling they have received from the Panel Executive, they may appeal to the full Takeover Panel. This means that the full committee is summoned to hear the particular point, and usually in very short order in view of the fact that speed is of the essence in takeovers. The hearing is not like a court of law and there is no formal process laid down. The full Takeover Panel gives its decision in writing soon after the hearing. It is possible to appeal against that decision to the Appeal Committee, either where the full Takeover Panel permits it or there is an allegation that it has exceeded its jurisdiction. The Appeal Committee consists of two senior judges and two Panel members not otherwise involved in whichever case is being appealed. It is technically the final port of call, subject to what is said about judicial review below.

More generally, it is important to be clear about the way in which the Takeover Panel handles the interpretation of the Code. This is covered in **8.8.4**.

8.8.7 IS THE TAKEOVER PANEL THE FINAL ARBITER?

Is there, in other words, any appeal from the decisions of the Takeover Panel after its own appeals process has run its course?

The Takeover Panel's decisions are open to judicial review (*R* v *Panel on Takeovers and Mergers, ex parte Datafin plc* [1987] QB 815), but only on a historical rather than a contemporaneous basis. What this means is that the Takeover Panel's decisions cannot be interefered with in the course of a takeover, only after the event as a way of ensuring that the Takeover Panel does not make the same mistake twice. The case has since been supported by a decision in the House of Lords and another one in the Court of Appeal. The basic thinking behind it is that, if parties could obtain judicial review through the courts in the course of a takeover battle, it would give enormous scope for tactical litigation, undermine the authority of the Takeover Panel, slow the whole timetable for a takeover down and make the transaction a great deal more expensive for the parties involved. The flexible and informal procedure which the Takeover Panel operates would be wholly overturned if takeovers began to end up in the courts. As it is, the effect of the *Datafin* case is to kill off judicial review in the context of takeovers: it is difficult to summon up the motivation (and hard to justify the cost) to resurrect points from a takeover when it is dead and buried, simply for the benefit of the next generation of takeover practitioners.

8.8.8 THE IMPACT OF EUROPE

The European Commission has proposed a Directive (the Thirteenth Company Law Directive) to place the City Code on a legislative footing. This has been resisted by the UK government and the Takeover Panel on the grounds that legislation will lead to 'strategic litigation' by bidders and targets as part of their bid conduct and strategy. This is characteristic of the US and French takeover markets in particular. Proposals for the Directive are the subject of current negotiations.

8.9 The Substantial Acquisitions Rules (the 'SARs')

Though not part of the City Code on Takeovers and Mergers, these are issued and administered by the Takeover Panel. Their purpose is to 'restrict the speed with which a person may increase his holding of shares and rights over shares to an aggregate of between 15 per cent and 30 per cent of the voting rights of the company'. The SARs achieve this under r. 1 by preventing a person from acquiring 10 per cent or more of a company's voting rights over a seven-day period if that would give the buyer more than 15 per cent (but less than 30 per cent) of those voting rights. This explains why buyers of shares frequently stop at the 14.99 per cent threshold. It also gives them the best possible position from which to initiate further share-buying – given the restrictions of the SARs.

The intention is not to prevent buyers from making substantial acquisitions of shares, simply to slow them down. This is in response to the old practice of the 'dawn raid', in which a buyer would 'swoop' on a target's shares when the stock market opened. Before the target had time to draw breath, substantial amounts of its equity would be in unwelcome hands. The SARs therefore give targets time to think and respond.

SAR 1 is supported by SAR 3, which obliges any buyer to disclose to the Stock Exchange when it goes through the 15 per cent threshold, and any further 1 per cent increases beyond that.

Sanctions are applied by the Takeover Panel in the same way as for breaches of the City Code (see **8.8.3**).

The SARs will not apply where purchases go through the 30 per cent barrier – this is governed by r. 5 (and r. 9) of the Code. More important still, *the SARs do not apply where a takeover offer has been made under the Code*. Hence, they are only relevant in the build-up to the announcement of the offer.

8.10 The Listing Rules

The Listing Rules are relevant in a number of ways in takeover work.

8.10.1 REVERSE TAKEOVERS

The Listing Rules require a company effecting a reverse takeover (and which is already listed) to obtain approval from its shareholders in general meeting for the transaction to proceed (LR, para. 10.39 – see also **8.6.2.5**).

8.10.2 TRANSACTIONS

We saw in the context of acquisitions the impact of the Class requirements on companies making disposals or acquisitions of companies, assets or businesses. The requirements apply equally to public company takeovers, and will catch a listed company making an offer to acquire all the shares in a public company: if the transaction is of a sufficient size by comparison with the value of the bidder, it may be a Class 1 transaction. Shareholder approval and a shareholder circular are then necessary. Section **5.6.4** contains further details on the Class requirements. Some of these, including the requirement to describe material contracts and litigation in the circular, require information to be included about the target as well as the bidder. This applies even to a hostile bid since the bidder is expected to make reasonable enquiry of the target's published sources of information.

8.10.3 LISTING PARTICULARS

In relation to some takeovers, listing particulars may be required. This is where all or part of the consideration being offered by the bidder consists of securities for which listing on the Official List will be sought. The listing particulars contents requirements (see **4.2.6.3**) will apply equally to a takeover as to an ordinary equity offering, and so these will need to be added to the list alongside the requirements stated in r. 24 of the Code (see **8.5.5.1**).

It is not necessary to issue the offer document and the listing particulars separately – the one may be incorporated in the other. If printed separately, listing particulars will generally need to be published at the same time as the offer document, and so it is important to ensure that the takeover announcement is not made until the listing process is well advanced (see **4.2.6.4**).

If the offer is recommended, and listing particulars are required, the target and its directors will have to accept responsibility in the listing particulars as well as the offer document for information about the target.

The final point to be made about the role of the UKLA in takeovers is that it is there to be consulted by companies and advisers alike if there are any doubts about the application of The Listing Rules to the transaction.

8.11 Companies Act 1985: Notification of Interests in Shares

These are provisions which apply in contexts other than takeovers but it is here that they are most frequently encountered.

The basic principle behind part VI of the Companies Act 1985 is that public companies (the only ones to which the sections apply) have an interest in identifying substantial shareholders on their register of members and in monitoring the sizes of their shareholdings. They are at least then put on notice if a potential predator should emerge.

The method for achieving this is to require a shareholder who acquires a 3 per cent interest in a public company's relevant share capital (essentially issued shares carrying a right to vote at general meetings) to notify the company within two working days. Failure to do so is an offence under s. 210. If the percentage of the shareholder's interest increases to a new whole number (for example, from 3.9 per cent to 4.1 per cent), that too requires disclosure. Disposal of an interest previously notified, or reduction of that interest from, say, 4.1 per cent to 3.9 per cent, must be similarly disclosed.

An interest in shares is very widely defined by s. 208 as 'an interest of any kind whatsoever in the shares'. It includes a beneficial interest under a trust or a right under an option. Some interests are exempt by s. 209, including that of a bare trustee or a market maker properly holding shares for the purposes of his market-making business. Some interests are defined as not 'material', for example, holdings by investment managers and unit trust managers, and they need to be disclosed only when they amount to 10 per cent or more of the relevant share capital: even if these interests are more than 3 per cent, no obligation of disclosure arises.

It would be tempting to circumvent these provisions by dividing an interest between a number of associates or subsidiaries, giving each less than 3 per cent. The legislation deals with this by requiring so-called 'concert parties' to amalgamate their interests for the purposes of disclosure. A concert party exists if two or more persons agree to buy and hold shares in a public company (whether in writing or not) and actually go ahead and make the purchase. Each member of the concert party is taken to be interested in the interests of other members of the party. The consequence is that they all need to notify the company if the accumulated total is over 3 per cent.

As for the use of subsidiaries, if a company controls one-third of the voting power of another company, by s. 203 it is taken to be interested in the interests which that other company holds in a public company: hence parent companies are interested in the holdings of their subsidiaries.

The provisions also give a public company the power to investigate the identity of any shareholder on its register of members. Section 212 enables a company to require anyone whom it *reasonably believes* either holds, or in the past three years has held, shares in the company to disclose whether he is interested in the company's shares. This may also be useful where an interest is held by a nominee company and the identity of the underlying beneficiary is unknown – the beneficiary only needs to make a disclosure where the interest is 3 per cent.

The use of s. 212 notices may become more widespread following the introduction of CREST (see **1.6.3**) since many shareholders will hold shares through nominee accounts on CREST.

The recipient of a s. 212 notice must reply within a reasonable time – taken to be two days in an urgent situation such as the middle of a takeover and five days at other times. Failure to do so may result in a court order under s. 216 interdicting the shareholder from selling his shares, voting on them or receiving a dividend. Some companies have automatic powers under their articles of association to impose such sanctions in the event of no reply (though the Stock Exchange has time limits which listed companies wishing to exercise these powers should observe). If a shareholder has an exempt interest under s. 209, he must still disclose his interest if he receives a s. 212 notice – effectively it overrides the exemption.

The effect of these provisons is that a target facing a perceived takeover threat will dispatch a flurry of s. 212 notices to establish precisely who is the enemy and how many shares it already has. During the course of a bid, the target will continue to send out notices to monitor the bidder's performance. The bidder must be careful to comply with these and particularly careful where it is acting in association with others (including advisers buying shares on its behalf) to stay within the concert party provisions.

8.12 Companies Act 1985: Financial Assistance for the Acquisition of Shares

You will already be familiar with s. 151 Companies Act 1985. Like part VI of the Act, it is not just in the context of takeovers that this becomes an issue (see also **7.2.4** on management buy-outs), but it is one of the more important areas where it becomes relevant in corporate finance work.

In essence, s. 151 prevents a company from giving financial assistance for the acquisition of its own shares. The policy reason is to help maintain the company's share capital for the benefit of creditors and shareholders alike. The financial assistance can take the form of a gift, a guarantee, indemnity or anything else which materially reduces the net assets of the company (anything over about 1 per cent is likely to be material).

Exceptions exist if the assistance is only an incidental part of a larger purpose of the company and given in good faith, or the assistance is for an employees' share scheme or by way of a dividend (for example). Private companies may take advantage of the 'whitewash' procedure under s. 155 provided the directors sign a statutory declaration that the company is still solvent, the company's auditors report to the same effect and the shareholders approve by special resolution.

In the context of takeovers, many s. 151 questions arise because it is a regular part of practice in these transactions for the bidder to instruct its merchant bank to acquire the target's shares in the market. The merchant bank will usually only be prepared to do this if the bidder indemnifies it against any possible losses it may suffer as a consequence. If the bid is a share-for-share exchange, there is the prospect that the merchant bank, having acquired target shares for the bidder, will accept the bidder's offer in respect of those shares, and so acquire the bidder's shares. Will the indemnity in these circumstances amount to financial assistance?

It seems bizarre that this was ever intended to be caught by the legislation; however, the words of the Act technically trap this sort of arrangement and it is important for the lawyers to be alive to it. In fact in this situation, the s. 153 'larger purpose' exception is almost always available as the assistance is given to facilitate the takeover (the larger purpose) and not to enable the merchant bank to acquire the bidder's shares.

There may be other circumstances in which these sections become relevant in the course of a takeover and it is important always to consider their application.

8.13 Companies Act 1985: Acquisition of Minority Interests

Where a bidder acquires 90 per cent of the target shares through *acceptances* of its offer (not including shares held when the offer was made), it can compulsorily purchase the remaining 10 per cent under ss. 428–30 Companies Act 1985. This will enable it to remove the potentially troublesome 'rump' of shareholders left who, for whatever reason, have chosen not to accept the offer.

The bidder's right to acquire arises only if it obtains its 90 per cent within four months of making the original offer. Once the 90 per cent has been obtained, the right to acquire the rest must be exercised within two months.

The bidder must send a notice to the outstanding minority offering to acquire their shares on the same terms as the original offer (s. 429). Shareholders can object to the court and the court may prevent the acquisition or vary its terms. In practice this is extremely rare. Occasionally it is difficult (if not impossible) to offer shareholders precisely the same terms as in the original offer: for example, as regards consideration, the bidder may not be able to offer the choice of a loan note alternative any longer. In this case, a cash sum equivalent to the value of a loan note alternative (if selected by the shareholder being bought out) is acceptable.

Should a bidder choose not to acquire the outstanding minority shares, the shareholders themselves (despite having declined the offer originally) may force the bidder to acquire their interests under s. 430A. They can do this only if the bidder has acquired 90 per cent of the shares *in total*, whether through acceptances or purchases. The buy-out must be on the same terms as the original offer. Section 430A sets out the timetable to be followed in these circumstances.

8.14 Insider Dealing

Insider dealing is now notoriously associated with takeover activity, but it may occur with any of the other transactions dealt with in this book.

It is now defined by Part V of the Criminal Justice Act 1993. The main offence is to deal as an insider in securities on a regulated market (essentially the Stock Exchange or the Unlisted Securities Market but extending also to other EC-regulated markets) while in possession of inside information, though off-market deals by or through professional intermediaries are also caught by the Act. An insider is a director or employee of the company or someone who has a professional or business relationship with it or someone whose direct or indirect source of the information is one of these. Inside information is basically any specific information not made public relating to particular securities or companies which is likely to have a significant effect on the price of any securities if known to the market. Securities are defined quite broadly and include equities, gilts, debt securities, options, futures, warrants and the like. It is also an offence to encourage someone else to deal in securities on the basis of inside information or for an insider to disclose inside information otherwise than in the proper performance of his job, unless he did not expect anyone to deal as a result.

There are exceptions where the insider did not expect to make a profit or avoid a loss through dealing, or where he reasonably believed the information was widely known, or where an insider who has inside information would have done what he did (either dealt or encouraged) even without the information in his possession. Nor will it be an offence for the insider to disclose information in the proper performance of his job.

The offences under the Act are triable either way. If a defendant is convicted in the magistrates' court, the maximum sentence per offence is a fine of £5,000 or imprisonment for up to six months or both. For more than one offence, the aggregate maximum imprisonment is 12 months. If a defendant is convicted in the Crown Court on indictment, the maximum offence is imprisonment for up to seven years and/or an unlimited fine. It would be open to the court to seek to confiscate the benefits of insider dealing under the Criminal Justice Act 1988 and to disqualify a director for an insider dealing offence.

As far as civil liability is concerned, there may well be liability for directors who use confidential information: they might be held liable to account to a company for any profits made as a result of using price-sensitive information for their own advantage.

Any dealing by a member of an SRO will inevitably constitute a breach of the relevant SRO rules. This means that if the dealing has caused loss, an action under s. 62 FS Act could result. It is important to note that, for the purposes of insider dealing, the right of action is not limited to private investors.

Any information about a target acquired through discussions with the target (perhaps with a view to a recommended offer which in fact never materialises) will be inside information. This will effectively prevent the bidder or anyone associated with it from buying shares in the target before the bid is announced: it could therefore be a useful defence tactic for the target to release such information selectively to potential bidders.

Care should be taken when seeking to obtain irrevocable undertakings from target shareholders as part of a bid. If there is any inside information of which the target shareholder is unaware, he should be told, so that the insider has the benefit of the s. 53(1)(b) Criminal Justice Act 1993 defence (a reasonable belief that the information has already been disclosed widely enough).

It is as well for the lawyers to ensure that everyone involved in the takeover is made aware of the restrictions imposed by this Act. The Stock Exchange monitors untoward share price movements and investigates any suspicious evidence of insider trading. Apart from the obvious risk of prosecutions and the fall-out which may result, it is highly embarrassing for all concerned to be subject to damaging investigations of possible infringements of the Act.

8.15 Financial Services Act 1986

Three sections of the Financial Services Act 1986 regularly affect the conduct of takeovers – ss. 47, 56 and 57. These have been covered extensively in **1.5.1.4**. You should refer to this section for the linguistic and legal detail of the provisions. There are a few points to be made in the specific context of takeovers.

In connection with s. 56 and unsolicited calls, these are a particular issue because either the bidder may wish to make calls on shareholders to persuade them to give irrevocable undertakings (see **8.5.4.2**) or to persuade them to accept the offer through a telephone campaign. Such calls are permissible under the section and accompanying regulations, provided they are made in accordance with the City Code. This requires the calls to be made by or under the supervision of an authorised person (for example, a merchant banker). Rule 19.5 of the Code regulates 'telephone campaigns': basically the caller must stick to an approved script. The authorised person must also comply with the provisions on cold-calling set out in its SRO rulebook.

Under the Financial Services Act 1986, the target and its advisers may call on target shareholders without inhibition (save in a recommended offer) as they will be attempting to persuade the shareholders *not* to enter into an investment agreement with the bidder. Given their common law duties, the directors will need to review whether such a telephone campaign is sufficiently in the company's best interests for the company to finance it.

In connection with s. 57, this is the status of the various documents issued in the course of a takeover:

(a) Press announcements are exempt as disseminations to the press.

(b) The offer document is an investment advertisement.

(c) Listing particulars are exempt under s. 58.

(d) The bidder's circulars to its own shareholders are exempt.

(e) The defence document is not an investment advertisement as it encourages target shareholders *not* to enter into an investment agreement.

(f) Section 429 notices will be exempt.

In all cases the regulations should be carefully reviewed. If a document is an investment advertisement, then it will need to be approved or issued by an authorised person. Generally in a takeover this will be the merchant bank, which is likely to be authorised by the Securities and Futures Authority. Its rules must be carefully checked by the bank when reviewing an investment advertisement for approval.

8.16 Merger Control

The objective of all merger control provisions is to prevent the accumulation of monopolies as these have an anticompetitive effect on the market, leading to higher prices and less choice for the consumer.

8.16.1 UK

The merger control regime in the UK derives from the Fair Trading Act 1973, which catches any merger that brings 25 per cent of a market in goods or services together in the new merged entity, or that has gross assets worldwide exceeding £70 million.

Such a merger qualifies for investigation by the Office of Fair Trading ('OFT'), which may recommend to the President of the Board of Trade that it is referred to the Competition Commission ('CC'). References to the CC are usually in circumstances where the President perceives an anti-competitive effect from a merger. Comparatively few mergers are referred to the CC in practice. The CC may prevent the merger, or authorise it subject to part of the merged business being sold off. The CC usually takes several months to reach a decision.

If a merger falls within the Fair Trading Act 1973 criteria, before the bid is announced it is possible to obtain what is called confidential guidance from the OFT to see whether it intends to recommend referral. This is usually reliable guidance but sometimes takes up to two months to obtain.

Alternatively, you can proceed to announce the bid. At this stage, there is no obligation formally to notify the OFT if your merger falls within the criteria, but it is normal practice to do so. If a merger is not notified, the OFT may investigate it regardless and refer it (though it must do so within six months of the merger taking place). Clearly this is a highly undesirable result for the bidder or buyer, hence the typical advance notification and condition to the bid or acquisition that no referral results. Notification is either by way of a submission for clearance of the merger or through the Companies Act 1989 merger notice procedure. The latter requires the OFT to come up with its decision within 45 working days.

8.16.2 EC

8.16.2.1 EC Merger Regulation

The Merger Regulation catches so-called concentrations with a Community dimension (CCDs). A transaction will be a concentration where control of an entity is acquired, and therefore takeover offers leading to a merger will almost always give rise to concentrations. A Community dimension arises where a merged entity has aggregate worldwide turnover of 5 billion euros (approximately £3.2 billion) and aggregate EC turnover of at least 250 million euros (about £160 million). The residence or nationality of the parties is not relevant, so in practice the Regulation has caught mergers between Japanese and US corporations with large EC interests. However, if each member of the merged entity (bidder and target) has two-thirds of its turnover in the same Member State, that will not be a CCD. That is a merger to be judged by the local regulator (in the UK the OFT). Where a merger threatens to create or strengthen a dominant position within a Member State, the local regulator may ask the EC to allow it to review the transaction under its own rules – even where the merger is a CCD. The OFT has done this once, and succeeded.

A CCD must be notified to the EC within a week of the bid being announced. The EC will decide whether to investigate the merger within a month, and if it decides to go ahead it will take about four months to decide what to recommend. To date, out of nearly 200 different notifications only 13 have been investigated in detail, and only one of those notified concentrations was blocked by the Commission. The EC may alternatively refer a merger back to the OFT for decision. Usually some consultation takes place with the EC before the bid to determine its likely position.

8.16.2.2 Articles 81 and 82 of the Treaty of Rome (formerly articles 85 and 86)

Article 81 controls anti-competitive agreements and art. 82 an abuse of a dominant position.

Article 81 strikes at arrangements between businesses 'which have as their object or effect the prevention, restriction or distortion of competition within the common market'. Its principal target is cartels, but the arrangements in connection with a takeover offer could technically fall within the article – a merger, after all, will generally fuse two competitors. It is possible to obtain a 'negative clearance' from the European Commission that the article does not apply.

Failing that, a breach of art. 81 renders void any offending agreement. Fines may also be imposed by the Commission.

Article 82 prohibits 'any abuse by one or more undertakings [businesses] of a dominant position within the common market or a substantial part of it'. A merger might amount to such an abuse, and certainly an abuse of a dominant position may be its effect. However, the European Commission has indicated that it will not seek to use art. 82 where the Merger Regulation applies. Nevertheless, negative clearance can be sought from the Commission in appropriate circumstances. Breaches of the article will attract fines from the Commission.

Articles 81 and 82 will of course also affect acquisitions and other transactions covered in this book, particularly joint ventures (see **chapter 6**). You should in those cases always consider their relevance alongside the Fair Trading Act 1973.

8.16.3 CONDITIONS

In view of these provisions, takeover offers will invariably be subject to a condition that the bid is not referred either to the CC or the EC for investigation. Any reference would then lapse the offer.

If for some reason the OFT takes an inordinately long time deciding what to do, the Takeover Panel may agree to freeze the bid timetable to await its decision.

8.16.4 PREPARING SUBMISSIONS

The success or failure of a bid may depend on whether the OFT or CC or the EC can be convinced either by the bidder not to interfere with the offer, or by the target to prevent the bid. Hence it is vital to prepare high-quality, detailed and well-researched submissions which have a thorough grasp of the economic, industrial, political and commercial implications of the bid and clearly present the relevant case on the effect of the bid on competition in the relevant markets. It is essential therefore to ensure that experts in the firm on merger control issues are brought in to advise at an early stage.

8.17 Common Law

There are a number of areas of common law which will be relevant.

8.17.1 CONTRACT

Clearly the law of contract affects the takeover offer. The principal concern, apart from ensuring that the offer document deals with everything necessary to bring a contract into effect (such as consideration and method of acceptance), is to spell out the conditions to the offer, and avoid any possible misrepresentations in the offer document. These may give rise to a right of action under the Misrepresentation Act 1967 (see **4.2.5.7**). Any failure by the bidder to perform its promises under the offer may also lead to actions for breach of contract.

8.17.2 COMPANY LAW

The duties of the directors at common law, both to company and shareholders, are of course always present in addition to the regulatory requirements imposed by the City Code and the Stock Exchange.

8.17.3 TORT OF NEGLIGENCE

Any misstatements in the course of an offer may be actionable if the maker of the statement owes a duty of care to the person relying on it. This has been covered in detail in the context of statements made in the course of an equity offering (see **4.2.5.7**). It is something which directors, the companies concerned and advisers need to be particularly cautious of.

8.17.4 TORT OF DEFAMATION

This is often a particular concern in takeovers. A takeover will depend for its success on the quality of the case made by the bidder and target respectively in convincing target shareholders either to accept or decline the offer. The bidder will rely on commercial arguments about the strengths it can bring to the target's operation. The target will try to show that it is making a good fist of the task entrusted to it by investors. The arguments may go further than this and seek to stress the negative about the other side. A bidder may wish to show that the target has performed badly because of failures of management. The target may attempt to warn shareholders of the weaknesses of the bidder in some of its ventures, and perhaps the lack of relevant ability to manage the target.

The risk is that in putting the negative forward, both sides may wrongfully blacken the reputation of each other and so be liable in defamation. Any imputation about the management or conduct of the affairs of either target or bidder runs this risk. Defamation proceedings are always best avoided as they are costly, cause significant embarrassment and are notoriously unpredictable in outcome.

If defamation becomes an issue, bear in mind the likely available defences:

(a) Justification, namely, that the defamatory statement is true.

(b) Fair comment, namely, that it is an honest expression of opinion on a matter of public interest.

(c) Qualified privilege, namely, that there was a duty or interest in publishing the statement and an interest in the recipient receiving it. This will generally not apply to statements released to the press nor to the offer document, but it will probably extend to the target's own document to its shareholders, as there is a pre-existing relationship based on a common interest (namely, the affairs of the company).

(d) Innocent dissemination, namely, where the defendant is a mere conduit (such as a distributor or seller) and did not know and had no reason to believe that he was contributing to any defamation.

Privilege will be overridden if the publisher acted with malice, or the statement is republished and republication was either intended or the natural and probable result of the original publication. This suggests that great care should be exercised when releasing any information to journalists.

Injunctive relief for defamatory statements is available but only where the case is clear-cut. If the document appears privileged or there is a defence of justification, an injunction is improbable. Summary relief is available by virtue of the Defamation Act 1996.

It is wise, if the statements being made appear defamatory, to research them thoroughly so that your defences are already prepared, but, better still, find some way of modifying them to avoid the need for legal action.

8.18 Takeover Checklist

This is a checklist in the form of a timetable of a hostile bid made by one Stock Exchange listed company incorporated and based in the UK for another, where the consideration is the bidder's own securities. The intention of the timetable is to alert you to the principal activities of bidder and target at the various stages of the transaction, so that you have a better understanding of what the parties are doing, and what you will therefore need to consider as their legal adviser. It is not comprehensive and should be read in conjunction with the timetable in **8.5.1** which sets out the key moments of the transaction defined in the City Code. The earlier sections of this chapter also expand on many of the activities referred to below.

	BIDDER		TARGET	
Time	*Activity*	*Document*	*Activity*	*Document*
Before announcing offer	Buying shares in target– see **8.5.3.2**		Defence planning, track share purchases, keep up investor relations, prepare defence strategy (e.g., OFT submissions, likely defence circular)	Defence Manual
	Planning structure and finance for the bid			
	Due diligence on target		If offer is imminent, watch general principle 7 and r. 21 – see **8.6.7**	
On and after announcing	Announce	Release press announcement	Communicate terms of bid to target shareholders	Preliminary circular
	Prepare offer	Offer document and listing particulars	Develop defence, influence investors	
	Continue share purchases			
	Begin lobbying regulators	OFT and EC submissions	Begin lobbying regulators	OFT and EC submissions
Posting offer and after	Offer document posted (by 28 days after announcing)	Offer document	Prepare first defence document (by day 0 + 14)	Defence circular
	Continue strategy from earlier			

	BIDDER		TARGET	
Time	*Activity*	*Document*	*Activity*	*Document*
First closing date (0 + 21)	Announce offer has closed or level of acceptances and next closing date	Press announcement		
After first closing date	Continue market purchases		Prepare any new information for shareholders	Day 39 circular
	Telephone campaign		Persuade shareholders to revoke acceptances (after 0 + 42)	
	Final offer (with increase – by 0 + 46)	Final offer document		
Final closing date (by 0 + 60)	Declare offer unconditional as to acceptances or announce failure	Press announcement		
0 + 81	Last date to satisfy all conditions			
0 + 95 and beyond	Settle consideration		Recommend remaining shareholders to accept	
	Exercise compulsory acquisition rights (s. 428)	Offer notice		
	Apply for de-listing of target	De-listing application		

NINE

CORPORATE CREATIVITY

The art of remaining competitive in the commercial world is principally about the readiness to change, to move with new markets, essentially to be a dynamic rather than a static entity. Corporate finance advisers are faced with clients needing new products for new times, and new corporate structures for new situations. This chapter is devoted to reflecting on the principal ways in which these demands manifest themselves in the work coming to lawyers.

Looking first at corporate reconstruction, a company develops over time a structural framework for its operations in the form of holding companies, subsidiaries, groups of associated companies and businesses, and **9.1** looks at some of the considerations relevant when establishing that structure.

But the structure can become rigid and unresponsive to change and market forces. Pressures sometimes emerge for a reorganisation of the status quo, for a variety of reasons (the most important of which are considered later in **9.4**).

9.1 Forming a Corporate Structure

Most large corporate enterprises are structured today around groups of companies. These groups invariably consist of a parent or holding company at the top of a pyramid, and underneath it a myriad of subsidiary companies which it directly or indirectly (through other subsidiaries) controls. Why do these groups exist? Why not instead construct one single entity to encompass all the different subsidiaries?

9.1.1 COMMERCIAL FACTORS

Groups are the usual product of expansion. As businesses develop, they spawn new businesses which operate *de facto* within the existing corporate stucture as separate units until eventually a business decision is taken that they should be represented as individual and legally independent entities. They will have their own management, employees and possibly premises – but of course they will remain linked to the original enterprise. Hence the subsidiary company is born.

Sometimes the same conclusion results from acquisitions or mergers. There may be benefits (particularly the preservation of goodwill) in keeping the name and notional existence of an acquired entity alive in the form of a wholly owned subsidiary rather than subsuming it within a lesser known acquirer.

An amorphous business unit can present problems of management and supervision. A group structure permits flexibility and the use of chains of command to improve efficiency in operational control and reporting.

9.1.2 LEGAL FACTORS

A separate subsidiary company is a different legal entity from the parent company which owns it. Following *Salomon* v *A. Salomon & Co. Ltd* [1897] AC 22, this means that the holding company owners have no legal responsibility for the liabilities accruing in the subsidiary. There are exceptions to this but that is the basic principle. As such, it provides a powerful rationale for enterprises to develop new (and possibly risky) business ideas through the medium of legally unrelated subsidiaries, where liabilities can be left to lie where they fall if the ideas fail.

9.1.3 TAX FACTORS

The tax legislation has developed to offer certain benefits to groups of companies so they can be treated as one entity. But what constitutes a group for tax purposes varies for the different taxes – so you should take care to check whether your group will qualify for the particular benefit sought. These are the most prominent examples of available benefits:

(a) A disposal of an asset between members of the same group does not give rise to a charge for capital gains tax purposes – though if the acquiring company were subsequently to leave the group, there might be a CGT charge on the value of the asset. The basic rule, though, allows assets to be moved around within a tax group with relative freedom. Stamp duty relief is also available for transfers of assets within groups.

(b) Trading losses, certain expenses and capital allowances can be surrendered between members of a group. Companies are often set up in group structures as 'sink companies' into which losses are poured, to be set off against taxable profits or acquired gains so as to minimise the resulting group tax bill.

(c) VAT is not charged on the supplies of goods or services between members of the same group.

These tax factors do not necessarily improve the treatment of a group over that of a single entity, but they at least help to equalise the treatment of groups so that there is no appreciable tax cost in setting up or running a group.

Assuming, then, the advantages of using a group structure, what factors are relevant when setting a group up?

9.2 What is a Subsidiary?

Since the introduction of the Companies Act 1989, there is now a distinction between a subsidiary and a subsidiary undertaking.

A subsidiary is defined in s. 736 Companies Act 1985. This definition holds good for the use of the term 'subsidiary' throughout the Companies Act 1985 (for example, s. 151 of the Act, which makes it unlawful for a company *or its subsidiary* to provide financial assistance for the acquisition of the company's shares).

A subsidiary undertaking is defined in s. 258 Companies Act 1985, and although these two definitions are similar, they differ in some respects.

The subsidiary undertaking is the accounting version of the subsidiary. Where a company has subsidiary undertakings, s. 227 Companies Act 1985 requires the preparation of group accounts, that is, consolidated accounts which deal with the state of affairs, and the profit and loss, of the parent and its *subsidiary undertakings* through a consolidated balance sheet and profit and loss account.

Looking first at s. 736, four conditions will make company X a subsidiary of company Z:

(a) If Z holds a majority of the voting rights in X.

(b) If Z is a member of X and controls a majority of the voting rights on its board.

(c) If Z is a member of X and controls a majority of its voting rights through a shareholders' agreement

(d) If X is a subsidiary of another company (W) and W is itself a subsidiary of Z.

As for s. 258, any of five conditions will make entity X a subsidiary undertaking of parent undertaking Z. The first three of these conditions are identical to (a), (b) and (c) above. The other two are:

(a) If Z is entitled to exercise a dominant influence over X either through a contract or by X's constitution. A dominant influence is exercised where X must act in accordance with Z's instructions.

(b) If Z has a participating interest in X and either actually exercises a dominant influence over it or Z and X are managed on a unified basis. Dominant influence is not the same as for (a): there is in fact no clear definition for it in this context. A participating interest is presumed if Z holds 20 per cent or more of the shares in X – otherwise it depends on whether Z is holding its shares in X on a long-term basis with the purpose of exercising control or influence through its interest.

Two things in conclusion. The first is that the definition of subsidiary undertaking does not just apply to companies. A parent company may have an entity (such as an interest in a joint venture) which is not incorporated which falls within the term 'subsidiary undertaking'. The second is the general point that essentially you should be guided not by majority ownership as your test of whether something is a subsidiary or subsidiary undertaking, but by majority control or influence.

9.3 Why Does It Matter whether a Company is a Subsidiary or Subsidiary Undertaking?

We have already seen why it matters whether or not something is a subsidiary – it then gets caught within the net of various Companies Act 1985 provisions. It may, for instance, be a helpful escape from a s. 151 problem if the intended financial assistance is given not by the company or a subsidiary but by a vehicle which does not fall within the definition of subsidiary. This will involve some creative engineering to manufacture a structure falling outside the s. 736 definition.

The definition of subsidiary undertaking is vital in establishing whether an entity needs to be included in the group's consolidated accounts. Consolidated accounts present financial information about the group's various members as if they were a single unit rather than as separate entities. The detailed requirements are in sch. 4A to the Companies Act 1985.

Before the Companies Act 1989, it was a good deal easier to create vehicles over which a parent company had effective control but which did not technically qualify as a subsidiary because the holding company's ownership rights were limited. The benefits of this to the parent were that these vehicles could be used to borrow money for the group when the group was already close to the borrowing limits in its articles of association. The vehicle, not a subsidiary, and therefore not a member of the group, would not be caught by the limits. This would also not aggravate the group's gearing ratio (its proportion of debt to equity).

Alternatively, a loss-making venture could be passed into such a vehicle so that its losses could not be seen to dent the group's consolidated profit figure.

Essentially, then, it was this process of so-called 'off balance sheet financing' (or 'window dressing', 'massaging the figures' or 'creative accounting', depending on how you looked at it) which the Companies Act 1989 was attempting to control with the introduction of the concept of the subsidiary undertaking.

There is still much creative energy exercised in finding a loophole in the legislation to achieve precisely the same objectives as before 1989, but of course these days it is somewhat harder. There are, though, a number of exemptions under which it is perfectly legitimate to exclude a subsidiary undertaking from consolidation in group accounts (see s. 229 Companies Act 1985).

A company's structure may of course start to present significant difficulties of cost and control – difficulties which the creation of further subsidiaries may not resolve. At this point a reorganisation, if you like, a root-and-branch reform, of the corporate tree may be needed.

9.4 Why Restructure?

There are a host of reasons for reorganising a company's structure. Very often they are quite individual to the specific needs of the relevant company. There are, though, some general themes that we can point to.

9.4.1 VALUE FOR SHAREHOLDERS

This is the prime mover behind any demand for change in the corporate structure, namely, that shareholders are not getting value for money from their shares, given the way the company is currently structured.

9.4.2 TAKEOVER DEFENCE

We saw in **chapter 8** some of the characteristic defence strategies which companies vulnerable to a takeover bid adopt. A change in structure by a company is another such method, particularly if it can anticipate the arguments of a would-be bidder.

9.4.3 RATIONALISATION

A company may need to slim down its operations because of toughening competition, expensive overheads, difficult national economic conditions and so on. This is likely to lead to a disposal programme (see **chapter 5**), which will generate much needed cash-flow, and accompanying this there will often need to be a reorganisation of the company's remaining operations to ensure they can be run more efficiently.

9.4.4 SURVIVAL

If the company mentioned in **9.4.3** is in particularly acute trouble, a reconstruction may effectively be forced on it as the only way of surviving in some shape or form – in other words, the only viable alternative to extinction as a going concern is to indulge in a wholesale reorganisation in the hope that something can be salvaged.

9.4.5 BREAK-UP

To some extent this is related to value for shareholders (**9.4.1**). The 1980s saw companies expanding through acquisition, often accumulating disparate businesses under one roof. The 1990s have seen some of these companies responding to leaner times by returning to their 'core' businesses, and so selling peripheral activities. Often this is also because the stock market tends to place a lower value on a group of companies which bear little relation to each other than on those companies as separate entities. An alternative to a disposal programme in these circumstances is a reorganisation in the form of a break-up of the group into individual enterprises. The 'core' businesses can be prised away from the rest so the company is free to concentrate on these, and the reorganisation carries the added benefit of improving the value of shareholders' investments.

9.4.6 FINANCIAL ENGINEERING

Occasionally companies are in the position that they have accumulated significant reserves of capital which they cannot employ in financing continued growth or expansion through acquisitions. They may consider returning that capital to shareholders through various mechanisms, including a reduction of capital (see **9.7**) or a purchase by the company of its own shares (see **9.8**).

A company may be motivated to begin a process of reconstruction by a number of these factors at the same time. An example in point is the demerger by BAT of two of the businesses under its parental control, Wiggins Teape and Argos. At the time (this was a process which began in 1989), BAT was a large conglomerate with interests in industries as diverse as tobacco, life assurance, insurance, paper and packaging and retailing. BAT was the target of a takeover bid from Hoylake, which eventually failed. One of the key factors behind the bid was the argument that BAT would be worth more to its shareholders in separate entities than as a single unit (see **9.4.5**). In response to that bid (see **9.4.2**), and the investor and market pressure which Hoylake's arguments over shareholder value generated, BAT initiated its demerger programme. In a sense, this was a necessary step to prevent the prospect of another bidder emerging, as well as to satisfy the shareholders' best interests.

Given these pressures exerting themselves on a company, what options exist to carry out a reconstruction? Some of the transactions we have already looked at may achieve some of the things mentioned above – for example, it may be better for a company's break-up plans for it to sell some of its businesses or subsidiaries (see **chapter 5**). Alternatively, the creative mind may prefer to toy with some of the ideas discussed below.

9.5 Demerger

As its name suggests, a demerger is a separation of two or more businesses currently operating under the same corporate roof: it is the opposite of a merger. The important point to note is that it is not simply a case of moving assets or businesses from one part of a company structure to another: it involves actual separation of the ownership of two or more parts of what is currently the same business empire.

The factors discussed in **9.4.1** to **9.4.5** tend to account for the majority of demergers. The commercial demands need to be strong to merit serious consideration being given to a demerger. The reason is cost. A demerger will inevitably eat quite heavily into the available time of hard-pressed managers, and most demergers will carry some sort of tax penalty: they are therefore not the sort of transaction to be undertaken lightly.

Demergers come in a variety of classic forms, which we will look at individually. Before we embark on that, though, we need to consider one common element of all these transactions, which is the preliminary preparation.

9.5.1 PREPARING FOR A DEMERGER

A demerger will involve separating a unified group of businesses or companies. This will require some shifting around of assets and businesses between a company's empire to ensure that, prior to the demerger scheme being announced, whatever is to be demerged has already been carved out of the existing corporate structure. The typical problem is that the business to be demerged is currently carried on, to a greater or lesser extent, by a number of subsidiaries, so that it needs to be brought together in one subsidiary and other aspects of that subsidiary's business taken elsewhere in the group.

In the ensuing examples, the subsidiary to be demerged is D, and its parent company (which wholly owns it) is P.

9.5.2 DIVIDEND IN KIND (OTHERWISE KNOWN AS A DIVIDEND *IN SPECIE*)

This is the simplest route (**figure. 9.1**). Currently, shareholders in P (S) have no direct shareholding interest in D. Under the dividend in kind method, shareholders in P receive shares in D by way of a dividend from P. The result is that shareholders in P now also have a direct shareholding stake in D, and D is no longer a wholly owned subsidiary of P at all. To achieve this:

(a) there needs to be power in P's articles to pay a dividend in kind to its shareholders, and

(b) P needs to have enough distributable reserves in its accounts to cover the value of D.

There is a major disadvantage. The dividend is a disposal by P for tax purposes and so will be subject to a capital gains tax charge. Furthermore, the dividend will be treated as taxable income in the hands of the shareholders (though they will qualify for a tax credit). The method is therefore expensive unless the gain is likely to be minimal.

9.5.3 THREE-CORNERED DEMERGER BY WAY OF DIVIDEND IN KIND

See **figure 9.2**. This is another dividend in kind route, but the differences avoid the tax disadvantages.

P sets up a new company (in this example referred to as Newco), to which it transfers the shares it holds in D. P meanwhile declares a dividend to its shareholders to be satisfied by Newco (currently its subsidiary) issuing shares in itself to P's shareholders. The result is that P's shareholders (S) now hold shares in P and Newco, and Newco is no longer a subsidiary of P.

The benefit of this is that the Inland Revenue treat this dividend in kind as an exempt distribution, provided various other conditions are satisfied, so that P is not liable to CGT on the disposal of D to Newco and the new shares received by P's shareholders in Newco are not treated as taxable income. P still has to have power in its articles to pay a dividend in kind to its shareholders, and have enough distributable reserves in its accounts to cover the value of D, but at least the tax problems of the first method are overcome.

Figure 9.1 Demerger – dividend in kind

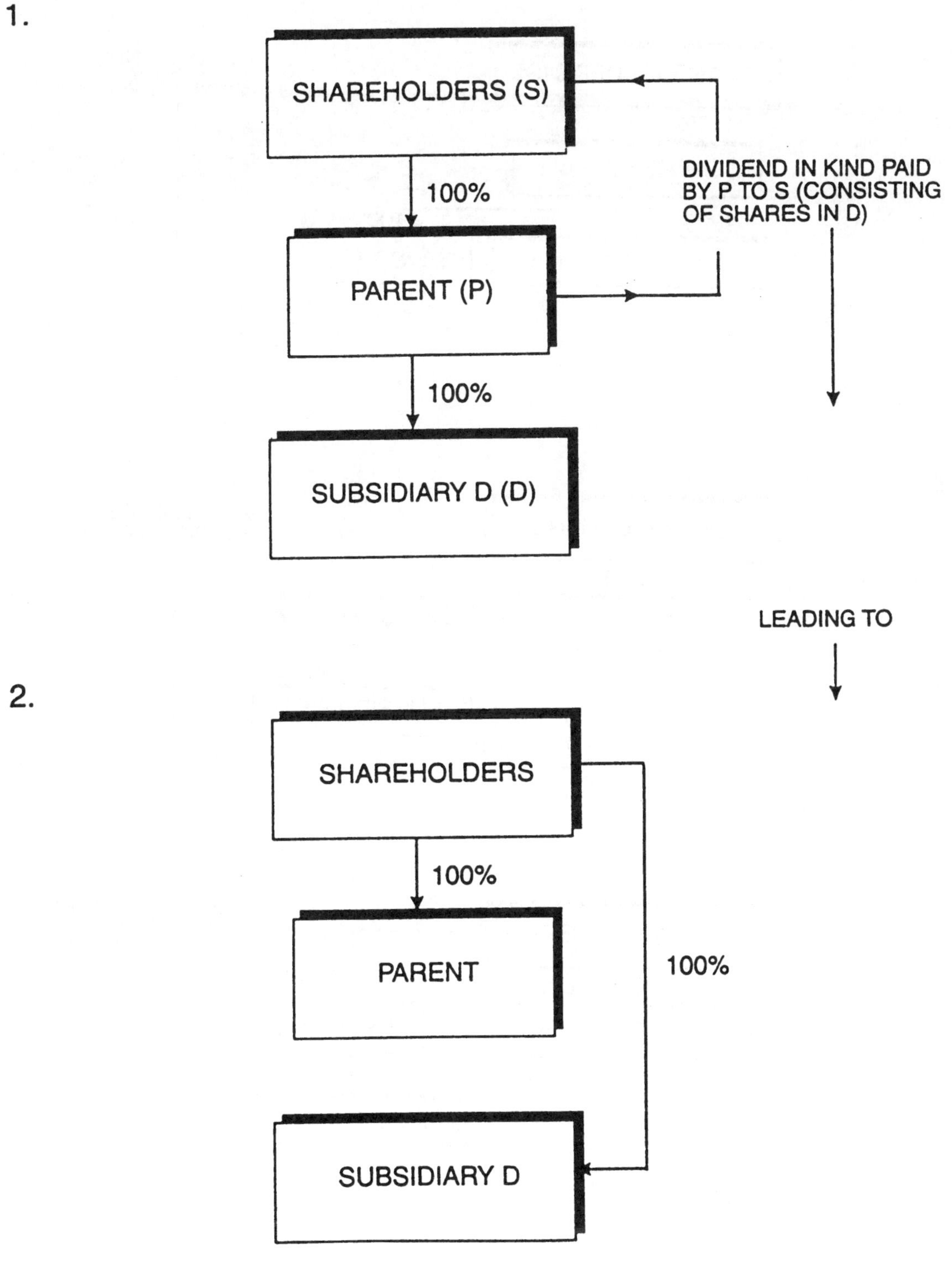

Figure 9.2 Demerger – three-cornered

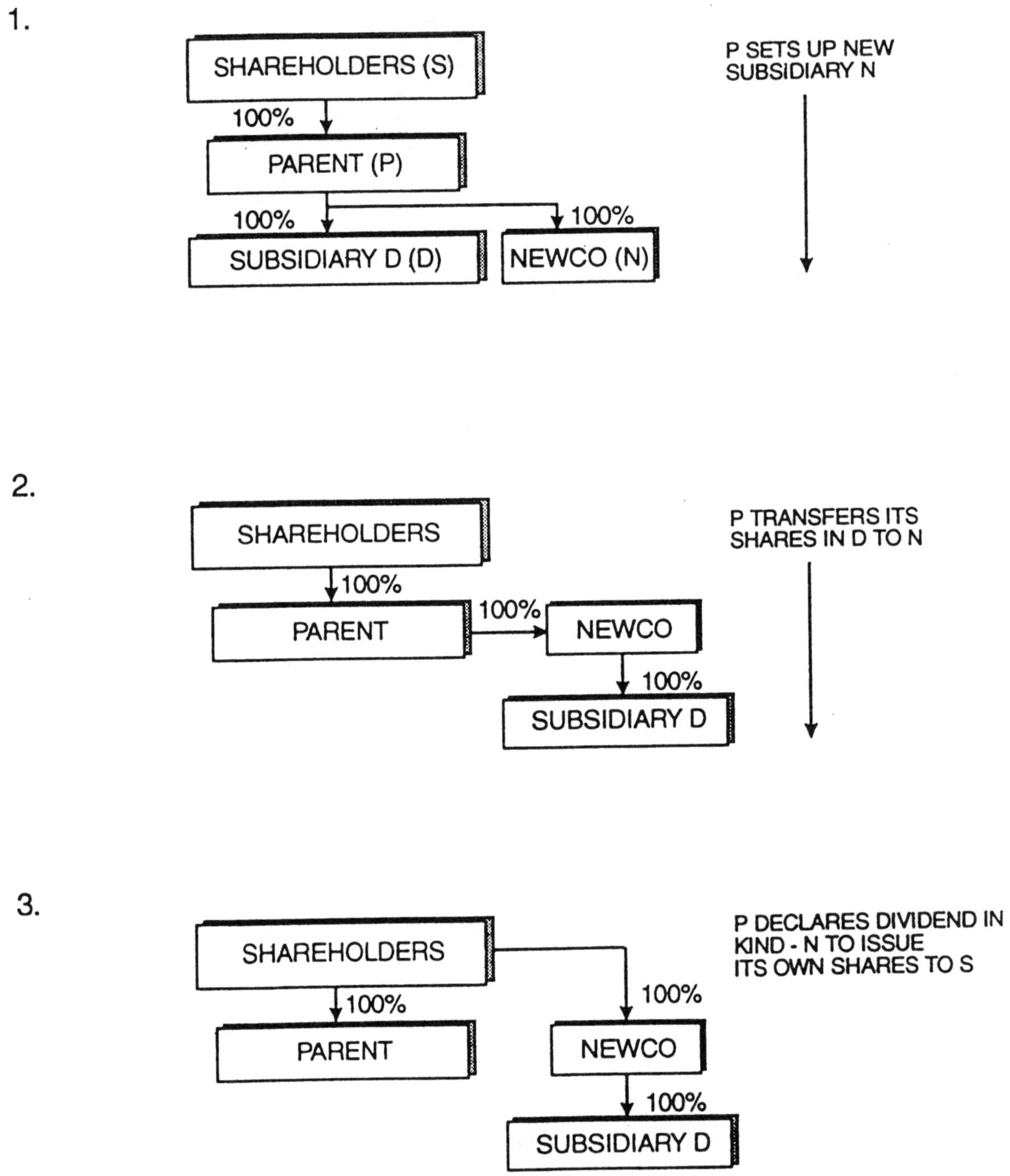

9.5.4 SCHEME OF RECONSTRUCTION

See **figure 9.3**. This is a method available under s. 110 Insolvency Act 1986.

P is liquidated. Its assets are transferred to two or more newly formed companies (Newco 1 and Newco 2 for these purposes). Newco 1 and Newco 2 then issue shares in themselves to P's shareholders, which satisfies their rights in the liquidation. P's shareholders therefore end up with shares in both Newco 1 and Newco 2 and lose their interest in P altogether.

This requires a special resolution of the shareholders in P to liquidate the company and authorise the transfer of P's business and assets to Newco 1 and Newco 2.

The principal benefit under the scheme is that, because it is not being effected by way of dividend, it is not necessary to have sufficient distributable profits available in P's old accounts to cover the stated value of the two new companies.

The main difficulty with this route is that dissenting shareholders can insist on a cash payment under s. 111 Insolvency Act 1986 in lieu of receiving shares in Newco 1 and Newco 2. In addition, the directors have to make a statutory declaration of solvency, which may give rise to personal liability on their behalf if it turns out to be untrue.

The tax implications are minimised as there is no capital gains tax charge on the disposal of the business and assets to the Newcos, and distribution of the Newco shares is not treated as taxable income in the hands of the shareholders.

9.5.5 SCHEME OF ARRANGEMENT

We have already encountered this in the context of public company takeovers (see **8.6.2.2**): perversely, it is a mechanism equally at home for demergers as well as mergers. It is a route governed by s. 425 Companies Act 1985. What is needed is a scheme – and the benefit of this method is that it offers great flexibility in the nature of the precise scheme. Usually, in the context of a demerger, the scheme will be along the lines of a scheme of reconstruction, namely forming two new companies out of one old one and issuing shares in the new companies to the shareholders in exchange for the cancellation of their existing shares in the old company.

The disadvantages are that shareholders need to approve the scheme by a majority in number voting at a general meeting and representing 75 per cent of the voting rights, the scheme needs to be accepted by the court, which can take time and is not something which can be guaranteed, and there may be tax liabilities otherwise avoided under the three-cornered demerger or the scheme of reconstruction – for instance, the issue of new shares to the shareholders may be treated as taxable income in their hands.

The scheme can be combined with some of the other methods (particularly the scheme of reconstruction under s. 110 Insolvency Act 1986) and in this way attract the tax benefits it will otherwise not qualify for.

9.5.6 PERVASIVE CONSIDERATIONS

In all these transactions, consider the following issues carefully in addition to the specific requirements of the particular scheme:

(a) The transaction may not be a disposal for CGT purposes (for example, if it is an exempt distribution under a three-cornered demerger) but it may nevertheless be regarded as a transaction under The Listing Rules (see **5.6.4**). This would require (depending on the relative scale of the new company to be established) a possible circular to shareholders or their approval if the company is listed on the Stock Exchange or quoted on the AIM.

Figure 9.3 Demerger – scheme of reconstruction

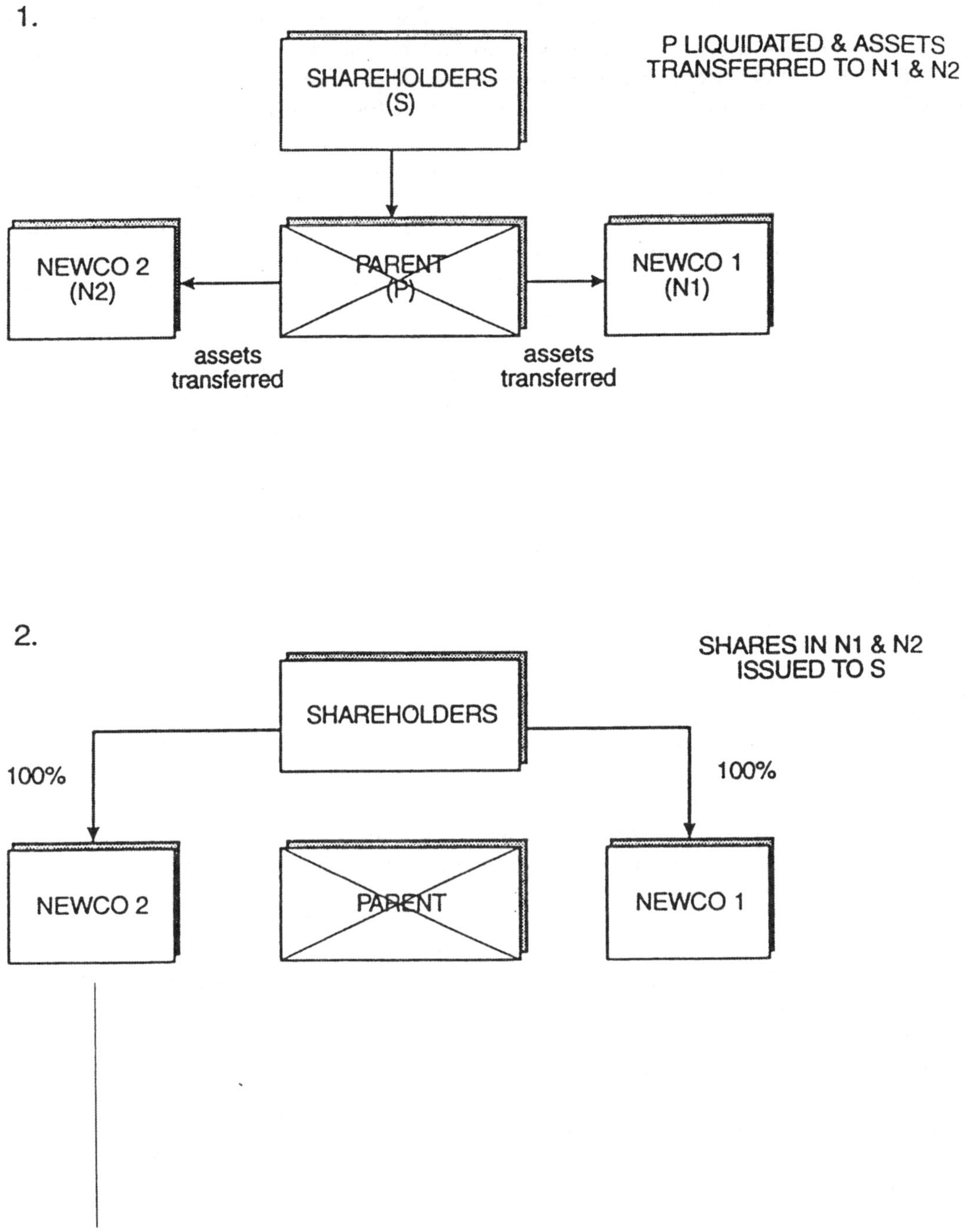

(b) If the parent company's share price is publicly quoted on either the Stock Exchange or the AIM and the dividend *in specie* route is used, the transfer of assets to the new company will cause the parent's share price to drop, as its value decreases. For the shareholders to feel as though they have received anything of value out of the demerger, the new company's shares will also need to be quoted on the same exchange so that the loss of value on their old shares is compensated by a marketable interest in the new company. Hence a demerger may also be accompanied by an application for admission to listing on the London Stock Exchange, or for a quotation on the AIM, of the new company's shares, and the consequent production of listing particulars or a prospectus (see **4.2** and **4.3**).

9.5.7 CONCLUSION

The dividend *in specie* routes are appropriate where the intention is to keep the existing parent company and create a new company alongside it in which the parent's shareholders also hold shares. The three-cornered demerger is the obvious procedure to select where the tax disadvantages of the simpler dividend in kind method are too great.

The scheme of reconstruction or scheme of arrangement are ideal where the intention is to create two or more new companies out of the existing parent and then remove the parent altogether. The reconstruction route is more tax-efficient and speedier but could be problematic where there are strong dissenting minorities or the company's future solvency is questionable.

It really is a question of 'horses for courses': it depends on your particular circumstances which route you would prefer to go.

9.6 Schemes of Arrangement under Section 425 Companies Act 1985

We have now looked at these in the context of mergers and demergers (see **8.6.2.2** and **9.5.5**). They are inherently flexible creatures available for use for any reorganisation, whether or not amounting to a demerger. An illustration would be changes to a company's capital structure including the alteration of special rights to shares, amendment of the terms of any loan or debt instruments or conversion of a class of shares from, for instance, ordinary irredeemable shares to redeemable preference shares. It is important to bear in mind, in this context, that s. 425 requires a 75 per cent majority in number of shareholders or holders of the appropriate class representing 75 per cent of the relevant voting rights to approve the scheme and make it binding on all.

A scheme can also be used for debt–equity swaps, where creditors substitute their secured debt holdings in a company for ordinary shares. This may be proposed as a way of relieving the debt burden on a company where this threatens to plunge it into insolvent liquidation: it will of course depend on agreement in this case of 75 per cent in value of the company's affected creditors and a majority in number voting at a general meeting.

9.7 Reductions of Capital

Reductions of capital by companies are permitted by s. 135 Companies Act 1985 provided there is authority in the articles, confirmation from the court in its role as protector of creditors, and approval from the shareholders by special resolution.

Why might a company contemplate such a method of reconstruction?

9.7.1 EXCESS OF WANTS

This means that the company is financially quite healthy but has more capital than it knows what to do with, for example, where the company has available cash reserves which are sitting idle. They can then be applied to repay shareholders their capital contributions and reduce the share capital account accordingly (see also **9.8** on purchases of shares).

9.7.2 CANCELLING LOST CAPITAL

A reduction of capital may be necessary where the company's financial position is unhealthy and its share capital no longer represents available assets but paints a misleading picture to shareholders of what is actually present to support their investment in the company. An example is a company with net assets significantly lower than the value of the share capital account. The share capital is then reduced to the level of the assets valuation. The court will usually be unwilling to confirm the reduction of capital in these circumstances unless it can be proved that the assets have declined to the stated value, so evidence of this will be needed. The court will also generally require an undertaking from the company that if any assets sold realise more than this stated value, the consequential profit shall be treated as capital for the benefit of the creditors.

9.7.3 ELIMINATION OF GOODWILL ARISING ON AN ACQUISITION

We have seen in **chapter 8** that goodwill arising on an acquisition must be written off against reserves immediately or through the profit and loss account over a number of years (see **8.6.3.6**). If the decision is taken to write the goodwill off straightaway, available share capital may be reduced by the same amount as represents the goodwill, taken to a reserve and then written off against the stated goodwill. They cancel each other out and both items are eliminated from the balance sheet. It is not just the share capital account which can be used for this: we saw in **8.6.3.7** that a merger reserve created as a result of the availability of merger relief under s. 131 Companies Act 1985 could also be used.

9.7.4 SHARES AT A DISCOUNT

Section 100 Companies Act 1985 prevents the issue of shares at a discount to their nominal value. If the market value of a company's shares is lower than their nominal value, a further issue of shares is impossible: you cannot realistically expect investors to subscribe new shares at a price higher than the investors can currently buy them in the market. One solution is to reduce share capital by reducing the nominal value of the shares to below market value – then a new issue can be made at a discount to market value but not nominal value.

9.7.5 REDENOMINATION OF SHARE CAPITAL INTO ANOTHER CURRENCY

If a company is changing the currency in which its capital is denominated, the existing share capital account must be extinguished, and a reserve established with the capital. This is converted to the new currency at the appropriate exchange rate and then used to pay up shares in the new currency to the existing shareholders. The share capital account is then restored, now denominated in the new currency. Consequently no capital is actually lost.

9.7.6 WHAT IS THE ROLE OF THE COURT IN THESE SITUATIONS?

The court's principal function in a reduction is to ensure that the interests of creditors are protected. If the reduction involves repaying capital to shareholders, creditors are entitled to object. A court will only confirm the reduction if it is satisfied that creditors are safeguarded. This will usually require some sort of a third-party guarantee (such as a bank guarantee) to pay the debts the company does not discharge, or evidence that the company's assets are still sufficient to meet the combined effect of its liabilities, the repayment to shareholders and its outstanding share capital. The lawyer's role in this kind of transaction, apart from ensuring the requirements of s. 135 are satisfied, will therefore be to make out a satisfactory case to the court that the company's creditors will not be left high and dry by the reduction.

9.8 Redemptions and Purchases of Shares

You are aware of the right conferred upon companies by statute to redeem and purchase their own shares (ss. 159–181 Companies Act 1985). We will look briefly at the rationale for such transactions as one technique for reorganising a company, and examine also some of the legal and practical issues which arise.

9.8.1 WHAT ARE THEY?

What do redemptions and purchases actually involve? Simply put, the company is buying back from its own shareholders the shares it has issued to them. The principal difference between a redemption and a purchase is that a redemption refers to a buy-back of shares which were issued as redeemable, and a purchase refers to the acquisition of any shares.

Purchase or redemption will generally be at a price which is at or close to market value. The company will therefore generally be paying a premium to nominal value to the shareholders to buy back the shares: hence it is not simply a question of finding the amount to cover the value of the shares as stated in the share capital account.

When the shares have been bought back, the shares will be cancelled and the share capital reduced by the amount of the nominal value of the shares acquired.

9.8.2 WHY DO THEM?

Private companies are generally motivated by considerations such as the desire to buy out a dissenting or minority shareholder, or to develop a 'market' for their shares (which can otherwise not be traded publicly): if the company is prepared to buy back shares, it enables shareholders to realise their investment and encourages new shareholders to invest.

Public companies' reasons tend to flow from the performance of their share price in the market (whether traded on the Stock Exchange or the AIM):

(a) A buy-back of shares restricts the supply of shares in the market relative to demand, and so tends to increase the price of those shares remaining; this enhanced value may be particularly useful if the company uses or intends to use its own securities to finance an acquisition (it has to issue fewer of the securities to obtain the same value).

(b) Because a buy-back reduces the number of shares in existence, it will lead to an increase in earnings per share, which is much beloved by market analysts as a benchmark against which to measure the comparative performance of companies.

(c) When companies find that their shares trade at a discount to net asset value, a buy-back of shares enhances the asset value per share of the shares left.

(d) A buy-back concentrates more voting control in known hands: provided these are safe, it will therefore help as a long-term defence strategy against unwelcome takeover bids.

Hence, both private and public companies can find buy-backs helpful in certain contexts. Sometimes, companies do not have a choice about whether or not to launch a buy-back. Some redeemable shares, under their terms, must be redeemed on a certain date. Some convertible securities are converted by being redeemed and cancelled first, before the appropriate number of ordinary shares are then issued to the holders of the original securities.

9.8.3 HOW DO YOU GO ABOUT A BUY-BACK?

The Companies Act 1985 (ss. 159 and 162) requires redemptions and purchases by private and public companies to be authorised in the articles, the shares to be fully paid up, and the cost of buying the shares to be paid out of distributable profits or the proceeds of an issue of new shares. Additionally, purchases under s. 162 must be approved by resolution of the shareholders. If the purchase is to be through the stock market (public companies only), a majority of shareholders in general meeting must approve; if the purchase is private (for example, a contractual deal with a particular shareholder), 75 per cent of shareholders in general meeting must approve.

A private company may also purchase shares out of capital (s. 171 Companies Act 1985). This involves an actual reduction of share capital – unlike buy-backs under ss. 159 and 162. Accordingly, the safeguards are more stringent, including the need for a special resolution, a statutory declaration of solvency from the directors and a report from the auditors confirming the purchase. Creditors additionally can object to the court to prohibit the payment.

The one further requirement is to set up a capital redemption reserve. An amount equal to the nominal value of the shares bought back must be attributed to this account, which is a capital reserve not available for distribution and so provides some financial security for creditors that the company is still properly capitalised. Money comes out of distributable profits and in reality is given to shareholders to buy the shares back. In accounting terms, that part of the money attributable to the excess over the shares' nominal value is a premium lost to the company, but the nominal value is treated as being transferred from share capital account (when the shares are cancelled) into the capital redemption reserve. Essentially an element of distributable profits is therefore being capitalised.

The accountants will advise the company on the accounting aspects described here: your role as the lawyer will be preparation of the appropriate resolutions, purchase contracts (if it is a private deal), and, of course, to check compliance with the articles and the Companies Act 1985.

9.8.4 UKLA REQUIREMENTS FOR LISTED COMPANY BUY-BACKS

These are set out in ch. 15 of The Listing Rules. Of course they apply only to companies with securities listed on the Official List. In summary, the most important obligations are:

(a) to notify the Company Announcements Office of the Stock Exchange of any purchase of listed equity securities as soon as possible after the buy-back (see The Listing Rules, para. 15.9 for the precise timing required);

(b) not to make a purchase at times when a director of the company would be unable to deal under the Model Code (LR, para. 15.1);

(c) where the purchase is of more than 15 per cent of the share capital of the company, to send shareholders a circular containing the information required by LR, paras 15.4 to 15.5; where more than 15 per cent is bought back in a year, the purchase has to be by way of a tender or partial offer made to all shareholders so they all have the right to participate, LR, para. 15.7 (see **8.6.2.4**).

9.8.5 TAX ON BUY-BACKS

If shareholders receive more than the nominal value of the shares in the buy-back, the excess over the nominal value (the premium) is treated as a distribution.

We have looked so far in this chapter at some of the more common forms of corporate reconstruction or reorganisation which may help a company respond to changing times and new demands. It is important always to bear in mind that all the transactions we look at in this book are forms of corporate reconstruction, whether it be a disposal, a merger, an acquisition, a management buy-out, a refinancing, a flotation, or taking the company private. There may be a number of different solutions to your client's longer term needs, so do not assume that only the methods of reconstruction described in this chapter are appropriate.

Some of the methods of reconstruction dealt with here may be particularly appropriate when a company is running into trouble: as we have seen, demergers and schemes of arrangement may be a way of keeping the company alive. We will look later at some of the other methods and techniques open to companies to help them survive – and what happens if they do not succeed.

First, though, one other aspect of corporate creativity: an alternative form of dividend.

9.9 Scrip Dividends

You will encounter these quite commonly with publicly traded companies. The traditional dividend is of course a cash payment. A scrip dividend offers shareholders a dividend by way of new shares in the company rather than cash. They choose which to take.

The company benefits from a scrip dividend as it holds on to its cash reserves (and so reduces the level of borrowings necessary). The shareholders increase their shareholding in the company at a cheaper cost than buying shares in the market (there are no broker's fees or stamp duty to pay), and this may increase their loyalty.

The main disadvantage is that a scrip dividend carries a relatively high administration cost: all shareholders need to be told about it, but generally only a small percentage of them take up the offer.

What do you need to think about if a company is interested in introducing this option for its shareholders?

(a) If the company is listed on the Official List, the UKLA requires that the company must explain the scrip dividend scheme to shareholders in the form of a circular (usually sent with the annual report and accounts). The shareholder must positively elect for a scrip dividend. Other contents requirements for the circular are contained in LR, para. 14.12.

(b) Do not forget that the company must have sufficient authorised share capital to meet the scrip dividend requirements, and directors' authority to allot the shares under s. 80 Companies Act 1985. The articles must also permit the scheme.

So, here you have a number of ideas in various contexts which may prove useful for companies dealing with changing markets and different demands. Your clients operate in a creative environment. They will expect similar standards from their corporate finance advisers.

TEN

COMPANY RESCUES AND FAILURES

This chapter looks in brief at what could be, and for some companies actually is, their own final chapter, and how they seek either to go on to write another volume or to bring their story cleanly to an end.

The first thing to make clear about this chapter is that it contains very little hard law. Company rescues tend to be a case of making the best of a difficult position, and so require expertise in the art of the possible. The skills of pragmatism are therefore paramount.

10.1 Circumstances of Financial Difficulty

These are often plain to see. Falling profits, falling asset values, excessive borrowing, boardroom tension – these are the stuff of which future company rescues are made. It is vital to understand the background to your client's problem to recommend the appropriate response. There is usually one phenomenon which brings about the inevitability of a corporate rescue plan – cash, or rather, the lack of it. Without ready cash-flow or the prospect of it, a company is unable to meet the interest obligations on its loans, to pay its staff or creditors, or to provide working capital for any corporate activity. Difficulties with cash-flow are the surest sign of hard times ahead.

10.2 Where Do You Begin?

Let us assume your client has a tight cash-flow position. The chances are he has approached you because he is on the verge of defaulting on the interest repayment covenants in his borrowing facilities and he realises something has to be done urgently or else the banks will call in the loans when the company defaults. Do you immediately recommend winding the company up? If not, what else do you have up your sleeve? Administrative receivership (i.e., calling in the bank's receivers to manage and sell off the assets which they have charged)? Or administration (appointing a company doctor to preserve what he can of the business)?

Of course, these may be appropriate, depending on the gravity of the client's cash crisis. They are, though, likely to be the measures of last resort, only to be employed when all else has failed.

The only way you can judge this is to get some information about the company's financial position. The first step, therefore (and you can usually expect your client to have initiated this before he speaks to you), is to instruct accountants, supported as necessary by you and other professionals (such as asset valuers like property surveyors), to produce some facts and figures about the company and give an idea of the prospects of recovery.

Let us look at what that accountants' report might find and what solutions therefore suggest themselves.

10.3 Possible Rescue Plans

10.3.1 NEGOTIATING WITH THE LENDERS

As default under the company's borrowing facilities is usually only a matter of time, and the company is hard-pressed to find any more cash, the company is forced to negotiate its financial future with its banks. This is both to improve the current state of its debt financing arrangements and also to see if further finance is available.

The banks will generally be very reluctant to commit new resources to an enterprise which is already ailing: it may literally be a case of throwing good money after bad. They may, however, be more cooperative about restructuring existing finance to give the company some breathing-space. Before you can begin to discuss this in earnest, though, bear in mind the following about these negotiations:

(a) They are likely to be protracted, particularly if there are a number of banks and creditors involved, and one thing the company will not have much of is time. It is therefore generally a critical first step when opening these negotiations to reach a 'standstill agreement' with the banks, under which they continue to provide essential banking facilities for a limited period of time (such as a month) while a longer term settlement or plan is being arranged. This will facilitate the company's short-term survival.

(b) Where a company has a number of borrowing facilities in existence, which is generally the case, it is pointless to try to reach agreement with the banks separately. The facilities are legally interrelated in that default under one loan will generally be a cross-default under all other loans. It therefore only requires one bank to take a different view for the company to be in serious trouble. Much the better approach is to negotiate collectively with the banks and get them to understand that they all face the same problem – namely, that they will not get very much of their lending investment out of the company if they do not cooperate to bring about its recovery (in practice often true where the company is highly geared). Unanimous support is an essential precondition to the company's survival and so is in their own interests. This is also an approach which the Bank of England advocates. It has issued guidelines suggesting that where negotiations with a number of banks are underway simultaneously, a lead bank be appointed to keep all lenders informed of developments. This also assists negotiations as otherwise the company is faced with a barrage of banking officials around the table.

So, assuming you have a standstill agreement in place and the banks are in agreement about what action to take, what possibilities exist when restructuring existing debt finance?

(a) Rescheduling (i.e., deferring) capital repayments under the loans, so that only the interest obligation is serviced in the short term.

(b) Extend the period of repayment of the loan (the interest and the principal) – obviously this reduces the size of each instalment.

(c) Convert some debt to equity to reduce the size of the company's debt mountain. This is becoming more common, but banks are generally unimpressed by this idea, unless every other avenue has been exhausted, simply because equity is of course a much riskier investment than a loan.

10.3.2 NEW EQUITY

The other method of raising additional finance is to tap the equity markets. There are only two options: either a rights issue or a placing of shares with institutions (see **3.6.4** and **3.5.6**). Against a background of financial instability, both will be difficult. The rights issue (in this context sometimes referred to as a 'rescue rights' issue) is the more likely, but suffers from two chief problems.

The first is that the rights issue circular has to make full disclosure of the company's current and prospective financial position (this is required by s. 146 Financial Services Act 1986, if the company is listed on the Official List – see **4.2.5.6**). This is not only likely to be embarrassing; it may deter anyone from investing. The circular will also have to tell a story, that is, what future the company sees and how it plans to use the money investors provide. It may be very hard to construct anything realistic.

The second is that, for much the same reasons as it will prove hard to attract investors in new equity in the company, it may be very difficult to persuade a merchant bank to underwrite an issue with the possible prospect of ending up with a huge volume of shares in a company with little future. The bank will want to hear a story which sounds credible.

10.3.3 NEW MANAGERS

Particularly where there have been boardroom difficulties, replacing existing directors, or at least the chief executive, may be beneficial. For a start, it promises a fresh approach and possibly new ideas to solve the crisis. Second, it gives the impression to lenders and investors alike that the company is prepared to be radical in tackling its problems, and this may enhance confidence in its future. Third, if the new managers have experience of handling similar crises elsewhere, this may be precisely the expertise needed. You may find you are approached for advice at such times on how to remove an unwanted director on a board.

10.3.4 DISPOSAL PROGRAMME

The only other realistic method of raising the much-needed cash quickly is to sell assets or subsidiaries. The disposals will have to be speedy and the price will probably have to be dropped (the emergency nature of such disposals means they are often referred to as 'fire sales'). Often the only bidder likely to appear for certain businesses or companies is the existing managers, simply because, of all likely contenders, they have a real interest in the survival of the enterprise. Hence an MBO (see **chapter 7**) is a likely outcome to one of these fire sales.

It will usually be the case that a combination of such solutions is adopted – for instance, that the banks agree to a standstill and reschedule the capital repayments on their loans in return for an undertaking that the company will initiate a disposal programme to generate cash to start repaying its debts again.

10.3.5 LAST RESORT

Sometimes, the accountants' report reveals a financial crisis which is so serious that none of the solutions discussed so far is at all realistic, and the only question is how best to salvage something from the wreckage. It is in these circumstances that insolvent liquidation, administrative receivership and administration enter the fray. These have been covered already in the *Business Law Guide* and you should refer to it for further guidance on their use. The point to note here is that generally these are options which are considered seriously only once everything else has been dismissed, or has been tried and found wanting. The main reason for this is that all three options hand the company's fate over to someone else – respectively, the liquidator and the court, the banks and their receivers, or the administrator. This is an outcome unlikely to be welcomed around the boardroom table – that is, unless there is no choice.

10.4 Legal Issues

10.4.1 ADVISING THE DIRECTORS

The most common problem you are likely to be faced with in this kind of situation is advising the directors and other parties on their most appropriate course of conduct. You will already be aware of the directors' position at common law and under statute when the company is in serious financial trouble. They have their duties at common law to act in the best interests of the company, the shareholders and the creditors and to act with reasonable care and skill. Section 214 Insolvency Act 1986 exposes directors to potential liabilities if they fail to take every step to minimise creditors' losses when there is no reasonable prospect of avoiding insolvent liquidation (wrongful trading). The banks and other professional advisers will be concerned about s. 214 too because of the risk that they will be regarded as 'shadow directors'. So what should they all do when the financial crisis arrives?

The first requirement is to decide whether the company can realistically survive – hence reinforcing, from a legal point of view, the practical necessity for a report on the company's finances from the accountants.

Let us assume the accountants are negative about the company's long-term prospects. The temptation for the directors is to walk away from the company while they still can, in the hope that their potential liability will then cease. Resignation, however, is not appropriate: this is hardly taking every step to minimise creditors' losses. The directors will have to stay on board and work on a strategy (whether survival or one of those described in **10.3.5**) which safeguards the creditors' position – which is why negotiating with the banks, as the most significant of the company's creditors, is also vital from a legal point of view.

As far as the banks and other professional advisers are concerned, to minimise any risk of 'shadow director' status, the key is to avoid being implicated in whatever decisions are made. This is quite different from not getting involved at all. A bank or other professional (such as an accountant or solicitor) will be negligent if it does not give advice in its professional capacity. It will stand every chance of wrongful trading liability if, on the other hand, it goes beyond advising and participates in the deliberations of the board. So, the banks and other professionals should stick to advice and consultation and avoid any inference that they have been managing the company's business. It would be sensible for the advisers, so far as it is possible, to ensure that any board minutes of the company reflect this.

10.4.2 SECTION 142 COMPANIES ACT 1985

This only applies to public companies. A public company whose net assets fall to half of its share capital must call a shareholders' meeting to consider what to do. Failure to do so is an offence.

10.4.3 FALSE MARKETS

Listed companies and those admitted to the AIM, under their Continuing Obligations, must avoid creating a false market in their securities. Section 47(1) FS Act makes it an offence to induce a person to acquire or dispose of investments by intentionally or recklessly making misleading, false or deceptive statements, promises or forecasts or dishonestly concealing material facts. Section 47(2) makes it an offence to do any act or engage in any course of conduct which creates a false or misleading impression about the market in an investment if the intention is to create that impression and so induce someone to buy or sell that investment.

So, a decision to defer telling investors about the state of the company's financial position so as not to panic them is in fact deliberately creating (albeit temporarily) a misleading impression and is certainly creating a false market. Taken together, then, these provisions effectively require the prompt and full disclosure of information regarding the company's position to the stock market and the world at large as soon as something coherent can be said – even if it is simply a holding statement. The usual language which gives the appropriate signals to the market is 'The company is in discussion with its bankers', although that may not always be sufficient.

There will of course always be a string of other legal issues to address – fraudulent trading, transfers at an undervalue where the company enters on a disposal programme, and so on. Those above are probably the most important. If you cannot help a company to survive, at least make sure it and its directors stay within the law.

ELEVEN

CASE STUDY

In this chapter, we look at two example transactions which illustrate some of the themes pursued in this book. These case studies do not look at the tax implications of these transactions, and you will need to consider these carefully when advising.

11.1 Acton plc

Acton plc has its ordinary shares listed and traded on the London Stock Exchange. Your firm acts for Acton plc. Three of its eight directors, Messrs Garden, Crescent and Lane, who hold 10 per cent of the company's ordinary shares, want to buy the rest of it, de-list the company and take it back into their own private hands. They say they have talked to Avenue Bank, which is prepared to provide the financial backing. They need your advice on how to proceed.

(a) Is this a preposterous idea which cannot be done? Why might they want to do it?

(b) Can you act?

(c) How would such a transaction be structured? What choices are there?

(d) What problems do you foresee? How can they be overcome?

(e) What documents would you expect to be necessary?

(f) What should the three directors do next?

Let us look in brief at how you might deal with the questions posed.

11.1.1 IS THIS A PREPOSTEROUS IDEA WHICH CANNOT BE DONE? WHY MIGHT THEY WANT TO DO IT?

This process of taking a company into private hands is the reverse of offering shares in a company to the public. A few individuals end up owning the shares previously held by the public. The de-listing this involves simply means the company is no longer officially listed or dealt in on the AIM (depending on which it is).

Why might this prove attractive? There are a number of factors:

(a) The benefits of public ownership and trading of a company's securities bring with them the disadvantage of onerous disclosure obligations and restricted freedom of movement under The Listing Rules. There are also the costs (both financial and in terms of management time) of maintaining a listing, and keeping institutional investors, analysts and brokers regularly informed of the company's financial and trading progress and future.

(b) Some companies find the stock market undervalues their traded securities relative to the net worth of their assets. This may be because the company operates in a number of different sectors of the market and is valued on the basis that the whole is worth less than the sum of the parts. Alternatively the market may not find the future trading prospects of the company as attractive as the company feels they are. This may also be costly for the company if it plans to use its securities as consideration in acquisitions. Private ownership means that the value placed by the market on the securities is irrelevant.

(c) The market tends to place a premium on short-term qualities of a company's performance, such as dividend pay-outs, and has less regard for its longer term investment strategy. The company itself may then find it is subject to criticism for reinvesting substantial amounts of its profits rather than distributing them to shareholders. If it is determined to stick by its strategy, and the market continues to dislike this, the only long-term solution may be a parting of the ways.

Whatever the reason, there have been a number of such transactions in recent years.

11.1.2 CAN YOU ACT?

Those who lead a bid to take the company private tend to be the company's directors (as here), sometimes in conjunction with its executive managers. Of course, their interests may not be the same as the company's. The company embraces not just the directors but the existing shareholders, employees and creditors. Solicitors who act for the company may therefore face a possible conflict of interests if they are asked to represent the directors here. The directors may therefore have to be told to seek their own independent legal advice.

The directors need always to be careful in such situations. Their duty of course is to the company (including all those parties mentioned above), and so any proposal on their part to take the company into their own hands must be based on their reasonable estimate not simply of their own best interests but also those of the company. Further, should they stand to profit from the transaction, they should be even more careful as any profits resulting from directors putting their own interests before their duty to the company belong to the company.

If the company and directors are to seek separate advice, who is then left to 'steer the ship' for the company? The independent and usually non-executive directors play a vital role here in representing the company's interests and consulting advisers. The Cadbury Code requires there to be a procedure under which such directors can obtain advice at the company's expense in such circumstances (see **2.2.3.1**).

11.1.3 HOW WOULD SUCH A TRANSACTION BE STRUCTURED? WHAT CHOICES ARE THERE?

Those wanting to take the company private are essentially proposing to buy a public company from its existing shareholders. As we saw in **chapter 8**, this will have to be done by way of a takeover offer. As discussed in **8.6.2**, there are a number of ways of doing this:

11.1.3.1 By general offer under the City Code on Takeovers and Mergers

This of course brings with it the City Code Rules (see **8.8**). In this case, the offer can be made by the directors acting as a consortium or by a company which they form (X Ltd) and in which they hold all the shares. In both cases, the objective will be to offer cash so that the existing shareholders are all bought out. Once all the target shares are acquired (assuming the offer is a success), the public company will be re-registered as a private company.

One benefit of the general offer is that, if the target shareholders acquiesce in it, it is likely to be concluded by the first closing date, which is 21 days after the offer document is posted. This is likely to be a much quicker timetable than that for the scheme of arrangement described below. The only fly in this particular ointment is that any outstanding minority will have to be compulsorily acquired first (see **8.13**) before the target public company can be converted to a private company, and this will extend the time it will take to complete the transaction.

Its major disadvantage is that it requires a 90 per cent acceptance level from shareholders, as contrasted with the 75 per cent acceptance needed for a scheme of arrangement.

There will also be a stamp duty cost of $\frac{1}{2}$ per cent of the consideration offered for the securities in a general offer.

11.1.3.2 By a scheme of arrangement under s. 425 Companies Act 1985 (see 8.6.2.2)

This will usually involve setting up a new private company (as with the general offer) and proposing a scheme whereby the target company shareholders agree either to transfer the securities they hold to the private company or to have them cancelled (which saves on stamp duty) in return for a cash payment. It will require approval from a majority in number of the shareholders representing 75 per cent in value of the shares, together with the sanction of the court. Court approval is sometimes a drawn-out process but once approval has been granted, the entirety of the target public company is bought out immediately (enabling speedy conversion to private company status), which means that there is no danger of the timetable dragging out.

Do not forget that the City Code applies equally to the scheme of arrangement as to a general offer.

11.1.4 WHAT PROBLEMS DO YOU FORESEE? HOW CAN THEY BE OVERCOME?

There are two particular problems which will arise, other than those already indicated (depending on whether the general offer or scheme of arrangement is preferred).

(a) The new privately owned vehicle (X Ltd) will need cash to buy the target shareholders out. The directors and managers will not have sufficient personal resources available. They will need to borrow the sums they need. An institutional lender such as a bank will require some form of security. The only form of security which exists is the value of the assets of the target company to be acquired.

The difficulty with this is s. 151 Companies Act 1985, which prohibits a company from giving financial assistance for the acquisition of its own shares either before or after that acquisition (see **8.12**). If the target company gives the banks security after it has been acquired and is owned by the directors' private company, that will be caught as financial assistance.

The only escape from this in turn is if the target company is converted to a private company and the so-called 'whitewash' procedure is taken advantage of (see **8.12**). This is why it may be of particular significance to the directors to complete the transaction as soon as possible, so that the company's re-registration can be effected rapidly.

(b) Acton plc has its ordinary shares listed and traded on the London Stock Exchange. As the company is to be bought by some of its own directors, will this be a related-party transaction under ch. 11 of The Listing Rules (see **5.6.4**)? The UKLA may take the view that it is in fact a transaction between the directors and other shareholders of the company, not between the directors and the company. If so, no issue under ch. 11 would arise. It is advisable to consult the UKLA on this issue. If the view is that ch. 11 does apply, the shareholders should be sent a circular and their consent to the transaction sought in general meeting.

If Acton plc were not listed (and even though it is), s. 320 Companies Act 1985 also requires the approval of shareholders in general meeting to what is a substantial property transaction in which the company's shares are being sold to some of its own directors.

11.1.5 WHAT DOCUMENTS WOULD YOU EXPECT TO BE NECESSARY?

Let us assume the directors choose to make a general offer to acquire the target company. These are the most important of the documents necessary:

(a) Offer document (this will also double as a circular to shareholders complying with the related-party transaction requirements) and any other documents required in connection with the offer, such as press announcements.

(b) Notice of extraordinary general meeting of target and resolutions for it (if necessary for approval of the related-party transaction).

(c) Loan agreement with bank(s) and charge.

(d) Special resolution, directors' declaration and auditors' report for s. 155 'whitewash' exemption (see **8.12**).

(e) Brokers' letters to the UKLA and Stock Exchange to de-list the target on acquisition.

11.1.6 WHAT SHOULD THE DIRECTORS DO NEXT?

After approaching different legal advisers, the directors should ensure the financing arrangements for their bid are secure and agreed with their lender. Thereafter, they need to determine how their bid is to be structured and put it into effect. Appointing financial advisers (accountants and merchant banks) is therefore a priority, particularly to obtain necessary tax advice. With these advisers, they will need to decide the timetable for the transaction and how the bid dovetails with any shareholder approvals (usually the bid is simply conditional on obtaining the consent of the target shareholders at a general meeting).

The directors will need to be satisfied they are discharging their duty to the company when making the bid. In support of that, as a matter of urgency, they will need to declare their interest in making a possible bid for the company at a board meeting of the directors (s. 317 Companies Act 1985).

11.2 Brentford plc

One of the difficulties with companies taken private as with Acton plc (now Limited) is that they take on a very high level of debt. This has a number of effects. It makes it harder for the company to raise extra capital (particularly now it has withdrawn from the equity market) and it will have a pressing cash-flow requirement to satisfy the interest burden of the debt.

In this case study, the assumption is that Acton Limited has found the interest payment obligation too exacting, and the director–shareholders (Garden, Crescent and Lane) have decided they must sell. Their urgent need is for cash to pay off the banks.

The assumption here is that the three selling shareholders hold the shares in Acton through the private company (X Ltd) which made the acquisition described above in the first place. This may be tax disadvantageous in that the first sale (of the shares held in Acton) may attract a capital gains tax charge, and then a sale by Garden, Crescent and Lane of their shares in X Ltd may attract another charge. Tax advice will be needed on how to mitigate any such potential problems.

Brentford plc would like to buy Acton. Brentford is listed on the Official List. It can offer only its own securities as it has no ready reserves of cash. It will have to issue half as much share capital again as it already has in issue to pay for Acton.

(a) How can the mismatch in the needs of the parties be met and what considerations need to be taken into account in resolving this mismatch?

(b) What statutory and regulatory controls and restrictions will impinge on the transaction?

(c) What documents will need to be produced for the transaction?

11.2.1 HOW CAN THE MISMATCH IN THE NEEDS OF THE PARTIES BE MET AND WHAT CONSIDERATIONS NEED TO BE TAKEN INTO ACCOUNT IN RESOLVING THIS MISMATCH?

Clearly the most appropriate method for resolving the parties' respective demands is through a vendor placing (see **3.6.5**). Brentford allots its securities to X Ltd as the shareholder of Acton. X Ltd sells the securities to a merchant bank, which has been appointed by Brentford to place those securities on behalf of X Ltd in the market. The cash provided by the placees passes into the hands of X Ltd, and, on receipt of the cash, Acton Ltd becomes Brentford's property.

There are a number of factors to consider with a vendor placing:

(a) Brentford will probably need to offer the securities to its own shareholders under The Listing Rules requirements. This would mean a clawback arrangement, and of the structures available a rights offer is the likeliest option (see **3.6.5.2**).

(b) The new securities will need to be listed alongside its existing securities. A prospectus or listing particulars will be required (see **4.2**).

(c) The point at which Acton will be transferred to Brentford will need to be interdependent with admission of the securities to listing. In other words, the sale of Acton will be conditional on admission to the Official List and the Stock Exchange of Brentford's shares, and the issue of shares will be conditional on the sale of Acton being completed.

11.2.2 WHAT STATUTORY AND REGULATORY CONTROLS AND RESTRICTIONS WILL IMPINGE ON THE TRANSACTION?

You will need to think about the impact of the following on the transaction:

(a) Companies Act 1985, s. 121 (does Brentford have sufficient authorised share capital in view of the size of the proposed transaction?), s. 80 (do its directors have the authority to allot?) and s. 89 (the need to issue the securities on a pre-emptive basis).

(b) Under the Financial Services Act 1986 and The Listing Rules, Brentford will need to issue a prospectus or listing particulars (see **4.2**).

(c) Under the Financial Services Act 1986, you also need to think about the possibility that any document being issued is an investment advertisement (s. 57) and the prospect of any exemptions which may apply to it (s. 58). The exemptions, for instance, cover a document which is also a prospectus or listing particulars (see **4.2.5.8**). You also need to be conscious of the criminal sanctions resulting from misleading statements or conduct in relation to the issue of shares as investments (s. 47 and see **1.5.1.4**).

(d) The Listing Rules will treat this as a Class 1 transaction for Brentford under ch. 10. Where that company is issuing equity as consideration for an acquisition, and that consideration is more than 25 per cent of its current market capitalisation, that acquisition will need to be notified to shareholders in the form of a circular and will be subject to their approval in a general meeting. If none of the other comparisons are above 25 per cent then The Listing Rules may allow you to treat this simply as a Class 2 transaction requiring only notification to the Stock Exchange Company Announcements Office and a press announcement.

You can ignore the City Code on Takeovers and Mergers as Acton Ltd is a private company and the Code only applies to the acquisition of public companies in the UK.

11.2.3 WHAT DOCUMENTS WILL NEED TO BE PRODUCED FOR THE TRANSACTION?

Some of the items in the list below have already been mentioned:

(a) Prospectus or listing particulars, incorporating the circular to shareholders required by the UKLA.

(b) Vendor placing agreement, under which Brentford will appoint a merchant bank to arrange the issue and placing of its shares.

(c) Sale agreement, under which X Ltd, as the seller of Acton, agrees with Brentford's merchant bank to sell the shares in Brentford it is allotted to the bank for placing in the market.

(d) Share purchase agreement between Brentford on the one side and X Ltd on the other. This will govern the sale of the shares in Acton to Brentford. This agreement will need to be inter-conditional with the vendor placing agreement. It will contain various warranties from X Ltd to Brentford regarding X Ltd's title to the shares in Acton, any changes in the financial position of Acton since the last audited accounts, any deterioration in asset values and the like (see **5.5.1.6**). The shareholders of X Ltd may feel it is difficult, particularly if they have only owned Acton for a very short period, to give extensive warranties, but given their former relationship as directors of Acton, Brentford is unlikely to be sympathetic.

(e) Various notices and resolutions required for a Brentford EGM.

(f) Share transfers for the shares in Acton to be sold to Brentford.

(g) Documents required for any UKLA and Stock Exchange listing of securities (see **4.2.6.5**).

(h) Documents required to discharge any security taken by X Ltd's banks over Acton's assets. The banks will be repaid out of the proceeds realised by the placing.

As ever, there will be a host of other supporting documents prepared for the transaction, including verification notes, board resolutions and the like. This list covers only the most significant documents you will need to consider.

INDEX